Black Puerto Rican Identity and Religious Experience

New Directions in Puerto Rican Studies

Florida A&M University, Tallahassee
Florida Atlantic University, Boca Raton
Florida Gulf Coast University, Ft. Myers
Florida International University, Miami
Florida State University, Tallahassee
University of Central Florida, Orlando
University of Florida, Gainesville
University of North Florida, Jacksonville
University of South Florida, Tampa
University of West Florida, Pensacola

New Directions in Puerto Rican Studies
Edited by Félix V. Matos Rodríguez

Vieques, the Navy, and Puerto Rican Politics, by Amílcar Antonio Barreto (2002)
The Phenomenon of Puerto Rican Voting, by Luis Raúl Cámara Fuertes (2004)
*Race and Labor in the Hispanic Caribbean: The West Indian Immigrant Worker
    Experience in Puerto Rico, 1800–1850*, by Jorge Luis Chinea (2005)
Humor and the Eccentric Text in Puerto Rican Literature, by Israel Reyes (2005)
Puerto Rican Nation Building Literature: Impossible Romance, by Zilkia Janer (2005)
The State and Small-Scale Fisheries in Puerto Rico, by Ricardo Pérez (2005)
Black Puerto Rican Identity and Religious Experience, by Samiri Hernández Hiraldo
    (2006)

Black Puerto Rican Identity
and Religious Experience

Samiri Hernández Hiraldo

University Press of Florida
Gainesville/Tallahassee/Tampa/Boca Raton
Pensacola/Orlando/Miami/Jacksonville/Ft. Myers

11 10 09 08 07 06   6 5 4 3 2 1

Library of Congress Cataloging-in-Publication Data
ISBN 0-8130-2924-4

Cover stamp design by Paul J. Fortier

The University Press of Florida is the scholarly publishing
agency for the State University System of Florida, comprising
Florida A&M University, Florida Atlantic University, Florida
Gulf Coast University, Florida International University, Florida
State University, University of Central Florida, University of
Florida, University of North Florida, University of South
Florida, and University of West Florida.

University Press of Florida
15 Northwest 15th Street
Gainesville, FL 32611-2079
http://www.upf.com

To my parents Irene Hiraldo and Josué Hernández

In memory
of a special caregiver, Delia Droz,
and of Tite Curet Alonso, Felipe Cruz, Father Antonio Hernández,
Toño Lacen, Fausto Pérez, Roy A. Rappaport, and Moisés A. Rosa.

Contents

Illustrations

Preface

"It is one thing to be black in Puerto Rico and another thing to be a black Puerto Rican from Loíza." This expression, which I heard on different occasions during my field study in Loíza, reminded me of comments I heard while growing up in Loíza's neighboring town of Carolina, comments such as "He is a black from Loíza" and "They look like blacks from Loíza." I understood my relatives and friends to mean that there is something unique about being from Loíza, something uniquely black, something even more than black. This all became clear during my first childhood visits to the town: most people on Loíza's streets were fairly dark skinned. I was enchanted by the local folklore, vibrant colors, loud street music, and dancers moving to the rhythm of the drums. From the open air eateries came the rich smells of *frituras* (fried traditional food), coconuts, and fish. I will always remember my first trip to the *ancón,* a rustic ferry that had become a symbol of the area. I remember feeling then that Loíza is both unique and yet close, familiar. Little did I know that day at the *ancón* that years later I would return to Loíza as a researcher to experience the uniqueness of its people again and to find a part of myself still waiting there.

Loíza is a town known in Puerto Rico for its long history of African tradition (represented best by the popular festival of Santiago Apóstol or Saint James) and its large black population. There are other towns and cities in Puerto Rico where African traditions are often celebrated (for example, San Juan, Ponce, Guayama, Carolina, and Hatillo), but in the common vernacular Loíza is seen as best representing the African/black component of Puerto Rican culture/society. Loíza is also known for its slow economic development; in the last several years it has gained much media attention because of its high crime rate and controversies surrounding entrepreneurial efforts to develop a strong tourism industry in Loíza, in what is a highly competitive area of Puerto Rico. The government sees the development of cultural and ecological tourism as a significant step toward resolving many of the town's economic and social problems, especially unemployment and crime.

The importance of old religious traditions in Loíza is evident in the festival of Santiago Apóstol. The continued significance of religion is evinced by the

presence of two parishes (each having several chapels in various neighborhoods); more than thirty-eight Protestant churches registered with the state
(most of which belong to Confraternidad de Pastores e Iglesias Evangélicas
de Loíza [Fraternity of Evangelical Pastors and Churches from Loíza]); and
small churches "on every corner," some of which are not registered with the
state. In Las Cuevas, a neighborhood of about 230 households and the focus
of my research, there is a Catholic chapel and five Protestant (mostly Pentecostal) churches. Here, as in the rural barrio where I grew up, the great majority of residents identify themselves by religious category and consider themselves from a religious perspective even though they might not attend church
regularly. However, the great extent of religion's influence on the Loízans'
daily lives became clear to me during my twelve months of fieldwork there
from 1996 to 2003. Most of the field work took place between 1997 and 1998
and consisted of historical, literary, audiovisual, and internet research. I also
conducted open-ended conversations, held formal and informal interviews,
carried out a census in Las Cuevas, distributed a questionnaire to individuals
in six churches in Las Cuevas, and acted as a participant-observer of rituals
and everyday activities in Las Cuevas and Loíza at large.

The significant impact of religion on Puerto Rican life has been acknowledged more publicly in the last two decades. Not surprisingly, this has also
been the case for Latino religion in the United States (Stevens-Arroyo and
Díaz-Stevens 1997). I am honored to be part of this widening discussion
through the writing of this book about religion in contemporary Puerto
Rico (and its relationship to Puerto Rican religious experience in the United
States) and also by addressing the topic of religion in my course "Introduction
to Latino Studies" at the University of Michigan. In previous years, religion
(as a separate topic) was not included in this course as a significant aspect of
the Latino experience. In Puerto Rico, one sign of this new openness about
religion is that current political candidates are proposing an executive cabinet
position to deal with religious matters. This proposal has been controversial
and prompts much discussion about the relationship between the state and
the church and about which religious interests will be represented in an increasingly religiously pluralistic Puerto Rico.

The greater awareness of the impact of religion in today's Puerto Rican
society is due to several factors: the rapid growth of Pentecostalism (traditional as well as nontraditional or neo-Pentecostalism); the dramatic move-

ment of historical Protestantism (composed of historical denominations that transferred from the United States) and Catholicism toward a charismatic experience; a growing access and control of the media by the church (especially the Pentecostal church); and an increasing cultural and religious pluralism caused by the growth of the Buddhist, Hindu, Jewish, and Muslim populations in the island, including immigrants. An important item here is the participation of religious leaders and church members from different religious sectors in the recent protests against the U.S. military presence in the small Puerto Rican island of Vieques. This experience has encouraged further ecumenical efforts to protect the country's social and moral fiber. During the protests, Coalición Ecuménica e Interreligiosa (Ecumenical and Interreligious Coalition) was founded. Because the U.S. government closed the military base in Vieques on May 1, 2003, May 1 was declared a national day of prayer. Also recently, the Catholic and Protestant communities have protested loudly against same-sex marriage and the repeal of the sodomy law. This has furthered open discussions about the moral role of the church in general and, maybe for the first time, encouraged systematic discussions about the church's position with regard to marginalized communities, such as blacks and homosexuals. The terrorist attacks against the United States on September 11, 2001 also led to a deep reflection on personal faith and the role of religion in society, both in general and in Puerto Rico. This reflective attitude was broadly covered in the religious and secular media. Views have ranged from fanatical religious fervor with pro–U.S. sentiments to anti-religious criticism flavored with anti–U.S. rhetoric. Playing into this new or greater awareness of the impact of religion are other factors: a big controversy, largely covered by the media in the late 1990s, concerning the proposition to sell property to the churches for one dollar; more recently, a new federal initiative to give funding to religious organizations that provide services to communities; and the rapid growth of the Christian music industry, which more and more is interconnecting Puerto Ricans across the island and across geographical borders through musical and evangelistic projects and events.

Similar to the effects that the Latino resurgence has had on U.S. scholars in the last several years, the Puerto Rican reality described above has hit members of Puerto Rican academia in the face, prompting a closer look at religion as a legitimate field of scientific analysis, a renewed appreciation of existing studies of religion (published and unpublished), and a recognition of the need for more studies on local and transnational (especially Latino) religion. According to Samuel Silva Gotay, professor of history and religion at the University of Puerto Rico (UPR), who I interviewed July 30, 2003, at least four factors have led to insufficient study of religion in Puerto Rico: (a) the belief that because religion is irrational it cannot withstand rational analysis; (b) Marx's view of religion as alienating; (c) the concept of religion as a clear-cut set of beliefs and practices; and (d) the belief that in a modern and pluralistic society religion should be considered a private thing. However, in the last several years some scholars have moved beyond the fear that too much subjectivity accompanies a personal connection with religion.

Two major events helped the study of Puerto Rican religion gather momentum in the 1990s. First, in 1993, the conference "El fenómeno religioso puertorriqueño: 550 años despues" (The Puerto Rican Religious Phenomenon: 550 Years Later) convened. It provided an opportunity for scholars to discuss Catholicism, Protestantism, popular religion, and the integration of indigenous and African religious influences. It was organized by the Oficina de Vida Religiosa (Office of Religious Life) of the Interamerican University of Puerto Rico (San Germán campus) and cosponsored by the Centro para el Fomento de la Fe Cristiana (Center for the Advancement of the Christian Faith) and also by the Association of Puerto Rican Historians. The second major event that brought about significant discussion of religion was the 1998 centenary celebration of the beginning of systematic Protestant missionary work on the island, which began with the U.S. invasion in 1898. The Equipo de Trabajo de Historia y Sociología del Protestantismo en Puerto Rico (Team of Historical and Sociological Work about Protestantism in Puerto Rico) was formed to develop a series of academic works, some of which were to be presented in public events related to the centenary celebration. Similarly, also in the 1990s, U.S. scholars founded a major organization called Program for the Analysis of Religion among Latinos (PARAL).

Since its founding in 1988, the Museo Puertorriqueño de Antropología Religiosa (Puerto Rican Museum of the Anthropology of Religion) has organized and sponsored at least seventy conferences and exhibitions about nontraditional Puerto Rican religions or belief systems that are growing in the country, such as Hinduism (Hare Krishna), (Zen) Buddhism, Islam, Santería, new age spirituality, new paganism, Satanism, and atheism. The main organizer of these activities is a nonprofit organization founded by its current director, Father Juan José Santiago, a Jesuit with a Ph.D. in theology who specializes in the phenomenology of religion. Father Juan José has worked in collaboration with various foundations and organizations, such as the Puerto Rican Foundation for the Humanities and the Medical Association of Puerto Rico, and with both secular and religious academic institutions, such as the UPR and the Evangelical Seminary of Puerto Rico. Plans are now being made to transform the museum into a center for interreligious studies and dialogue and to combine it with the Centro Católico Universitario (Catholic University Center), directed by the Jesuit order. For decades this Jesuit center has offered pastoral services primarily, but not exclusively, to the Catholic university community.

Catholic and Protestant universities and colleges continue to offer undergraduate courses in religion on a regular basis. The number of Protestant schools offering graduate theological studies is increasing. According to Rubén Pérez Torres, this is especially true for Pentecostal schools. (Pérez Torres was the executive secretary of the Evangelical Council of Puerto Rico and a Protestant pastor. He is currently a popular writer, the founder of theological schools and programs, and a professor of religion at the Interamerican University.) From time to time secular institutions such as the UPR and the Center for Advanced Studies of Puerto Rico and the Caribbean offer courses on different religions or various aspects of them. Still, according to Silva Gotay, the relatively small number of religion courses offered by the country's main collegiate institutions and a lack of participation by the nonacademic religious and the nonreligious academic communities in the events of the 1990s demonstrate that, despite increasing interest in the analysis of Puerto Rican religion, this study domain has a long way to go. I agree with Father Juan José, with whom I spoke on October 9, 2003, that the analysis of cross-cultural or comparative perspectives is even more neglected.

A number of things can be done to develop further an interest in the discussion and analysis of religion. There needs to be a consistent and open exchange (national and international) of information and resources to record the existing data; to identify areas needing further research or those still largely unexplored (such as everyday life, popular religion's interactions with formal Christianity, and other world religions); and to determine how these areas can be analyzed more appropriately. Reaching the general public is crucial and can be done more effectively by making good use of mass media.

Also, the information needs to be more accessible both in terms of the physical location of materials and in terms of writing style. This book responds to all of these concerns.

This project could have not been possible without the collaboration of many Loízans. To those who are not public figures, I give my apologies for not including their real names as some of them requested. However, I have tried to maintain the integrity of their stories and narratives as much as possible. I would like to draw special attention to Mayor Ferdín Carrasquillo, Laura Meléndez, Serafina Dávila (with whom I stayed in Las Cuevas), Micaela Dávila, Luis Rodríguez's family, Pastor Juan V. Salgado and his family, Anacleta Dávila, Rosa Ortíz Pica, María Córdova, Carmen Rodríguez, Felipe Cruz, Carmen M. Ortíz, Marcos Peñaloza, Toño Lacen, Jacinta Rodríguez, Pastor Luis Ruiz and his family, Marcelino Dávila, Juan de Dios Lacen, Fausto Pérez, Cecilio Casanova, Father Antonio Hernández, Father Marco Antonio Sánchez, Father Francisco Conkle, and Pastor Rafael L. Osorio (now in Massachusetts). I would like to thank Kevin Díaz and Menén Osorio Fuentes from FLECHAS (Fiestas de Loíza en Connecticut en Honor al Apóstol Santiago), Father William Burbank from Saint Rose of Lima parish in New Haven, and Maureen Montross from Business New Haven, all in Connecticut, and also Blanca Irizarry from the organization Hermanos Fraternos de Loíza Aldea in New York.

The staffs of the Puerto Rican collection room at the Graduate Library at the UPR, under the supervision of Maritza Ordoñez of Loíza's municipal government offices and of the Catholic Church's headquarters, helped this effort as did David Ramos (from the Pentecostal Church of God), Reverend Moisés A. Rosa (from the Puerto Rican Evangelical Council), Shirley Font (from the Church of the Fountain of the Living Water), Reverend Margarita Sánchez De León (from Amnistía Internacional and Movimiento Ecuménico Mundial in Puerto Rico), Esterla Barreto (from Alianza Anti-Racista Puertorriqueña and the UPR), and Doris Quiñones (from Unión de Mujeres Puertorriqueñas Negras [UMUPUEN] and the UPR). Samuel Silva Gotay, Rubén Pérez Torres, and Father Juan José Santiago contributed current information about Puerto Rican religion, and Luis R. Juarbe and Waldemar Reyes contributed information about (Christian) music in Puerto Rico.

I am very appreciative of financial support from various institutions at the University of Michigan: the Department of Anthropology, the Horace H. Rackham School of Graduate Studies, the Latin American and Caribbean

Studies Program, the International Institute, and the Office of Multicultural Affairs. I am also grateful for the opportunity provided by the Department of Sociology and Anthropology at the UPR and its director David Hernández to teach two courses while doing fieldwork, which helped cover research expenses for stipends for students Eva Villalón, Zulem Echevarría, and Sundra Arroyo from the Departments of Anthropology and Geography at the UPR. These students rendered valuable assistance with the census used in this study. I am indebted to Lilibet Rodríguez, who also helped with the census. I am very thankful to my parents, Josué Hernández and Irene Hiraldo, and my brother, Josué Hernández Jr., for their hospitality, for their accompanying me to the field, and for their great emotional support. Iris Jové and José F. Colón also gave me emotional support during my stay in Puerto Rico and provided much support during my long hours reviewing microfilms at the UPR main library.

I would like to thank members of my dissertation committee at the University of Michigan for their contribution to this book: Gillian Feeley-Harnik (chair), Sueann Caulfield, Daniel H. Levine, Bruce Mannheim, and especially the late Roy A. Rappaport (former chair). I specially thank Carlos Buitrago for his academic mentoring during my years at the UPR and for providing significant information. I thank Morgan Liu, Katherine L. Hinds, Margaret Baker, Mary Anderson, Mike Martin, Matthew L. Fortier, and Frederick Sleator for their editorial assistance in the earlier stages of the book and Christine Sweeney for her editing in the book's final stages. I value greatly the questions of students at Florida State University, where I presented an earlier draft of chapter 2, and the comments and discussion about chapter 2 that took place in a session of the Program for the Analysis of Religion Among Latinos at the 2004 Annual Conference of the Society for the Scientific Study of Religion. I appreciate the comments of my students at Washtenaw Community College and at Eastern Michigan University, who read earlier versions of chapters 6 and 9. Reviews of several chapters—chapter 9, published in *Revista de Ciencias Sociales,* and chapter 2, accepted for publication in *Latin American Perspectives*—have proven very helpful. I am very thankful to anonymous reviewers from the University Press of Florida and especially Anthony Stevens-Arroyo for his very perceptive observations and suggestions, most of which were incorporated into the final work. Amy Gorelick and Susan Albury of the University Press of Florida, and Félix V. Matos Rodríguez, series editor, skillfully facilitated the publication of this book and fielded my many inquiries.

My deepest gratitude goes to my husband, Paul J. Fortier, for his editing work, encouragement, patience, and love, and to my children, Rafel Constantine, Adriana Antonette, and Erin Juliette, for being my greatest inspiration. Finally, I am eternally grateful to God for allowing me to be part of this experience.

Abbreviations

CC	Church of Christ
CFDC	Church of the Faithful Disciples of Christ
CFLW	Church of the Fountain of Living Water
HDEC	Heavenly Doors Evangelical Church
ICP	Instituto de Cultura Puertorriqueña (Institute of Puerto Rican Culture)
JP	Junta de Planificación (Planning Committee)
PCG	Pentecostal Church of God
PIP	Partido Independentista Puertorriqueño (Puerto Rican Independence Party)
PNP	Partido Nuevo Progresista (New Progressive Party, pro-statehood)
PPD	Partido Popular Democrático (Popular Democratic Party, pro-commonwealth)
UPR	University of Puerto Rico

Significant Participants/Interviewees

"Carlos," chapter 3

"Manuel," chapter 3

Father Antonio, Catholic Church, chapters 4 and 5

Father Marco Antonio, Catholic Church, chapter 5

"Rosa" ("Tapia" extended family), Catholic Church: Chapel San Antonio, chapter 5

Pastor "Correa," CFLW, chapter 6

"Luisa" (co-pastor and Pastor "Correa's" sister), CFLW, chapters 6 and 7

"Pablo," chapter 7

Pastor "López," PCG, chapter 7

Pastor "Febres," CC, chapter 7

"Elena" (Pastor "Febres's" niece), chapter 7

Pastor "Tapia" ("Tapia" extended family), CC, chapter 7

"Delia" ("Tapia" extended family, Pastor "Tapia's" sister), chapters 7 and 9

"Lydia," chapter 8

"Alfonsina," chapter 8

"Bartolo," chapter 9

Introduction

Catching Identity and/or/in Religion

One of the sermons that caught my attention during my stay in Las Cuevas was delivered during one of my early visits to the mission of the Church of the Fountain of the Living Water (CFLW). The sermon became representative of other sermons I heard there while staying in Las Cuevas. The CFLW is a Puerto Rican Protestant denomination that was founded in the 1980s. In the last few years it has become one of the fastest growing and most financially prosperous churches in Puerto Rico. The CFLW has been strongly criticized by Catholics and Protestants (both non-Pentecostal and Pentecostal, who together are usually referred to as *evangélicos*) because of its emphasis on material prosperity and an alleged imitation of U.S. evangelism and sympathy with new age ideas. In Las Cuevas, this emphasis on material prosperity might be considered obvious because a small store selling authentic Puerto Rican food is attached to the church building and is administered by the co-pastor of the church, who is also the pastor's sister. Pastor Correa is the founder of the CFLW mission in Las Cuevas, the only one of its denomination in the town of Loíza. Although the Correa extended family grew up in Las Cuevas, most of the family members have moved out and live in other towns. Most of them are socioeconomically stable and have had professional careers. The sermon was delivered on a Sunday morning before a congregation of thirty-seven individuals, most of whom were members of the Correa family, originally from Las Cuevas but living elsewhere at the time.

Pastor Correa began the sermon by mentioning an article in the day's newspaper about Mormons. He said, "Brothers, I do not understand how there can be people in Loíza who even listen to the Mormons. Do you know the Mormons believe that being black is a punishment from God? Racists are not smart. Any Loízan who listens to the Mormons deserves to be hung." ("Deserving to be hung" is a common expression in Puerto Rico and it can be said with a humorous or serious connotation.) Then, in another section of the sermon, he claimed that the existing religions and traditions in Loíza have not helped the town to get away from its poverty and backwardness.

"Brother," he said, "you ask some Christians how they are doing and they answer, 'the way God wants.'" While he spoke he made gestures to ridicule that kind of poor or conformist attitude. Then he asked the congregation, almost screaming, "What is that?! What kind of Christians are they? I should ask, what kind of god do they serve? Their religion does not make sense." Later he said, "Loíza, in particular, urgently needs another message!" At this moment the congregation responded with verbal and bodily expressions of affirmation.

Loíza's Physical, Social, and Historical Location

Loíza is located fifteen miles from the capital of San Juan, on the northeastern coast of Puerto Rico. The town is bordered on its north by the Atlantic Ocean, on its east by the town of Río Grande, on its south by the town of Canóvanas, and on its west by my hometown of Carolina. When one drives to Loíza one has a sense of going to an isolated place because of a large empty, or undeveloped, piece of property—some of which is used for cattle breeding—that surrounds the town's main living area. Loíza is known as a tourist spot. Its river, Río Grande de Loíza, the second largest in Puerto Rico, is well known because of a poem written by the famous poet Julia de Burgos during the 1940s; it is also quietly alluded to in Puerto Rican literature. The town covers an area of twenty-five square miles. During my field study, Loíza had a mostly rural population of approximately thirty thousand people, a population density per square mile of around fifteen hundred (putting the town in eighth place on the island), approximately eight thousand households, and an average of almost four members per household.[1]

Loíza was a Taíno Arawak Indian settlement at the time of the Spanish conquest. The area of Loíza was attacked during the conquest by neighboring Carib Indians and then again in the early eighteenth century by English soldiers. At the beginning of colonization in the early sixteenth century, Loíza became an important area of economic activity based on Indian labor. Later, labor was performed by slaves originating from the west coast of Africa and belonging to the Yorubas, the Congos, and the Angolos, among other ethnic groups. Fugitive slaves to whom the Puerto Rican government granted freedom, also populated Loíza from other Caribbean, especially English, islands. After the Haitian Revolution in the early nineteenth century, fugitive black Haitians settled in Loíza. Later in the century, Loíza, with its use of slaves and wage laborers, became one of the most important areas of sugar production in the country. The early economic significance of the area helped Loíza to become a town officially in 1719. Loíza reconstituted itself as a municipality in 1971 and separated from what is today the town of Canóvanas. This separation left Loíza—in relation to other towns (including Canóvanas)—in the worst socioeconomic condition of all of them, except for the small island of Culebra. Many Loízans think they are still trying to recuperate from the terrible effects of the separation.

During my field study, the percentage of Loízans living in poverty was nearly 68 percent, 9 percent more than the total percentage for all Puerto Ricans. The percentage living in inadequate housing was a little less than 20 percent. By 1989, the per capita income had increased only $79.00 from that of a decade earlier, when it was less than half of the country's per capita income of $4,177. In 1990, the unemployment rate in Loíza rose to 33 percent, up from 19 percent in 1980, which means that it was higher than the overall unemployment rate in Puerto Rico, at the time estimated at more than 20 percent. Still today, about 90 percent of Loíza's employees work outside the town, doing mainly technical and vocational work. At least two-thirds of Loíza's households depend completely or partially on welfare. During my research, the illiteracy rate was a little less than 10 percent, slightly under that of Puerto Rico as a whole. But in 1990, it was calculated that of the people between eighteen and twenty-four years of age, only 46.1 percent had graduated from high school and only 2 percent had attended college. In 1997–98, the total municipal income was $5,182,275.00. This municipal income was derived mainly from unbudgeted income, municipal taxes, and federal funding. However, the municipal expenses were $5,270,775, leaving the town with a deficit of $88,500.[2] The town's principal products are leather, paper, electronics, cane sugar, and minor crops; to a lesser extent the town also depends on fishing and cattle breeding. The municipality's main goal continues to be to hasten its development by promoting tourism, which is seen as creating many employment and business opportunities, thus helping to lower the high rates of crime and drug use while increasing the municipal income through municipal taxes.

The Theme at Hand

In this context, Pastor Correa's managing of identity in his sermon presents itself as a necessary means by which Loízans must deal with and transform their difficult reality. This book's main argument is that although Loízan experience cannot be reduced to the issue of identity, identity is highly significant to many Loízans. Religion's management of identity is both the cause and the result of this central role of identity. Religious pluralism and an increasingly uneven economic development both in relation to Puerto Rico and, importantly, in Loíza itself, are significant factors in the development of various consciousnesses or multiple logics in regard to the role of identity and its relationship to sociopolitical action; these logics manifest themselves in personal experiences and different spheres of social interaction. Even more so, in this book I show how Loízans' management of identity is (intentionally or unintentionally) strategic: by involving different dimensions of human experience; by involving various identities (individual, family, community, town, national and transnational, socioeconomic, religious, cultural, racial, generational and gender); by involving different relationships among these dimensions and identities (antagonistic, supportive, and hierarchical); and by involving small- and large-scale competitive social, political, economic, and religious agendas. Here, I am more concerned, first, with the Loízans' use of identities (as specific characterizations and representations) than with their accuracy and, second, with the way Loízans reconstruct identities than on how these identities originated. This book makes it clear that even though Loízans' forms of managing identities are not unique, they do have a specific meaning and significance. Whether these managements are social and politically effective or not is an open-ended question.

General Theoretical Framework

This book presumes, in accordance with Connolly (1991: 64–65), that identity requires socially recognized differences in order to be and that identity implicates otherness, including, as Cornell states (1993: 41), the otherness that marks the boundaries of the self "within," such as the unconscious. Therefore, identity is not autonomous but consciously and unconsciously contextual. However, as Butler (1993: 12) asserts, it is precisely in this contextual nature of the process of identification where the possibilities of agency (or purposeful and reflexive action) are found. For the purpose of analysis one therefore has to ask: How can the social context be delimited? Here, Juan Flores's (2000: 14, 20) preferred approach on popular Latino culture is very helpful. According to this approach, popular culture is a system of relations, an exercise of traversing and transgressing boundaries and spheres of cultural practice. Thus, what is in front of the researcher is the "catching," the interplay between practice and theory, between the people as subject and as object of knowledge, between the lived and observed social reality. Considering this interplay and the timing and historical relationship between the people and the writer can help the concept of popular culture as *local* be rescued from its relegation to archaic and residual roles in today's global modernity and mass media. With this in mind, it makes sense in this book to stress the local and the particular in the Loízan experience of identity and religion in order to approach the global and the general.

Moreover, this book considers identity as a dynamic map of power (Butler 1993: 117). Along these lines, Lorentzen, who studied issues of identification in Chiapas, Mexico (2001: 91, 98), argues that to overemphasize the impact of the global economy on the situation of Chiapas, while ignoring the internal dynamics of power, is to leave the explanation at the level of abstraction. This is why this book, similar to Morris's (1995) and Guerra's (1998) studies of Puerto Rican identities, considers different interrelated identities. Here I look at national, town, ethnic, racial/color, community, family, religious, individual, gender, and generational identities.

Pastor Correa's sermon points to an exercise of using identity for religious purposes and vice versa. This strategic relationship, sometimes contradictory or ambiguous, has been demonstrated by Kipp (1993) in her study of the Karo people in the multicultural/multiethnic country of Indonesia and by Burdick (1998) in his study of popular Christianity in Brazil. This book's perspective on religion and the great significance identity and religion have for many Loízans explain why I focus on religion to explore identity. Rappaport (1999: 1, 8, 16), inspired by cross-cultural ethnographic data, argues that religion is a fundamental structure of human nature. According to him (1999: 30, 375) certain meanings and effects can best, or even only, be expressed or achieved in ritual, the main component of religion. He also establishes that ritual structure and religious form are specific to society, to church or religious community, and to the individual (1999:111). At this point, Comaroff and Comaroff's (1993) view of ritual, based on data from countries in Africa, is incisive. They argue that ritual works and is constituted within the framework of everyday interaction. However, the Comaroffs' insistence on considering ritual as an integral dimension of everyday life does not mean one has to sacrifice the analysis of ritual on its own terms. Therefore, as Taylor (1995: 242) states in his study of Irish Catholics, it is necessary to be aware of a possible balance between religion as already given and "out there" and religion as "an act by people, a process."

Once one knows where to look for the different forms of the religious quest, the next step is to look at how these forms are made up to work for people. I believe this question can be answered by following Caldwell's advice, in her study of religion in Kerala, India (1999: 2–3, 275–76), to adopt a "multi-layered perspective" to understand the religious meaning as a whole. By this she means a perspective that integrates the social, feminist, psychological, performative, and indigenous theoretical perspectives or layers. In this book, however, a multilayered or multidimensional perspective is that which integrates the following layers of human experience: the cognitive (see Rappaport 1999); the physical-emotive; the verbal and nonverbal ritualistic elements (see Csordas 1994b); the body practices (see Obeyesekere 1981); the transcendent; and the social context, particularly religious pluralism and a marginal socioeconomic status. Let me clarify that I am not discrediting a researcher's preference for focusing on one dimension. I maintain, however, that by following a multidimensional perspective one can achieve insights into functions, motivations, and experiences (performative/linguistic, symbolic, psychological, social, and political) that have been overlooked by others, and one can see more precisely the various arrangements among religion's dimensions that make religion, in relation to identity, work for people in their personal experiences and various spheres of social interaction.

Studies of Puerto Rican Religion (and Identity) in Context

After considering the theoretical perspectives and analytical steps outlined above, one realizes that despite the great contribution of Puerto Rican religion studies to this research (some of them touching briefly or indirectly on the issue of identity), they have left us with little ethnographic description of the processes by which religion is reaffirmed and simultaneously contested in everyday life in order to work for people. These studies have also fallen short in presenting other explanations for the religious phenomenon besides descriptive and the functionalist (psychosocial and sociopolitical) ones. In addition, as Duany (1998: 184) has observed, most of the existing studies are specific to one religion or religious group and do not use a comparative or an integral perspective. (It is important to distinguish these two perspectives, because we can compare two religious experiences that are not necessarily connected, and we can study the interaction of two religious groups within a geographical area without comparing them directly.) For instance, works on Spiritism (*espiritismo*) in Puerto Rico or among Puerto Ricans in the United

States—by Saavedra de Roca (1969), Koss (1970), Matos Salgado (1974), and Nuñez Molina (1990)—concentrate on its psychosocial and psychotherapeutic functions in situations of poverty, family conflict, and migration. Cook's (1965: 34) study about the religious movement known as Las Profetas (The Prophets), which originated in the 1950s among the working class, demonstrates the way it "serves to cushion" the impact of social and economic deprivations. Zayas-Micheli (1990: 206) and Díaz-Stevens (1993a) interpret popular Catholicism as "fundamentally" political: as national affirmation and as resistance to the Spanish and North American colonial systems, respectively.[3] López Sierra (1994) affirms the use of religion by black and mulatto Puerto Ricans as political protest and as a form of vindication because of their status of double alienation in their capacity as laborers and as citizens. Similarly, Camayd-Freixas (1997) sees the Mita cult, centered on a female prophet and originating in Puerto Rico in the 1940s, as responding to or protesting against a national sense of orphanhood while vindicating subordinate women.

In relation to the tendencies just described in studies of Puerto Rican religion, it is hard to ignore Craig's (1982) observation that the nature of Caribbean studies has been typically conceptualized in terms of rigid characterizations. Along the same lines, Brusco (1995: 4) has indicated that conceptualizing religion at the macro social and political levels, while forgetting the multidimensional information and experience of individuals, has been characteristic of many studies of religion in Latin America. Also, several scholars have recently observed a pervasive emphasis on the social aspects of religion at the expense of considering the very motivation of relating to the sacred or the supernatural (see Míguez 1999: 230 and Stevens-Arroyo and Díaz-Stevens 1997: 12 [based on their studies of Latin American and Latino religions, respectively]; Torres Vidal 1998: 111; and Díaz Quiñones 1998: 127 [based on Quintero Rivera's 1998 work on Puerto Rican popular religion]). I believe this kind of realization would help researchers avoid making quick assessments such as that of Castro Flores (2001: 60), who held that attraction to Spiritism in Puerto Rico and to religions of African origin among women in Cuba owes more to utilitarian concerns than to mystical-spiritual convictions. My point is that through systematic and close interaction with participants one can better grasp the whole picture of religious motivations. This interaction can also help our understanding of the complex relationship between ordinary experience and transcendence. Here too, we can avoid jumping to the conclusion, as I think O'Neal (1999: 12) does using data from the African-American church, that ordinary experience "mimics" transcendence.

However, Stevens-Arroyo's (1995), Romberg's (2003), and Nuñez Molina's (1994) studies of noninstitutionalized Puerto Rican religion such as the Taíno religion, witchcraft, and Spiritism, respectively, have all contributed to the study of Puerto Rican religion. Stevens-Arroyo combines biological, sociohistorical, and psychological arguments to determine the Taíno influence on contemporary religion. (The psychological component of this argument posits a human collective unconscious charged with emotional force specific to each time and society.) Romberg situates witchcraft in a web of local, transnational, and global forces and relationships in a collapsing (or "merging" or "disruption") of time, space, religious, and ethnic distinctions. Nuñez Molina emphasizes the experiential approach in its varied social and psychological dimensions, while including the experience of the researcher. Agosto Cintrón's (1996), Mintz's (1988), and Silva Gotay's (1997) studies about Protestantism in Puerto Rico strictly tie the phenomenon to larger political, economic, and social processes. At the same time, each also represents an advance in the study of Puerto Rican religion: the first through its attention to local processes of transformation in relationship to larger changes; the second through its attention to individual experience; and the third through its attention to specific religious elements or mechanisms and to religious competition. Studies about Latin America and the Caribbean diaspora such as those of Levine (1992), Brusco (1995), and Rodríguez Toulis (1997) have raised significant ideas to be adopted when studying religion as a force of social change, one such idea being that the relationship between religion and the actors (here I include the researcher) is manifested in everyday life experience and may follow multiple logics.

Loíza (and Its Representations) in the Forming of Puerto Rican Culture

The fact that the participants in this study are from Loíza requires a brief discussion of some of the existing literature about the town so that the contribution of this work will be fully grasped. Basic information about Loíza is found first of all in studies of Puerto Rico's history and national culture, with attention to the African tradition, slavery, and issues of race and color in Puerto Rico at large. Most of these studies can be understood from the point of view of the "invention" of Puerto Rican national culture around the time of the creation of the commonwealth of Puerto Rico (Estado Libre Asociado or Free Associate State) under the U.S. government in 1952. Under the administration of the Partido Popular Democrático (Populist Democratic Party or PPD) and Governor Luis Muñoz Marín (the first governor elected by the Puerto Rican vote, who held office until 1964), the idea of "Puerto Ricanness" (*puertorriqueñidad*) was developed. As Dávila (1997: 4–5) has stated, during the 1950s the government made a concerted effort to define and advance Puerto Rican national culture.

This idea of national culture was based on a conceptualized harmonious coexistence of the Spanish, Indian, and African components (Dávila 1997: 4–5). *Jíbaro* also officially became the archetype of Puerto Ricanness. *Jíbaro* normally refers to the light-skinned peasant, often colored brown by the sun, who lives in the rural mountainous area and who is mostly influenced by the Spanish folk traditions. Catholicism has been another significant aspect of Puerto Rican culture. The minimalist view of Catholicism as just "a main ingredient" of Puerto Rican identity and of other competitive noninstitutionalized religious practices as "secondary ingredients" has limited the understanding of the complex role of religion in Puerto Rican society and at the level of individual experience. This view has influenced the perspective of Puerto Rican Protestantism as a logical result of U.S. imperialism and, therefore, as "another main ingredient" of Puerto Rican identity.

A big concern is posed by the idea that the word "identity" automatically refers to a self-contained national identity with no multiple fissures and fragments, something postmodernist writers have already pointed out (Duany 2002: 23). Here it is good to refer to Quintero Rivera's (1998: 45) suggestion with respect to national identity that it is not enough to acknowledge the components of Puerto Rican identity as blocks encountering each other, but rather to view each of them as a process. At the same time, there is also the problem of thinking that religion and identity are two completely opposite things and that these elements are fluid and extremely individualized.

Going back to "inventing" and advancing Puerto Rican culture, the concept of "invention" follows Anderson's (1991:6–7) popular idea of nations as "imagined communities," as both inherently limited and sovereign regardless of inequality and exploitation. Anderson prefers "imagined" to "invented" because these communities are distinguished by the style in which they are imagined and not by their falsity or genuineness. This makes relevant Duany's (2002: 21) indication that previous generations of government officials, anthropologists, and other scholars, writers, and artists contributed to the commonwealth's representation of the Puerto Rican national culture. With this is mind, I still prefer the word "invention" because it carries the idea of a project. This cultural (re)invention and the creation of the commonwealth, which granted Puerto Rico its own government under the federal government's tutelage, were part of a big plan during the 1940s to enhance the country's progress through fast industrial production. Today it is common knowledge that the country is almost completely dependent on U.S. imports and that a majority of the country's exports are to the mainland United States. The new status encouraged a massive migration of Puerto Ricans to work in the country's urban areas and also on the mainland, especially after World War II. During my field study, it was estimated that more than 3.4 million Puerto Ricans lived in the mainland, while 3.8 million were estimated to live on the island. Puerto Ricans are involved in a back-and-forth migration pattern. Something else affecting the cultural and religious landscape of Puerto Rico awaits future research: the migration of people from different parts of the world, many of whom see Puerto Rico as a physical or symbolic trampoline or bridge to the U.S. mainland or the U.S. lifestyle.

I agree with Duany's (2002: 281) argument that inventing national culture was the response of Puerto Ricans to the American rationale for occupying the island (officially, since 1898), which was based on the Puerto Ricans' incapacity for self-government and a lack of a well-defined cultural identity. However, I would like to emphasize that (re)inventing Puerto Rican identity also responded to an internal atmosphere of concern and tension regarding the new status of dependency, the difficult reality of social inequality, and the threat of modernization to morality and traditional Puerto Rican ways. Puerto Rican tradition was adamantly, but not exclusively, defended by the left—even to the point of an assassination attempt on the U.S. president—which at the time was composed of independence advocates—nationalists, socialists, and communists (the three often being indistinguishable) and against whom the federal and state governments took serious repressive measures.

In his analysis of building nations and nationalism, Anderson (1991: 163–85) also paid careful attention to instrumental ways of reproducing nationalism. Three years after the commonwealth was created, the Legislative Assembly approved the creation of the Instituto de Cultura Puertorriqueña (Institute of Puerto Rican Culture or ICP), a governmental organization with the mission to promote and disseminate national culture. The three components of Puerto Rican national culture are in the seal of the ICP and have been reproduced everywhere: a Spanish man is at the center with a grammar book in his hand, an Indian man is on the Spanish man's right, along with a carved stone god surrounded by plants, and an African man is on the Spanish man's left, along with a machete and a drum. Cultural centers in each municipality were also created to help the cause of the ICP at the local level (Dávila 1997: 79).

There are tendencies in the studies discussed above to acknowledge and describe the African or black side of Puerto Rican culture and society (Babín 1973; Zenón Cruz 1974; L. M. González 1993); to argue such things as the existence of social discrimination and mild rather than oppressive racism in Puerto Rico (Blanco 1975 [1942]: 63); to demonstrate that the African or black tradition has been marginalized (Dávila 1997: 43, 71–73, 177–82; Morris 1995: 103); to maintain that the African component is more basic than the other components (J. L. González 1993); and to claim that Puerto Ricans are "really really black" (Torres 1998). The unique character of Loíza, particularly of the barrios Medianía Alta and Medianía Baja, has been pointed out in linguistic studies (Mauleon Benítez 1974), in studies about Loíza's festival of Santiago Apóstol, which originated in Medianía Alta (Alegría 1954; Zaragoza 1995), and in studies about witchcraft in Puerto Rico (Vidal 1989). (Not surprisingly, Alegría and Vidal were members of the board of directors of the ICP. The former was the first president of the ICP and served longer than any other president.) The works of Alegría (1954), Zaragoza (1995), and Vidal (1989) suggest that Loízan religion plays a resistant role. At the same time, the "unmistakably" African character of Loíza's traditions has been questioned (Steward et al. 1956). Also, LaRuffa's (1966) work suggests that Loízans are not devoid of African ancestry because of their affiliation with Protestantism. With data from the community of Piñones (on the very northern coast of Loíza), two other ideas have been challenged: that the high black population in Loíza is exclusively due to high sugar production with the use of slave labor and that Loízans went from peasantry to proletarian work in a linear manner (Giusti 1994).

My study challenges common ideas and stereotypes about Loízans' identity/experience by illuminating the complex processes involved in the way they manage their identities (emphasizing the plural), mainly within the religious framework. This book issues these challenges by building on previous theoretical perspectives to study religion as it is related to identity in different geographical areas. It therefore fills a gap in the studies of religion in Latin America, the Caribbean, and especially Puerto Rico and Loíza.

Organization of the Book

Each of the book's chapters is a unit in its own right: each emphasizes the overlapping of themes, applies a multilayered perspective, and considers both the collective and the individual, the ritualistic and the mundane in its areas of investigation. At the same time, the chapters complement one another by concentrating on a theme and the theoretically and cross-cultural approaches surrounding it; by more or less favoring one perspective or layer over the others; and by privileging the collective or the individual, the ritual or the commonplace areas of investigation.

In the first chapter I construct a trajectory of the significance of Loíza during my upbringing, which I consider illustrative of the experience of other Puerto Ricans. I also comment on the close relationship between religion and identity and on my experience doing anthropology in my home country while questioning "otherness" or the idea that anthropology studies a distant subject.

To better understand Loízans' promoting and contesting identities in religious discourse and practice, in chapter 2 I look at the way Loízans manage identities mainly "outside" the religious realm: through daily interactions, including those in which the researcher is involved; through racial classifications in response to a census; and through the efforts of Loízans in Loíza and in the state of Connecticut to promote their culture with the festival of Santiago Apóstol. In the last section, I explore strategies of dissociating from and reassociating with tradition or national identity and religion, on the one hand, and with color and cultural/ethnic background, on the other.

In chapter 3, I briefly examine the historical trajectory of the religious restructuring of Puerto Rico in an atmosphere of intensely religious competition. This competition is basic to an understanding of the various ways in which religious groups and individuals manage identities in Loíza and Las Cuevas. Here, I focus on Catholicism and Protestantism, the two predominant religions in Loíza and Las Cuevas, while looking closely at the experience of Protestantism in the last few decades.

The fourth chapter treats the Catholic Church's retreat from identifying itself as the state religion and its advance toward identifying itself as the national, as well as the Loízan, religion. I conclude that although these movements were critical for the Catholic Church and Loízan Catholics, many parishioners found them insufficient. Using the experience of Las Cuevas's Catholics, in chapter 5 I examine the church's progress toward a "more meaningful" or "more spiritual" Catholic experience, which gives less importance to or tries to leave behind cultural and black identities, while giving greater significance to the guidance and work of the Holy Spirit. I insist, though, that this happens precisely to give legitimacy to Loízan identity and its religion.

In contrast, in the chapter 6, I examine the church's tactic of directly addressing Loíza's black identity, socioeconomic "backwardness," and conformist attitude in order to validate the need for a "new" Christian message of self-esteem, prosperity, and self-determinism. Since the Church of the Fountain of the Living Water insists this message is urgently needed in Loíza, I also draw attention to other verbal and nonverbal mechanisms employed by the CFLW's preacher to validate his church's message.

The interaction of religious, family, economic, and spacial identities is highly pertinent to the CFLW and the other churches in Las Cuevas and forms the focus of chapter 7. Here I look particularly at the simultaneously positive and challenging implications of this interaction for family relationships and socioeconomic stability, for ideals of social and sacred space, and for religious motivations and religious experience.

Family and community relationships are two of the most significant factors behind the managing of religious personal identity for two women from Las Cuevas, one Pentecostal and the other Spiritist. They form the focus of chapter 8, in which I look at the interplay of unconscious and conscious motivations manifest in these women's everyday lives and through their physical appearance. I also draw special attention to the motivations of sexual maturity; relationships with significant male figures; affirmations of self (as mothers and women) and as community members; adoption of specific doctrinal stands; and strong convictions of personal social mission.

The ages of these two women plays a big role in their capacity for a kind of managing of personal religious identity. Thus, in chapter 9, I focus on the way religious identity is reaffirmed and re-formed as it is reexperienced through the witnessing of two Pentecostal elders of each gender, each a resident of Las Cuevas. I argue that this reenactment of religious identity is possible because of certain linguistic mechanisms and physical-emotive and cognitive process-es and that it carries special spiritual and social implications for individuals of advanced age.

In conclusion I briefly reflect on the situation of Loíza and the sociopoliti-cal role of religion, while making a call for serious attention to Loíza's prob-lems in relation to the country's larger sociopolitical issues and agendas. I also call for future research in the area.

"But it isn't just about Loíza"

Encountering Loíza

Choosing the content of this chapter and using myself as an informant in this and the following chapters came about after feeling forced to abandon all notions of myself as an unengaged and immutable observer (to paraphrase Tweed, 2002: 68). Although many anthropologists have tried to probe "immersion" in the culture they are studying while trying at the same time to be objective, I found myself trying hard to demonstrate my capacity for objectivity by keeping my distance. Similar to Davidman's (2002: 25) experience, I also felt initially that I could not afford the risk of explicit self-reflection in this book for fear that my work would be considered too subjective, and even therapeutic, while advocating religion.

Caldwell (1999: 3) has argued that despite much reflection about the significant role of "inner experience" by anthropologists since the late 1970s (and later by other disciplines), "inner experience" is still constrained by coherent ethnographic presentations (or deep and systematic descriptional and analytical accounts) with no use of the analyst's personal experience as method and data. In the same vein, Mannheim and Tedlock (1995: 13, 15) have stated that ethnography is a peculiar zone of emergence of culture, a form of "culture making" through interaction between the ethnographer and the research participants, without ignoring differences and dynamics of power (Spickard 2002: 250).

How Loízans and I encountered each other in our mutual play of representation, in this peculiar zone of emergence of culture, in this form of "culture making," which this research represents, is understood by looking at some of my personal and academic development. Therefore, let me start by saying that I will always remember sitting as an undergraduate in the main theater at the UPR in 1988 and watching a professional music and dance performance that celebrated our Puerto Rican African and/or black roots and emphasized the religious aspect.[1] (Members of this group were wearing the same African-style clothing that my professor of sociology often wore. One of the members of this group was from my hometown, where years later he founded Clave Tres, a musical group that emphasized Caribbean rhythms using a lot of percussive instruments, especially drums. He also wore African-style clothing during this group's performances. Percussionist Waldemar Reyes, whom I will mention later in this chapter, was a member of this group.) Just as many of us Puerto Ricans got used to hearing the U.S. national anthem and saluting the U.S. flag in elementary school, we constantly heard that Puerto Rican national culture was a mix of the Spanish, the Indian, and the African elements and that *jíbaro* was the most authentic Puerto Rican. The performance at the university's main theater encouraged me to open myself to something I had considered hidden to me and other Puerto Ricans or that we had been denied the opportunity to experience fully and to celebrate: the "African" element, particularly in its folkloric version. I would like to propose three other versions of the African element: the historical, represented by slavery; the everyday, represented by habitual or quotidian social and economic circumstances; and the modern-cultural, represented by the music of salsa.

Looking further back, I can construct a kind of trajectory of my relationship to Loíza and what this town has represented in relation to the Puerto Rican culture. In constructing this trajectory, I agree Boyarin's argument (1994: 2) that memory is about the past filtered through the present or that it is really about the present. Watching the performance at the university made me realize that, while I was growing up, my life had moved through two interacting but different worlds that were more or less related to the three components of the Puerto Rican national identity: the *jíbaro* archetype and the North American element. My father's family was "white" and resided in Barrazas, a mostly "white" barrio where I was born and raised. The family was Northern Baptist. This characteristic and the family's strong church leadership role brought family members into association with important Baptist officials, from the island and mainland, and moved them toward identification with North American culture. This did not prevent them from also identifying with the *jíbaro* lifestyle and traditions, which we proudly demonstrated for North Americans, residents of urban areas in the Baptist community, and members of my extended family who had moved to the United States.

In contrast, my mother's family was mostly *trigueño* (mixed color) and "black" and was raised in Cacao, a "black" barrio next to my father's barrio. Family members were mostly Catholic and had some beliefs in Spiritism, although some members, including my grandparents, converted later to a very traditional Pentecostalism. My mother, however, became a Baptist as an adult, after my father invited her to his church during one of his evangelistic visits to her community. My mother's family was involved in activities that, according to my father's family's perspective, were considered secular, such as listening and dancing to Afro-Caribbean rhythms such as plena, bomba, and salsa.[2] During my fieldwork, I found out that one of my interviewees, Toño Lacen, who was one of the main Spiritist leaders in Loíza (the number one Spiritist in Loíza some people say), had visited my mother's parents' home to organize Spiritist meetings (*sesiones* or *veladas*). For many years, my grandfather operated a stand in the farmers' market downtown and dealt with local farmers and fishermen as well as people from the town of Loíza where, I was told, many black people lived who were superstitious and practiced witchcraft, Spiritism, and Santería. I learned that these practices were considered characteristic of black people in general. I also remember that during evangelistic "tent meeting" events sponsored by my church, held in locations within the interior parts of my mother's barrio, many sermons, broadcast by loudspeakers to the neighborhood, condemned these "wrong" or "false" beliefs.

There had been many instances in which I thought of my father's family as superior to my mother's, although at the same time I had enjoyed the type of freedom that my mother's family represented. Visits to my mother's family provided a kind of liberation from a relatively strict Baptist doctrine. The performance at the university helped me to develop a deep appreciation of my mother's side, as did my exposure to the claim in my first anthropology class that humans of all colors share biological and intellectual traits. In our university classes, we students were also exposed to different lifestyles and worldviews and to an atmosphere of critique against U.S. imperialism. This critique and a leaning toward Marxist ideology seemed to be fueled by left-leaning groups on campus. We were often reminded of the martyrdom of two leftist students who were killed by state police, backed by federal agents. These students were seen as defending the national sovereignty of Puerto Rico. The genocide carried out by Spaniards against the native Indians was also regarded with contempt, although this was not directed at Spanish colonialism in general. I was not the only one who slowly began to notice the marginal position of African themes and that discussing them was less significant than critiquing the United States and the genocide of the Taínos. (This awareness had an immediate effect on me; I stopped wearing Indian-style jewelry and started wearing African-style instead, and I began to collect African art.)

My personal experience with religion spurred me to write a paper for my first course in anthropology about the role of religion in different peasant societies. This was my first consideration of the cross-cultural significance of religion and how it relates to the political and economic system. I joined a Christian university group called La Escalerita (literally, the little ladder), which was associated with historical Protestantism and the Catacumba movement. I made this move after attending a few meetings of La Confra (Confraternidad Universitaria de Avivamiento or Revivalist University Fraternity), which had a Pentacostal and pro-status quo majority. La Confra was doctrinally conservative and charismatic, while La Escalerita was less conservative and more willing to experiment with the arts, for example, by incorporating classical dance and Afro-Rican rhythms during worship. La Confra was perceived to have more socioeconomically deprived members than La Escalerita, and it had more dark-skinned members, including Loízans. This fact confirmed what I learned when I visited the Baptist church of Medianía Alta as a member of my church's children's choir: not all Loízans were witches, Spiritists, or Santeros. I also realized that Loízans were willing to surrender aspects of their identity in the name of Protestantism.

At the university we were also learning about the controversial aspects of Christianity, for example, how both Catholicism and Protestantism had supported colonialism and exploitation. Liberation theology was a response to these aspects of imperialism and social injustice in Latin America, and during my membership in La Escalerita I participated with other groups' members in presentations and discussions of this very subject, which connects Puerto Ricans with other Latin Americans. At the final stages of my bachelor's degree and in an effort to develop even further an objective perspective, I decided to study colonization, development, and globalization and to leave behind my interest in religion as this topic was too familiar and therefore too subjective (personally troubling).

Unexpectedly, in my first anthropology courses at the University of Michigan, students were encouraged to consider and criticize the classical view of anthropology as an objective study of the *other* or a distant subject. The works of Clifford (1983), Said (1989), and Fabian (1990) are part of a body of literature we covered that touched upon an ongoing argument that *otherness*, or what we think and represent of the other, is a bias fabrication.³ This point was confirmed many times during my research when I felt "othered by the other" (using Juan Flores's expression, 2000: 21–22), when Loízans demanded as many answers to their questions as I demanded answers to mine. By sharing with Loízans the many experiences included in this chapter, I was able to confirm Spickard's (2002: 240) conclusions that when a researcher reveals herself she is better able to know the research participants. I also confirmed the fabrication of otherness on the many occasions I caught myself having an intolerant, critical response to the Christian experience when I participated in a Hare Krishna meeting, a *puja* (a Hindu ritual celebration), or a Muslim service.

Nevertheless, I became convinced of the importance of studying my home country after realizing that, even if I studied another country in the future, I should first address the scarcity of in-depth anthropological studies about Puerto Rico and assist the future development of a comparative or "broader" perspective. After my second year of graduate school (summer of 1994), I conducted two months of preliminary fieldwork in Adjuntas, a town in the central mountainous area of Puerto Rico that is very representative of the *jíbaro* culture. This town is also known for its long pro-independence history. I had done some work in Adjuntas as a research assistant and as a teaching assistant of Carlos Buitrago, professor of anthropology at the UPR. Much of the collaborative research work was on the origins of capitalism and slavery in this town. My decision to return to my former interest in religion was prompted by classroom discussions of otherness and of religion per se and by intellectual discussions about religion in special events sponsored by the Graduate Christian Fellowship at the University of Michigan. The two months of field study in Adjuntas convinced me of the importance of religion in people's lives at the local level and for developing personal and national identities. But after this field study I became interested in doing a comparative study on the topic of religion in a very different town in Puerto Rico. For reasons already mentioned, Loíza immediately came to my mind.

Where Is the African Element?

I heard the following comment several years ago from a musician friend: "You feel brainwashed into believing that Puerto Ricans are a mix of the Spanish, Indian, and African elements, so you expect that these three elements are treated as equally significant." During my time in grade school (from 1975 through 1980), we learned more about Indians, Spaniards and Spain than about Africa and Africans in Puerto Rico or other Caribbean countries. The category "Caribbean" has been mostly used by Puerto Ricans to refer to Cuba and the Dominican Republic, while excluding English and French Caribbean islands and the Caribbean regions of eastern Central America and the northern part of South America. This may have something to do with Morris's (1995: 103) finding that, to many Puerto Ricans, Caribbean and Latin American identities share a lower position compared to Puerto Rican identity. Furthermore, many Puerto Ricans consider the island to be physically in the Caribbean, but historically and culturally related to Latin America. But the African connection was not overlooked entirely. In school we learned a famous poem illustrative of the African influence in the Puerto Rican culture. One of the phrases, "Y tu abuela, a ónde está?" (Where is your grandmother?), was recited in the "African" or "black" type of pronunciation. The idea behind the question is that the African component is somewhere in your family roots. A group of us once recited a poem with African words written by Luis Palés Matos that begins "Calabó y bambú, bambú y calabó." We learned popular African words such as *mondongo* (a stew with pork parts) and *mofongo* (a plantain dish).

On the one hand, during my elementary and middle school years (1980–83) there was an emphasis on the *jíbaro* figure in various activities held at my school and through my family's strong involvement in the pro-commonwealth party or PPD, especially my father's side. The ensign of the party was a red head with a red *pava*, the hat most characteristic of the *jíbaro* peasant worker. Dávila (1997) has demonstrated the successful use of the *jíbaro* theme as a marketing strategy by foreign and local corporations during the 1970s and 1980s. Many Puerto Ricans can remember commercials that used the *jíbaro* theme to advertise products such as Don Q rum, Old Colony soda, and Winston cigarettes. On the other hand, the word *jíbaro* has been used negatively, mainly to refer to an ignorant, shy, and conformist person. Years later, during my studies at the UPR, we developed a critique of the *jíbaro* as static, usually excluding the female *jíbara* and the dark-skinned worker of the coast.[4]

Generally, there was a lack of or a stereotyped representation of the black sector in local and foreign commercials and programs (mainly North American and Mexican). One of the few and most popular commercials that directly represented the black sector was that of Yaucono, a brand of coffee produced on the island. In this ad a heavy black woman dressed as a cook and wearing a handkerchief on her hair danced the African–Puerto Rican style— moving her butt—while singing "En Puerto Rico tomamos café" (We drink coffee in Puerto Rico)—coffee being considered an icon of Puerto Ricanness. This portrayal of an African–Puerto Rican woman clearly contrasts with my memories of the commercial for the corn oil Mazola, in which Indians were portrayed as spiritual ambassadors, a portrayal that was consistent with grade school descriptions of the Taíno Indians as good and pacifist in contrast to the wild and aggressive Carib Indians from other Caribbean islands, who were also darker or more reddish. Additionally, there was an exceptionally famous character on television called Chianita, who was a black woman with political aspirations. She had a segment on a popular local show on weekdays at noon, in which she commented on the news and the social and political systems, although people were not supposed to take her seriously. Although Chianita was black, she was played by a white actress—probably because there were so few black actresses at that time.

Many Puerto Ricans learned about slavery in the United States and about how it could have occurred in Puerto Rico while watching *Roots,* the famous North American television miniseries about slavery. We learned the basis of discrimination against blacks in the United States. Watching the North American music show *Soul Train,* we learned that blacks constituted a distinct group and culture in the United States and that they were talented. The successes of Roberto Clemente, the famous Puerto Rican baseball player, taught us that black Puerto Ricans were also talented and could compete with black and white North Americans. In the last several years, the local comedy show *El show de Raymond Arrieta* has brought up the issue of discrimination based on color as something happening at home. One episode used satire to make a point: when a white person is dressed in a white gown people immediately think she is a doctor, but when a black person is dressed in a white gown people think he is a butcher. Another famous comedian, Sunshine Logroño (who is known for his pro-independence stand), has addressed the tensions between *roqueros* and *cocolos* in the section of his program entitled "La guerra urbana." The former term normally refers to upper- or middle-class, young, light-skinned people, who prefer rock music. The latter term refers to lower-class, young, dark-skinned people, who prefer salsa music.

Sacred music was another area where one could experience the greater significance given to the *jíbaro* theme over the African theme. In Las Cuevas I heard a few stories about how some young individuals, most of them from Pentecostal churches, were encouraged to think that plena (which is considered an urban, Afro-Rican rhythm, though it is now performed more by light-skinned Puerto Ricans) and bomba (which is considered the genre closest to the Puerto Rican rural black community) were secular and pagan music rhythms that were therefore almost prohibited to them. In the early 1980s, *jíbaro* rhythms and instruments had entered the repertoires of a good number of Pentecostal and Baptist churches, including the churches in Loíza and in my barrio. The *jíbaro* theme was emphasized in my Baptist high school (1983–1986), which was located in the urban area of Carolina. We performed *jíbaro* music at both secular and Christian events. The repertoire included native music from Latin America, some of which was directly inspired by liberation theology and considered representative of the Puerto Rican situation. This occurred during a time when Marxist ideas and liberation theology were influencing the Baptist community (although we did not know it then). The implicit message many of us received was that *jíbaro* music was "Christian" and "good," while Afro-Boricua music was "too worldly" and "risqué."

Still, this growing musical experience in the Baptist school encouraged music students to experiment with Afro-Rican rhythms and to develop a personal appreciation for this music. Similarly, by participating in the church's music ministry, individuals from Las Cuevas recognized the existence of such "secular" rhythms in the church's repertoire and began consciously to incorporate them. As they engaged in a process of musical growth and experimentation, they redeveloped a taste for outside-the-church or secular rhythms such as bomba, plena, and salsa, and later merengue (from the Dominican Republic and in a great rivalry with salsa), rap and jazz (from the United States), and reggae (from the Caribbean). According to a recent newspaper article about the development of Christian music in Puerto Rico, the fact that the rhythms of *nueva trova* (once considered *jíbaro* subversive), plena, and salsa were finally adopted by the Christian church in the late 1980s also had a lot to do with the conversion of secular groups characterized by this music. Also, after some time, Christian groups were formed using these rhythms and met with great success (*Diálogo* [March 1994]: 13–14).[5]

Some of my interviewees developed a critical outlook about the church's music and about the church's world position in general. They became aware of the role religion plays in forming (national and local) identity. For example, they drew attention to the fact that members of their churches had criticized their use of the rhythms of secular songs (especially in salsa, plena, and bomba) with Christian lyrics, while forgetting that many Christian songs they learned in church originally had North American secular lyrics.

We all agreed that in the Christian church today, bomba is the least popular of the three. Not surprisingly, bomba was not mentioned in the aforementioned article, and I believe this absence relates to the fact that only recently have bomba and other rhythms commonly associated with black people, such as merengue, rap, and reggae, been consciously incorporated by the young Christian community. As Soto Torres (2000) recently pointed out, bomba is the rhythm that Puerto Ricans most often deny. To my interviewees this statement applies more to the Loízan style of bomba. However, as the professional percussionist Waldemar Reyes argues (interviewed September 3, 2003), bomba, mixed with other rhythms such as jazz, is gaining popularity in the secular sphere thanks to people such as William Cepeda, a popular musician, composer, and arranger originally from Loíza. Cepeda is internationally known for his compositions that mix jazz with bomba and plena and for his award-winning CD entitled *Afro-Rican Jazz: My Roots and Beyond.* He also directed a CD of the Loízan bomba group, Balet Folklórico de los Hermanos Ayala. This increase in bomba's popularity has been gradually affecting Christian music. Nevertheless, bomba does not have legitimacy on its own, as evidenced by the music of Reyes himself. Reyes is a member of Latin Jazz Antillano, a group that mixes bomba with jazz (Latin jazz and *jíbaro* jazz are other existing hybrids) and has accompanied internationally known singers.

In addition to their experimentation with music, the young residents of Las Cuevas reoriented their personal religious experiences toward their Puerto Rican and Loízan identities, as they felt that connecting with God was better accomplished from a genuine perspective of who one is or where one comes from. At some point, they took a step further by placing their Puerto Rican and Loízan identities in a larger cross-cultural or global framework, and they began to see themselves outside the exclusive contours of the Puerto Rican and Loízan identities. Some indicated that this evolution had a lot to do with access to better communications and technology. They acknowledged having faced criticism and lack of understanding from a secular perspective—because of their apparent lack of Puerto Rican and Loízan identities—and from a religious perspective, because of their secularism. As a result of the latter, some have left the church (but not their faith in God, as they explained to me); some live their lives by compartmentalizing church experience and "other" activities; and others have stayed "inside" the church in order to encourage changes in the music ministry and in the church's perspective in general.

Also, in this discussion it is hard to ignore the controversy during the 1980s surrounding the naming of the Centro de Bellas Artes Luis A. Ferré, considered by many Puerto Ricans as the most important performing arts center in Puerto Rico. One strong popular opinion was to name the center after Rafael Cortijo, a black singer and composer who made the rhythms of plena and bomba very popular during the 1950s and who, according to many opinions, became the representative icon of the "revolution of the Puerto Rican black" at the time (Aparicio 1998: 35). However, this option ended up being rejected in favor of naming the center after Luis A. Ferré, a former governor from the pro-statehood party, the PNP. Ironically, he is known on the island as one of the biggest advocates of a universal and progressive/liberal idea of Puerto Rican culture oriented in Europe (even after his own party adopted the populist discourse and embraced Puerto Rican folklore and the black sector in order to compete with the PPD). In fact, Ferré was the founder of the Museo de Ponce, one of the most prestigious museums in the country, if not the most prestigious, which has a predominant and permanent Western artistic exhibit. The museum is located in the city of Ponce, on the southern coast of Puerto Rico. Ponce is known as one of the most representative towns, architecturally speaking, of the European-Spanish style. It is also the cradle of the Ferré family, which is one of the richest in the whole country. In addition, Ponce is known for having a large concentration of African descendants and for its carnival with strong African elements. The controversy around naming the art center was covered extensively by the media and it promoted a spirit of critique and a reawakening of the African and the black consciousness on the island, if only for a while.

In graduate school at the end of 1994 I decided to take courses on Africa and the Caribbean and to begin digging into some of the "black" or "African" material in Puerto Rico. I thought seriously about Buitrago's (1982: 103–6) observations regarding "indigenizing" anthropology in Puerto Rico. He observed that after many years of highlighting the Spanish component of Puerto Rican national culture, a strong interest in Indian material was born during the 1950s within the discipline of anthropology, particularly through excavations. Then, the so-called black interest surfaced, but with less respectability as a legitimate area of study. According to Buitrago, the "black interest" in Puerto Rico has survived thanks to the discipline of history, to the interest in slavery, and especially to folk studies and to popular artistic expressions. Buitrago's observations and my experience of three months of preliminary field research in Loíza in 1996 convinced me to focus my study on Loíza alone, rather than doing a comparative study of Loíza and Adjuntas. Thinking back, however, I can also see myself trying to recapture a process of self-discovery or identity redefinition, which I had begun at the time of the performance at the university. Perhaps I wanted to compensate for thinking negatively of the world that my mother's family represented and which I had begun to associate with Loíza. I wanted to compensate for the fact that the critique against the marginal position of the African theme was less significant than the critique against North American imperialism in the university's circles. Interestingly, I noticed a greater interest in my research and greater opportunities for financial funding when I made the switch from Adjuntas to Loíza, once the characteristics of the latter were known.

Going back to the issue of self-discovery, I cannot ignore the possibility of being part of the process described by Marrero (1997: 155) that is happening in U.S.-Cuban literature, particularly that written by white women, in which the treatment of (religious) African tradition as mysterious and exotic has become the strategic avenue for Cuban cultural identity and survival. Coincidentally, a similar process leading to self-discovery in the Puerto Rican female writer Rosario Ferré (the sister of former governor Luis A. Ferré, whom I mentioned before) has been discussed by Aparicio (1998: 45–61). In one of Ferré's novels, an upper-class white woman, who represents the lady/danza music (more in the position of the author), encounters her own truth and her own self through the presence of the racialized other: the lower-class black woman representing the whore/plena music. Aparicio (56) notes that the white woman's desire to be like the whore may be a sign of racism, because she stereotypically views the racialized other *as* whore while ignoring her oppression.

The Use and Abuse of "Lo Africano"

Regarding the process described by Marrero and Aparicio, it is important to clarify, however, that what is considered "African" is not always interesting, exotic, and welcoming. (Indeed, simply getting to the point of considering something "African" or "African influenced" can be problematic or controversial.) According to Juan Flores (2000: 177–79), in the United States Puerto Rican literature in general has not been as good a "cultural capital" as

Cuban-American literature. I believe that this helps explain the fact that the African theme under the Puerto Rican experience has not enjoyed the popularity of the African theme under the Cuban or Cuban-American experience in literature and other media.

With great intention, white and especially *trigueño* and black Puerto Ricans on the mainland have used Africanness (*lo africano* or *africanidad*) to defend what I refer to as "Puerto Rican nationalism at the very bottom" and to protest against an Hispanophilic and/or Indian emphasis carried in the idea of Puerto Rican identity. When considering the use of black and/or African elements for affirmation and protest in general in the United States, one cannot ignore the common experience of Puerto Ricans and African-Americans with discrimination and hard socioeconomic conditions. This brings to mind Felipe Luciano's poem "Jíbaro My Pretty Nigger" and Roberto Angleró's song "Si Dios fuera negro" (If God were black), a song with which many Loízans identify. (The name of this song was also chosen as the title for the next chapter.) The song was written in response to the discrimination the composer, like other Puerto Ricans, especially *trigueño* or black Puerto Ricans, and also African-Americans, suffered while in the U.S. Air Force during the Korean War. In the last few decades, these common experiences have been vividly expressed in various types of social and political movements and in hip-hop and rap music. According to Juan Flores (2000: 82, 176), these common experiences and their significance for the Puerto Rican and the Latino identities are often denied or ignored in the literature about the Latino experience.

Somewhat relatedly, Carlos Flores recently (2001) brought up the issue of racism within the Latino community and the way it has been demonstrated in daily social interaction, in political and economic participation, and in the Hispanic media. He illustrated the latter with the publication of a pamphlet by Dr. Juan Andrade Jr., which invited the general public to attend the seventeenth annual conference of the United States Hispanic Leadership Institute, of which Andrade is the president and the founder. The image on the cover was supposed to represent the Latino/Hispanic community, but none of the twenty-four Latinos on the cover were black. These experiences on the mainland are important to note because even though they are influenced by experiences back home, in turn, they have an effect on the island.

I witnessed subtle stereotyping back home when I decided to study Loíza and its religion. Some Puerto Rican scholars and non-scholars suggested to me that the African or black theme in Puerto Rico was not as significant as in other Caribbean countries or the United States. Some indicated that placing too much emphasis on this theme gives too much credit to the North American influence. Others indicated that everything about Loíza had already been said, while others insinuated that just by choosing Loíza my study would be less scientific. Similar to common opinions about my mother's barrio, some comments established a correlation between Loíza's religious practices and its marginal economic status and high rate of crime and drug abuse. This is also similar to the correlation normally established between Haitian Vodou and Haiti's serious economic and political problems (Hurbon 2001: 121). The idea behind these comments seems to be that Loíza is an anomaly and that its religion is an irrational response to social dislocation (to paraphrase Spickard and Landres [2002: 7]). Also, relatives and friends cautioned me against study in Loíza out of concern for my spiritual safety. Consider, for instance, the comments: "Loíza is full of witches" and "Pentecostalism in Loíza is a masked Spiritism." Their cautions immediately transported me to the times when we church members were trained in evangelism in my mother's barrio.

At the beginning of my research I confirmed once more that these comments were not completely representative of the Loízan experience; indeed, the situation of the Loízans was more complex than the comments allowed. Many times I noticed a defensive attitude when I approached the subject of religious identity; some residents even showed a subtle or an exaggerated attitude of denial about Loízan identity in general. It did not take me long to realize that, for Loízans, clarifying Loízan religious identity was an important reason to participate in my research. One of the expressions that summarizes Loízans' defensive attitude and their need to clarify their real identity and which reveals the relationship between identity and religion is "no more witches."

"No More Witches?"

In Loíza, as in other towns, witchcraft is associated with an event or a behavior that involves supernatural powers (forces or energies). It is seen as something that cannot be explained naturally or logically. For this reason witchcraft is considered synonymous with belief in the intervention of (ancestor) spirits in human society. This perspective harks back to the beliefs of native Indians and of some Spanish arrivals, who practiced a Spanish folk Catholicism. Generally this event or behavior alters or disturbs the normal social order and is influenced by conscious and unconscious (or involuntary) human involvement. Ritual (or ritualized action) or envy are examples. During colonial times, these events were seen as clearly outside the Catholic institutional codes or standards. They were, therefore, considered to be direct attacks against the church as well as the colonial system the church both endorsed and was a part of. Church and political leaders accused each other of practicing or associating with witchcraft during times of disagreement or conflict (Romberg 2003: 34–35). In Loíza I learned of accusations of witchcraft among and between Catholic and Protestant lay leaders and members of different socioeconomic classes and skin color groups. Loízans, like other Puerto Ricans, generally believe that witchcraft influences events or people in two ways: by imitating what one wants to happen and by affecting a person by affecting something directly associated with him or her. One might expect that these two principles were also part of the religious systems of earlier inhabitants of the island.

As I will discuss in chapter 3, the coming of European Spiritism at the end of the nineteenth century brought about a public distinction between folk Spiritism and scientific Spiritism as well as a distinction between Spiritism in general and witchcraft in particular, although these practices have been mixed with Santería and other Afro-Caribbean religious elements. This has happened more openly in the last decades for reasons discussed in the chapters ahead. Loízans recognize that these beliefs have been mixed precisely because they have been distinguishable (at least to some extent). The persistence and mix of these religious traditions has caused the term "witchcraft" to continue to be used by Christians and non-Christians as a generic term for any non-Catholic and non-Protestant religious practice and as something anti-Christian, evil, or Satanic. Many Loízans agree that this generic and negative use of the term is more applicable to Loíza because of the town's strong African and/or black heritage, which, for a large number of Puerto Ricans, is a negative thing. This is the reason why many Loízans keep these practices secret and why "no more witches" is a common phrase in the town. I found that when a person mixes Spiritism and witchcraft, that person tends to call him- or herself a Spiritist. This is more because of witchcraft's negative connotation and less because Spiritism is considered to be a more coherent or structured religious system than witchcraft. This situation is similar to that of Las Cuevas's black residents who, when responding to a census, reject classification under the category of "black" and of Christians who reject classification under the category of "religion" (as discussed in following chapters).

In Loíza the actual practice of witchcraft has declined over the past decades owing to a stronger and more definite Catholic and Protestant campaign against it and to the advance of modernity and technology. Nevertheless, a sizeable number of Loízans do not keep their beliefs and their practices secret; in some instances, this is a sign of pride and a clear statement of protest. They have no qualms about mixing specific elements of witchcraft with Spiritism, Santería, astrology, the belief in extraterrestrial beings, and with the doctrines of Catholicism or even with Protestantism. Some individuals even take advantage of the marriage of modern technology and these practices. According to Loízans, some of them practice witchcraft genuinely and with good intentions, while others use it to increase their assets or to intimidate or frighten others (as was the case with gang members). In Loíza there are many people who do not adhere personally to witchcraft, but admit that it is real and effective. This is the case with several Pentecostals I spoke with to whom the Pentecostal message was first presented in a "black and white" way (as many of them say) and who continue to accept the truth of that message. About a similar Pentecostal attitude in Africa, Meyer (1994: 64) has argued that if Satan became the Lord of the known gods and ghosts, "It is in no way unique or surprising that, as a result of diabolization, Christians take the demons seriously."

It took me a while to understand that the use of the phrase "no more witches" is also intended to deemphasize the negative view of Loíza or to emphasize its positives. The phrase was used to describe a change in the Loízans' view: In the past anything negative or tragic (such as losing a job, a sudden death, or a serious conflict in the family) was usually attributed to witchcraft. However, over the years Loízans have become more aware of the many social causes behind their difficult reality, such as discrimination and a conformist attitude in many of them. Still, these two causes are used in combination to argue that inequality, uneven development, and materialism in general have brought about more bad intentions and jealousy or a lack of a sense of community and social commitment and subsequently more witchcraft (as a personal belief or as part of the outside reality). For some Loízans, thinking that greater social forces are responsible for everything in society without considering the role of the individual is as bad as attributing all the responsibility to witchcraft. Given these different attitudes, "witches" have become both a symbol of brainwashing or a lack of collective and individual consciousness and a symbol of awakening or alertness.

Thematic and Methodological Issues

At the beginning of my insertion into the Loízan community, I was convinced of the significant and strong relationship between religion and identity. I must confess, however, that before beginning the fieldwork I had decided to overlook that issue for fear of reducing religion to identity. I resented the overemphasis placed on the identity issue by Puerto Rican scholars and the elite (especially from the left) on the island and on the mainland. The latter, according to Juan Flores (2002: 52), have tended to defend Puerto Rican identity more passionately than Puerto Ricans on the island. I also considered the issue of identity to be esoteric and unpractical. Therefore I found myself with a great sense of responsibility: I had to avoid the trap of rescuing Loíza from its marginal position and from negative or false stereotypes, while also avoiding the trap of forcing the experience of Loíza (or what the town is supposed to represent) onto the entire Puerto Rican experience. I also accepted the challenge of not reducing Loízan religion to identity, while at the same time demonstrating the practical nature of identity.

This book is committed to providing an accurate, although not exhaustive, portrayal of Loízans' experience with identity. First, this book is really about my interpretation of Loízans' management of identity, even after I have made a conscientious effort to elucidate Loízans' own interpretations while trying to safeguard objectivism to the best of my abilities. It offers partial accounts because, as Davidman (2002: 19) reminds us, the (biographical) construction of identity inside and outside religion is an ongoing process. Also, some personal information has been altered or left out to avoid negative ramifications for the research participants. Here I must clarify that the main interviewees in this book were chosen because most of their personal experiences were known in the community. These participants had no concerns about making some of their personal details known publicly. Many of their experiences were similar to those of other members in the community. Nevertheless, I used false names (even though many participants requested I use their real names) in order to protect their privacy.

Moreover, this book's commitment to the most accurate portrayal possible of the Loízan experience comes with the theoretical framework previously discussed and twelve months of systematic fieldwork in Loíza, primarily in Las Cuevas, a community I chose because of its rural and urban characteristics, a better organization of households (which allowed me to look at space issues), strong family settlement patterns, a greater variety of incomes than in many other communities, and safer research conditions. However, Las Cuevas did not have as much religious variety as I had expected. Because of the element of secrecy in Santería and a prejudice toward its practice and toward Spiritism, I was initially confident that I would find a large number of devotees of these practices as I got deeper into the study and gained the participants' trust. I was expecting these findings to make my study more interesting. At the same time, I share concerns similar to Scherer's (2001: 164) about scholars ignoring Chinese identity and religion in Cuba. As a result, I want to respond particularly to a disproportionate obsession with Afro–Puerto Rican religion in Loíza and also to a tendency to limit black experience to the study of Afro-religions when a majority of Loízans practice various versions of Christianity (with some Afro-religious aspects).

2

"If God were black, my friend . . ."

Loízan African Identity in the Puerto Rican Experience
Here and There

Early in my fieldwork I saw that Loízans were trapped in stereotypes of themselves even more than I had envisioned. This chapter is devoted to understanding this "entrapment" by looking at the various ways Loízans manage identities, mainly outside the religious foci and under a variety of circumstances. One of the first things I realized in Loíza was that people there are accustomed to tourists and individuals who want to investigate their town because of its archaeological sites, unique historical roots, folklore, and cultural traditions. In Loíza, this understanding also has to do with the archaeological and historical research conducted in the area by the well-known Puerto Rican archaeologist Ricardo E. Alegría (mentioned earlier as the first director of the Institute of Puerto Rican Culture). Initially, the people of Loíza expected me to study the "usual." My affiliation with the discipline of anthropology worsened the situation because of a common misconception in Puerto Rico that anthropology is exclusively about archaeology or about the study of folklore and traditions. To obtain other kinds of information, I told them initially that the goal of my study was more like that of a social worker who investigates an individual's and a community's social, economic, ideological, and psychological condition. Sometimes to help people make more sense of my research, I explained my work as that of a historian. However, even these strategies were not enough for some individuals because neither social workers nor historians live in the communities they study or participate in everyday activities for a long period of time, as I did.

When I returned to the field in March of 1998, after having left in December of 1997 to pursue more funding in Ann Arbor, there were rumors that I was a police agent. One afternoon, I visited people in their homes as usual. This time Carlos, whom I will talk more about in the next chapter, responded hesitantly to my greeting, but he opened his gate and asked me to enter his house. As I approached him, I noticed signs of anger and disbelief on his face. He told me loudly that he hated hypocrites. Then he asked why I had deceived him after he had come to trust me. He told me that he had found out my real identity: police agent. His son and his friends had learned of my identity from the police itself. This experience reminded me that "while our 'presentation of self' is part of the field researcher's method and deserves to be reported, we cannot control the identities and roles that others impute to us" (McGuire 2002: 200).

At that point I realized I needed to contest that identity for my own safety and to be able to continue with my project. I told him he could verify my real identity, but he continued accusing me. Finally, Carlos's daughter allowed me to show her a family photo that included my parents. Carlos's daughter, a teacher, immediately recognized my father as her co-worker in the Head Start program in Carolina. As Carlos's wife said, "It was not chance but God's hand." A big change came over Carlos: he looked embarrassed and was almost without words. Carlos's daughter suggested that I stop the study in Loíza for my own safety while Carlos made sure that I understood his reaction and explained the reason for the rumors: right before I left Loíza for Ann Arbor in search of funding there was a drug raid in the neighborhood involving teenagers and young adults. Carlos also indicated that people had been deceived and taken advantage of by outsiders, including researchers. As I will discuss in the last section of the next chapter, his reaction was also influenced by the fact that many people think Loízans are stupid or ignorant.

Other members of the community expressed their disappointment and embarrassment for what happened. As the information spread beyond Las Cuevas, I heard expressions such as "this is why people think negatively about us [Loízans]." Many residents of Las Cuevas promised their protection and support for the project and after a while even those whom I learned later were my accusers seemed apologetic given the way they began to approach me. Soon I heard comments such as "Miss, let me know if you have any problem" and "Miss, we are here to serve you." My experience through the end of the project proved McGuire's (2002: 202) statement, based on personal experience in the field, that the researcher's vulnerability pays off in terms of bonding and commitment to the research. I sensed that the participation of new and repeat interviewees in the project, after the situation became known, was a direct response to this specific event. Many comments led me to believe that the new or renewed interest in participating in this research was the way the residents of Las Cuevas showed their "good" side or repaired their image. Still, some individuals remained suspicious of me throughout the project.

The aforementioned experience made me aware of the error of not reaching out to the teenagers and young adults. They spread the rumors about me first. Looking back with fresh eyes, I am almost certain that I dismissed them because I felt intimidated around them. Although I did not really know them I considered them to be lazy, disrespectful, suspicious, and even aggressive. Later, I was proved wrong by some of these young people: every now and then I found one of them waiting in the streets to be called for manual work (to get money for his household's basic needs) or a few of them discussing relevant issues in a critical and positive manner, and I was given the chance to interview them after they had determined my sincerity.

Countless hours of conversations and different interactions alerted me to the various ways individuals, consciously or not, manage identities for different reasons and under various circumstances. As I approached, I found myself moving back and forth between identities, making it difficult at times to articulate the ideas in my head in any coherent manner. In Las Cuevas negative stereotypes such as laziness, conformist attitude, dependency mentality, backwardness, isolation, poor education, lack of trust, a high crime rate, and drug abuse were used at the very beginning of my insertion into the community to scare me in order to test my motives. A few of Loíza's municipal workers cautioned me about where to walk and what to eat when I visited people. Without denying their good intentions, I was convinced that they were concerned that a wrong doing to me would bring bad publicity to the town. They did not expect me to stay in the area or develop close ties in the community.

Similar to the Hispanic marketing strategy of alternately emphasizing differences and similarities among the Latino community in the United States (Dávila 2001: 41–42), Loízans pointed out differences and similarities, both negative and positive, as a form of self-criticism and self-acceptance, as well as a means to justify conflictive situations. I heard residents of Las Cuevas making fun of the style of speech and the superstitious and backward mentality of the people from the barrio of Medianía Alta. The people of Las Cuevas described them as very black and associated them more with Santería than with Spiritism for reasons I will explain later. Because of these characteristics, some residents of Las Cuevas blamed them for the slow development and difficult spiritual and social situation of the whole town.

At first I listened politely but disinterestedly to experiences of prejudice against whites. My attitude changed when I heard three white residents of Las Cuevas raise the issue vividly. They remembered being rejected immediately after moving to Las Cuevas decades ago and being criticized for marrying black women from the neighborhood. They described their experiences in the community and within the family as "very difficult," a description that is be consistent with Burdick's (1998: 43) reaction to the common idea that Brazil's family is the arena of racial democracy. These white residents also remembered neighbors making fun of any white person who visited the area. Some of the white visitors were local politicians and actors who came for a *trabajito* (a spiritual favor). North Americans (which they mostly referred to as *americanos* or *yanquis*) also visited the town as federal officials and as tourists. While doing the census one day, my assistants and I walked near a group of teenagers and young adults. Some of them were whispering to each other while looking especially at one of my assistants, who is white, almost blond, and green eyed. She became the subject of these teenagers' (and some elders') fascination and curiosity as they thought she was North American, when she is really Puerto Rican. I also experienced this ambiguity toward my person in my mother's barrio and in Las Cuevas, which was exemplified when some residents referred to me as "la muchacha blanquita" (the [diminutive] white girl).

Conflicts among teenagers involved in sports and gangs in Las Cuevas have related to community origins and skin color. Similar to what I witnessed in my middle school back in the early 1980s, in Las Cuevas boys confronted each other verbally and physically, addressing openly their community origins. Among girls, conflicts related to physical appearance tended to be more common but were manifested in a subtle manner, as in an exaggerated way of touching and combing the hair to mark differences in hair texture and by pointing out differences in body odor (because of the idea that black girls and boys tend to have bad body odor). I witnessed conflicts between the children of Las Cuevas and other neighborhoods in which references were made to their community origins. There were fights among children from different areas of Loíza during children's Friday night activities at the Heavenly Doors Evangelical Church (the first Pentecostal church founded in Las Cuevas). The situation seemed so out of control that I offered to put the pastor in touch with a group from my former church that addresses the issue of fighting through puppetry. Additionally, in the school where Mildred, a resident of Las Cuevas, was teaching, the children of Las Cuevas called the children of Piñones, in the very northern coastal area, "piñoneros" in a negative way. The children of Las Cuevas thought of themselves as better and lighter than the kids from Piñones. This caused Mildred to ask her students to bring to class information about their grandparents' places of origin. To their surprise, some of their grandparents and parents were originally from Piñones. After the homework assignment, Mildred noticed some changes in her students' attitudes, at least in her classroom.

It became less likely that these conflicts were a recent thing. For example, fights broke out among the children from various Loízan communities while they were participating in a Christian children's ministry that began more than twenty years ago. This ministry, which was well known in the area, had been under the direction of a North American missionary couple (he was a retired physician and she a retired Navy official). At the beginning of their ministry in Loíza they were highly criticized by many Pentecostals, who, for example, pointed out the fact that the missionaries wear shorts. The missionaries and their local crew tried to stop the fights between children and between teenagers through community activities, games, Christian songs, and Christian literature about God's love and loving one another, although the couple told me the situation was not as bad in the past as it is now. (At the time of my field study the missionaries were preparing to return to the United States, both as an expression of their understanding of God's will and for reasons of safety. It was painful for them to admit that they were afraid of becoming victims of a major crime committed by one of the children they had helped in the past. Indeed, they had been robbed on various occasions.)

Many Loízans quite often associated the lack of respect, discipline, and morals with young adults and teenagers and attributed these characteristics to the influences from outside Loíza. I often heard expressions that indicated that Loíza keeps itself distant or even separated from the rest of Puerto Rico. According to the two priests of Loíza, this explains in part why some parishioners do not want to participate in church activities outside Loíza. Many individuals pointed out the hospitality and sense of community that still exist in Loíza, which they contrasted with the selfish and individualistic mentality in many parts of Puerto Rico. Loíza's *a lo natural* lifestyle was contrasted with the polluted air, many cement buildings, and a preference for "artificial" food outside Loíza. However, the residents of Las Cuevas, especially the elders, stressed the negative characteristics of Loíza to illustrate how things have changed. A good number of them indicated that Loíza had been contaminated by modernism and *libertinaje* (extremist liberal behavior) and established a correlation between Loíza, the past, and a *sana* lifestyle (one that is morally healthy or innocent). Some of them associated this *sana* lifestyle with a religious common ground, although they admitted that they did not think deeply or appreciatively of religion's role when they were young and when they first became born-again Christians.

Federico, who was ninety-three years old when I met him, said that the new laws and government systems are contributing to *libertinaje* and crime. According to Don Federico, parents cannot discipline their kids because of the fear that the state will punish them and will take their kids away from them. Every time I visited Don Federico it was a struggle to get inside his house because of the moldy old bars he had on his windows and doors that were hard to open. Many cement and wooden homes in Las Cuevas have bars to protect them against robbers and other criminals, whom residents normally think are young people from Loíza itself. Some residents install bars on the inside of the house fearing the bars themselves would be stolen. Don Federico told me that in the past you could leave your house unlocked and with the front door open and that you really knew your neighbors. "We all lived like God's family," he said.

"The beautiful faces of my black people": Contesting a Racialized Otherness

I found in Las Cuevas an extensive vocabulary of racial and/or color terms, even in the same household (as in many Puerto Rican households), many of which referred to other physical features besides color. In addition, there were instances in which some lighted-skinned participants identified themselves, collectively, as black or as Loízan black with words such as "We Loízan blacks." It is important to point out that since colonial times in Puerto Rico as in other Latin American countries, such as Nicaragua (Olien 1980), there have been social factors that have contributed to the fluidity of racial classifications. Additionally, my experience in Las Cuevas was similar to Duany's recent research experience (2002: 236) in barrio Gandúl in San Juan, Godreau-Santiago's (1999) in Ponce, and Kottak's (1992: 68–69) in Arembepe, Brazil. In Las Cuevas, my assistants and I asked participants about their color, which many considered to be synonymous with race. A few indicated they were from the black race (instead of the African race), but refused to classify themselves as black. Others indicated that although their color was black they could not say they were completely from the black race because they had some white and Indian blood. I consider their classifications to be primary, even after considering Burdick's (1998: 17) caution of having long lists of color terminology. According to his experience in Brazil, the terms individuals use most consistently are the terms by which they classify themselves; the terms they use less consistently serve as secondary or complimentary classifications.

The residents of Las Cuevas utilized color classifications inconsistently, sometimes during the same conversation. However, I was able to confirm most of these terminologies a second or third time during the same conversation. I do not want to ignore completely Burdick's call for caution, but neither do I want to ignore the need of Las Cuevas's residents to use a given terminology during a certain interaction. Of course, one may expect these classifications to be secondary if the standard is one of the few classifications used in the U.S. census. Having said all of this, the most common primary classifications found in Las Cuevas, from 603 participants, were *trigueño,* which refers to a mix of black and white that is more on the darker side (mentioned 342 times), *negro* or black (mentioned 147 times), *blanquita* (a diminutive form of white mentioned 12 times), and *jabao,* which refers to a person who has light skin and black people's features (mentioned 7 times). Other primary classifications were *prieto, claro, clarito, trigueñito, grifo, prieto-moreno, negrito, negro-jabao, indio, blanco-trigueño, trigueño-jabao, negro-trigueño, trigueño o negro, amarillo, marrón, colorao, de los indios, entre blanco y negro, moreno de Piñones, negro-mulato, más oscuro, ni blanco ni prieto, natural, de color, chocolate,* and *mestizo.*

Moreover, while answering the question of color, participants used expressions that were in agreement with Guerra's (1998: 233) observation that different expressions represent different strategies, some of them contradictory or subliminal, for enforcing allegiance to racial/social hierarchies. Most of the participants who used these expressions were women, which parallels Johnson's (1998: 430) experience growing up in the United States, where the women of his family, contrary to the men, lived in a state of denial of their Mexican identity while exaggerating their Spanish heritage. However, contrary to Blanco's (1975 [1942]: 64) statement that prejudice is more notable in women than in men, I would not equate this obviously manifested attitude with prejudice. In fact, I found Loízan women with this kind of attitude showing great affection to "racialized" others within the Loízan orbit, even more so than their men who did not verbally manifest a prejudiced attitude.

For instance, according to Guerra (1998: 236), Puerto Ricans make statements among themselves to excuse or explain the fact that a person might be educated, kind, or well mannered as well as black. She asserts that the point of these sayings is that some people of predominantly black ancestry defy expectations by being morally good despite the "handicap" that their physiognomy presents. Accordingly, the residents of Las Cuevas used expressions such as the following: "I am a negra de caché" (sophisticated); "I am negra but beautiful."As was the case when I was growing up, in Las Cuevas I wondered why in many instances the words *trigueño, moreno,* and *de color* were substituted for the word *negro* when I understood *negro* to be applicable or even the most appropriate word. This is evident in expressions such as "I am trigueña, the same as negra, but I would rather say trigueña" and "I am trigueñita; black sounds ugly."[1] In the last expression, the use of the diminutive "ita" doubles the sense of closeness and kindness and softens the action of saying the words "negra" and "trigueña." The following expressions also show a kind of softening through ambiguity: "I am trigueño? You tell me . . ."; "I do not know . . . I guess I'd better say trigueñita." Another expression indicates less of a softening and more of an acceptance: The statement "I am negro and I cannot help it" gives the impression that being black is bad luck.

In Puerto Rico a fluid system of classification is not indicative of a lack of prejudice against blacks and other "racialized others" (Kinsbruner 1996), such as Dominicans (Duany 2002: 20, 246). Thus, Kottak's (1992: 68–69) argument that a variety of racial classifications is due to the minimal significance of racial differences in establishing social differences becomes problematic, even when he is referring to the situation in Brazil, as opposed to the situation in the United States. Taking together the above findings—Loízans' apparent denial of their blackness, Guerra's idea that the referred language expressions are strategies for enforcing allegiance to racial/social hierarchies, and the fact that these expressions come from Loízans themselves—makes it easy to conclude that Loízans are in complicity with a racial/social hierarchical system that is so internalized that it has become natural or standard. Such complicity seems to be related to my experience of hearing black people, including relatives from my mother's side of the family, making jokes about blacks. At the time, I thought that this was a way to separate themselves from other "real" black people, as they saw themselves as less black. But according to Santos Febres (1998), these jokes are something more: they are a source of empowerment and agency because blacks joking about other blacks is based on the idea that black people should laugh at themselves before white people do. Here I want to add the fact that entertainment has been one of the most important avenues for blacks to improve their economic and social status in the long run. This function of entertainment can occur momentarily, as when during one of my visits some elders of Las Cuevas, in a manner similar to that of my grandfather, took center stage by telling the rest of us jokes about blacks.

Following Santos Febres's line of thought, I propose that a fluid system of color classifications and the language expressions referred to above are a significant way for many Loízans to protest a general view of themselves as the "racialized other" (using Dávila's [2001: 210] term). These classifications and language expressions are a creative form of contesting the existence of a social/racial hierarchy: by playing with it, laughing about it, altering it, and best of all, by reappropriating the very act of classifying themselves. They are also a way of detaching a nomenclature from the essence of a person. At the same time, I take seriously Santos Febres's position that blacks should not use these hidden avenues of agency and empowerment, but should show clearly their indignation instead. A third way also presented itself in Las Cuevas, wherein I found a "more affirmative" attitude in the following expressions: "Write it there: I am N-E-G-R-A" (the speaker spelled the word *negra* aloud); "I am a very proud trigueña"; "No matter who likes it or not, we are black and that's it!"

However, many of my interactions with the people of Loíza confirmed my initial thought that there was not a strict correlation between these apparent more "affirmative" verbal expressions and active involvement against discrimination based on color and cultural ancestry. Given the lack of correlation, one has no alternative but to question the meaning of "hidden" and "affirmative" and, more importantly, to place Loízans' racial approach in a larger sociohistorical framework in order to confirm it, as do the studies by Williams (1972: 291, 334–35) and Díaz Soler (1965). The next section touches briefly upon Loíza's situation in order to clarify the social/racial restrictions that exist despite a fluid social/racial classificatory system. This exploration will help explain a common phrase in Loíza: "It is one thing to be black in Puerto Rico and another to be a Puerto Rican black from Loíza."

Competing Taíno and African Heritages

One of the first things I learned when I arrived in Las Cuevas, which means "the caves," is the actual existence of caves in the area. Today these caves make up a public recreational and tourist spot, although during my field study the area was in bad shape. According to historical accounts and to archaeological research conducted by Alegría, part of the area of Las Cuevas included an Arawak Indian settlement at the time of colonization. Indeed, residents of Las Cuevas used this information with much pride to probe their Indian heritage. Immediately, I thought the residents of Las Cuevas took such pride in their Indian heritage because they held a romantic view of Indians, as do many other Puerto Ricans(Duany 2002: 261–80). This has been the case in other Caribbean countries, such as Guyana (Moore 1999) and eastern Nicaragua and Honduras (Helms 1977). I also thought about the need of the people of Las Cuevas to feel better than other Loízans, such as the people of Medianía Alta, whom the residents of Las Cuevas described as being very influenced by or more attached to the African traditions.

Later, I realized that this identification with Indian heritage also belied a need to compete with Canóvanas, a town that derived from Loíza in 1971. The separation was approved under the PPD administration and followed the recommendations of the governor's Junta de Planificación or JP (Planning Committee). The JP assigned fewer funds and less land to Loíza than to Canóvanas, despite the larger population and greater needs of the former. These developments gave Loíza a lower financial status than any other town in Puerto Rico, except the small and almost completely uninhabited island of Culebra. Loízans ended up accepting these conditions because of the state government's promise of aid, Canóvanas's promise of a gradual separation, and the future possibility of a strong tourism industry. The JP seemed to justify these changes by using a description of Canóvanas and Loíza, part of which was allegedly based on the opinions of their residents. Canóvanas was described as more economically developed and geographically closer to the metropolitan area. The people of Canóvanas were characterized as self-sufficient, distant from traditions, independent, practical, less subordinated to the social group, and puritanical. Canóvanas's socioeconomic progress was associated with the faster growth of Protestantism in the area since the beginning of the century. In contrast, Loízans were described as subordinated to the social group (which is cohesive, integrated, homogeneous, and isolated) and inclined to a bohemian lifestyle, use of alcohol, carnal pleasures, and free love (Puerto Rico, Estado Libre Asociado, Junta de Planificación 1968: 21–26). Here is a clear example of what Kipp (1993: 6, 19) argues: that identities take form through a conceptual process of contrast that marks differences as well as hierarchies of value and power.

Similar to Brow's (1996) findings about the development of negative opinions between two rural communities in Sri Lanka because of the uneven effects of development, the difficulties suffered by Loízans before 1971 (while the barrio of Canóvanas was enjoying economic prosperity) and the terrible situation brought about by the separation from Canóvanas exacerbated the tensions between Loíza and Canóvanas. As explained by a resident of Las Cuevas, the people of Canóvanas have thought of themselves as "blanquitos" (here the diminutive form of "white" is used sarcastically) because they have had more white residents than Loíza, although the vast majority of Canóvanas's residents are not white. According to this resident, the people of Canóvanas have also thought of themselves as better than Loízans. According to many elders, this has been the case since they were young, when at dance parties there was one dance area for the people of Canóvanas and another area for the people of Loíza. This sense of superiority is given as the explanation for why the people of Canóvanas have appropriated the Indian identity as if they were the only ones with Indian ancestry. At the main entrance of the town of Canóvanas there is a big statue of an Indian couple and the people of Canóvanas commonly refer to themselves as the Indians of Canóvanas, although I knew residents from Canóvanas who did not identify with the Indian heritage. Referring to the people of Canóvanas, another resident from Las Cuevas made the following comment: "They want to blacken us so much that they forget our Indian heritage." This resident, like many others, indicated that an awareness of the Indian heritage was old in Loíza. A poem written by Stevens (1902: 4), in which she described Loízan children at the beginning of the twentieth century playing that they were Indians indicates that children knew about Indians. The author said that they wore crowns on their heads or flame-tree blossoms and the tallest child carried a whip.

Stevens-Arroyo has used psychological premises to substantiate the argument of a persistent Taíno influence in contemporary Puerto Rican religion, although he uses historical evidence as his point of departure and as the basis for his statement. At the same time, he has indicated that Taíno beliefs in Puerto Rico "have been identified with African religion so as to obscure for the unwary their origins in Taíno belief" (1995: 131). This statement may conflict with my earlier reference to the fact that for many decades there was greater significance given to the Taíno Indian component than to the African component of national culture. However, it is one thing to demonstrate and give great significance to the Taíno presence in Puerto Rican history and another to demonstrate its influence on various aspects of contemporary Puerto Rican life, at both the conscious and the unconscious levels. Following Stevens-Arroyo's analysis, there can be agreement about an unconscious persistence of the Indian influence in contemporary Loíza and an understanding that we must wait for future research to confirm this with systematic data. What is clear is that in Loíza, and in Las Cuevas in particular, there has been an effort to claim the Indian heritage. This is in response to the residents' belief in an attempt to deny or ignore the Loízan Indian heritage and to overemphasize the African component as a negative thing. At the same time, residents resent the fact that some people think that Loízans still live in *bohíos* like the Indians did in the past. Every now and then I encountered a Loízan who did not like it when people referred to Loíza as "Loíza Aldea" (literally meaning "village Loíza") because of a common association of the word "village" with a primitive or backward lifestyle.

Consistent with this affirmation of Indian genealogy, Indianness was literally represented in Las Cuevas's *comparsa* (community parade) during the festival of Santiago Apóstol, which originated in Medianía Alta. As usual, the children were dressed up like "real" Indians, representing the Indian innocence and the Indian spiritual role mentioned above.[2] Africanness was also represented, but (as in other parades) in a broader, more folkloric, and symbolic way. Such representation was accomplished by dressing up like the ritual characters of the festival. The *caballero* (gentleman) represents the warrior saint and wears a mask with Spanish facial characteristics; his clothing is very colorful, which to many represents the African element. The *vejigante* represents the evil force that Santiago has to fight; it wears a colorful three-horned coconut-husk mask and a brightly colored bat-like costume. (The name comes from the *vejiga*, which is an inflated cow or goat stomach used by these characters to scare people.) The *viejo* (old man) and the *loca* (crazy woman) are additional participating characters. This type of representation of the African identity in the festival of Santiago supports Dávila's (1997: 93) statement that Loíza is regarded as the embodiment of Puerto Rico's African tradition in its most folkloric version. This treatment of the African or black component in a way that is not related to the crude reality of slavery is reminiscent of the reluctance of many Loízans to talk about slavery and Dávila's

(2001: 121) observation about the Hispanic marketing and advertisement agencies' view of black Latinas as not representative of generic *Latinidad*.

Nevertheless, in his analysis of the festival of Santiago Apóstol, Zaragoza (1995: 55–56) points to the great social, political, and psychological potential in the symbolic and folkloric character (which he describes as ambivalent and liminal) of the festivals' ritual figures or "clowns," as they generally stand apart from the main figure of Santiago. According to Zaragoza, the symbolic and folkloric character of these ritual clowns allows Loízans to maneuver their interpretations in order to make them closer to their day-to-day reality. Zaragoza (108) elaborates this point further when he argues that *locas* and *viejos* reiterate the tension between the *caballero* and the *vejigante* but at the more domestic level.

Samuel Lind, a well-known Loízan artist, recently commented that Loízans have identified with Santiago or the *caballero* as the warrior of their cause, especially since the end of the nineteenth century. He made this comment in a recent music video entitled *Raíces* (2001), one of a series of annual musical productions that began in 1993 and which was dedicated for the first time to the rhythms of bomba and plena.[3] Alegría (1954), however, has stated that the devotion to Santiago Apóstol, who is portrayed as a warrior, goes back to the fights between the Spanish and the Arabs or Moors. In fact, in the parish of Santiago Apóstol there is a large mural of Santiago with his sword on his horse fighting a Moor. This devotion to Santiago has also been related to the fights between the Spanish and the Indians and Africans and between settlers and Carib Indians from neighboring islands. All of these experiences of the past are retold during the festival in honor of Santiago.

More precisely, Zaragoza (1995: 42) has argued that the strong devotion to Santiago Apóstol in Loíza had to do with an attitude of resistance and protest against the state and the church that went back to the times when festivities among slaves, both free and fugitive, were regulated. Slave owners thought such festivities were opportunities for planning rebellions: the revelries had to be visible to the slave owner, sexes had to be separated, alcohol was prohibited, free blacks could not speak to slaves, and there was a reward for slaves who informed about a conspiracy. Favoring Santiago Apóstol over Saint Patrick, who for centuries had been the official patron saint of Loíza and whose celebration fell within the Lent season when nothing else was supposed to be celebrated, is by itself a protest against the social and religious hierarchies. This is even more the case when considering the connections established by some Loízans (some of whom are strong devotees of Santiago) between this saint and the deities of Changó and Ogun from the religion of Santería. These were spread by Cuban migrants and then by local residents from the area of San Juan. In addition, could it be a coincidence that Santiago is one of the most important personified deities (as the warrior Ogou) in Haitian Vodou, which is believed to be closer to its African roots than most other forms of New World African religion (see McCarthy-Brown 1991: 93–139)? Here it is worth noting the number of Haitians who have moved to Loíza in the last few decades and the Haitian migration that happened centuries ago. Here it would be good to ask: Is the devotion to Saint Santiago simply a means to an end—the affirmation Loízan (or Loízan-African) identity—or part of the end itself?

According to Samuel Lind's interview in the video *Raíces* and many other town residents, Loízans have identified even more strongly with *vejigantes,* who really represent the free spirit of African roots that needs to be expressed, unhindered, even when these African roots are not readily identified. In fact, the term "African" is often used abstractly to mean a tradition or practice that is obscure, unknown, or unofficial. At the same time, when I asked Loízans to define the word "African" many of them mentioned their black color, their beliefs in different deities with different personalities, their taste for loud and rhythmic music that includes the use of drums, their taste for bright colors, and so forth. Some mentioned specific language expressions, words, food, and personality traits such as spontaneity, a close connection with nature, and a highly sociable personality. Some Loízans seemed reluctant to connect the Puerto Rican African experience with Africa itself, as if to say that whatever is African began when African slaves arrived on the island. However, the search for Africanness rooted in Africa and Africanness that developed on the island continues to be relevant to a good number of Loízans, such as Samuel Lind. The latter view clearly opposes Duany's (1998: 184) opinion that scholars should abandon the search for African roots in the popular religion of the island. Mention should be made here of the association, whether or not all Loízans acknowledge it, of *vejigantes* with the figure of *mojiganga* of the medieval Spanish carnivals. (Quintero Rivera [1998: 15] also mentions this association in his essay on the psychosociological significance of saints.) I encountered a few Loízans who acknowledged the Spanish influence in the festival and in Loíza in general, even though they all agreed it is not as obvious as the African influence. A few of these individuals vacillated between the Spanish, the Indian, and the African identities when I asked them which one was the most significant in the festivity. All of the factors mentioned above led me to believe that what really makes the festival in general and the figure of the *vejigante* in particular so significant is their summarizing symbolic powers. According to Ortner (2002: 161), "summarizing" symbols (as opposed to "elaborating" symbols) are seen as summing up, expressing, representing for the participants in an emotionally powerful and relatively undifferentiated way what the system means to them. This undifferentiated way of summarizing symbols opens space for the ambivalent or the liminal and for identity creativity.

Samuel Lind was born in Mediania Alta, across the street from the property of the Ayalas, an extended family known for its business making *vejigante* ensembles and other local crafts and also for the famous group of bomba called Balet Folklórico de los Hermanos Ayala. Samuel told me during a meeting in his art studio that he also likes to emphasize the three components of Puerto Rican culture because emphasizing the African elements in conjunction with the triad has been shown to be more effective than highlighting African elements alone (Dávila 1997: 71). This strategy not only benefits his work but also the festival of Santiago Apóstol because his art is exposed during the festival in exhibitions and in the festival's brochure and program.

"Loíza, the capital of tradition": Culture Sells at a High Price

As previously indicated, Puerto Rico is a good example of the success of exploiting national culture for economic gain. The successful selling of folklore during the 1970s is part of the folklorization of culture, including folk religion, that began at this time. The media and the ICP played significant roles in this process (Dávila 1997: 64–69), which was spurred on by an economic recession during the 1970s. Especially since this time, informal economic activities, including those related to the country's folklore, have become a means of survival (Scarano 1993: 815–16). An article in *El Mundo* (July 13, 1968, 1, 3, and 5), the most important newspaper at the time, highlighted Loíza's folklore and credited it as a source of pride for the town's people as well as an important means of survival for Loízan families.

This emphasis on the town's uniquely African traditions in the last several years has much to do with the municipal government's interest in promoting the idea that Loíza is "the capital of tradition" (the words on the town's logo) to encourage a tourism industry and to improve the town's socioeconomic situation. The festival of Santiago Apóstol is seen as greatly serving this purpose. Neighboring coastal towns are moving fast to advance tourism, using nature (the beach) as the main attraction in restricted and very secluded areas. Famous foreign personalities, including actors, have bought property in these areas. Loíza is trying to market both open and restricted nature tourism and especially its folklore. Towns such as Ponce, with a significant black population, have events and activities with characteristics similar to Loíza's folklore; however, they are not attributed to the town as a whole as is the case with Loíza. Accordingly, at Loíza's main entrance there is a big welcome sign with a *vejigante* mask. In spite of the fact that *vejigante* represents the evil force that Santiago has to fight against, it has become representative of the festival and a national and international symbol, as is evident in a good number of websites. The festival, which is also known as the festival of the *vejigantes* and which today competes, with the Carnival of Ponce (a celebration of the Afro-Puerto Rican traditions in this town) and El Gran Bombazo in San Juan (a celebration of the Afro-Rican rhythms of bomba and plena), has gone from three to ten days, while attracting national and international tourism (although more national than international). In the last few years, the festival has received much attention by local and international media (including the Discovery Channel and the program *Caminante* on the Hispanic channel Galavision).[4] It counts on the financial support of local and international business and requires a complex team to coordinate various shows, competitions, pageants such as Miss Piel Canela (Miss Cinnamon Skin), marathons, caravans, and parades representing different communities.

The festival of Santiago encourages broad-based support by including one day that is dedicated to Loízan absentees, or those Loízans who no longer live in the town. This is an important strategy given the fact that a significant number of Loíza-born professionals have left Loíza.[5] Along the same lines is the idea of "friends of Loíza," which mainly refers to non-Loízan residents who participate in activities related to the town. They are recruited before events and activities and given credit during these events and activities. In general, some residents participate in the festival of Santiago directly while others prefer to watch the parades from their balconies, accompanied by relatives and visitors for the occasion. Many church members, some of whom adamantly oppose the festival, use the occasion to pray and fast. These Loízans are convinced of a relationship between African traditions and evil forces.

They are also concerned about the many acts of violence related to the festival. (The year I was in Loíza the festival was safer in comparison to previous festivals because of some precautionary measures taken by the municipality, such as the registration of individuals who were going to use costumes and an intensive program of police patrolling in the community at large. In contrast, there were at least five deaths related to the festival in 2003. In any case, intensive police patrolling has become routine in Loíza. During my fieldwork I got used to seeing the police make stops to check for illegal guns, speeding, and alcohol abuse and to a strong security system they put in place during weekends on the main roads of Loíza. Most Loízans agree with the use of an aggressive police security system, but some are concerned that too many policemen gives an exaggerated impression that the town is not a safe place.) In addition, a group of people, mainly Catholics, would like the festival to continue, but with a serious and spiritual tone, even though the fact that the festival is a traditional celebration without spiritual overtones allows many people to participate. Most Loízans, however, agree that Loízan heritage and tradition is something that deserves to be celebrated and preserved and that the festival of Santiago Apóstol helps this purpose to a great extent.

The festival of Santiago is not the only event in Loíza that faces contention. The town's development efforts in general continue to confront opposition. This ongoing opposition is more about what course Loíza's development should take and who gets to control it. Constructing tourism facilities in the area of Loíza has led to the opposition of environmentalists, such as the group Misión Industrial (originally ascribed to the Episcopal Church), which some Loízans, especially from the organization Emancipación de Loíza (Emancipation of Loíza) and the mayor himself, have referred to as racist. These environmentalists have also been accused of brainwashing the minds of many well-intentioned Loízans in the name of the environment. Emancipación de Loíza and the mayor's office have even denounced the efforts of the Association of Piñones Residents against development. The area of Piñones is well known for it beach and its kiosks, which are small and rustic stores that sell traditional Puerto Rican dishes and are the residents' means of survival. Emancipación de Loíza has sustained its accusation of racism against the state government with the fact that Loíza, unlike any other town on the island, is submitted to a profound investigation by the legislative committee every time it is going to do a development project. Here it is relevant to note that Emancipación de Loíza is composed of professional, nonresident, and white individuals and that this opposition has been largely covered by the local media.[6] Mayor Ferdín Carrasquillo told me in one of our interviews at his office that he does not want Loíza to encounter problems similar to those in Africa, where there are many natural resources but people are starving. (I found interesting this seemingly sarcastic comparison of Loíza with Africa.) Along the same lines, those who want to preserve the town as a museum of African tradition have been accused of a racism mixed with a condescending attitude.

This is not the first time that the issue of racism has been associated with Loíza's slow development. During the process of separation of Loíza and Canóvanas (the late 1960s to early 1970s), Loíza, which was receiving the media's attention, had the advocacy of the Partido Nuevo Progresista (New Progressive Party or PNP). This advocacy was seen as opposing the support of the PPD for Canóvanas, which leads us back to earlier decades when the majority of the people of Canóvanas favored the Republican Party and the majority of Loízans, like many blacks and mulattos on the island (López Sierra 1994: 71), voted for the Socialist Party. At the time, the PNP was a new party; it, even more than the pro-independence and Socialist parties, quickly became the greatest challenge to the PPD, which was in power. The pro-statehood stand exemplified by the PNP had been popular since decades earlier. Over time it has gone by different names, including Partido Estadista Republicano (Statehood Republican Party or PER). The pro-independence stand also went through a few transformations and during the 1950s it suffered a major division between the PIP and the Movimiento pro Independencia (Pro-Independence Movement or MPI). The latter joined in a radical anti-colonial effort with the Federación de Universitarios pro Independencia (Pro-Independence University Federation or FUPI), which was founded in 1956.

The PNP's advocacy of Loízans' interest represented a critical step toward identifying with a marginal sector of Puerto Rico on the basis of color and ethnic background. The party's use of the concept of "jíbaro statehood" shows that the leadership of the PNP also tried hard to be inclusive because the figure of the *jíbaro* was supposed to represent the Puerto Rican people. Many individuals from the barrio where my mother grew up became members of the PNP during the 1970s, as the party not only embraced the black community but also presumably opened the doors for black leadership. The PNP's attention to the issue of color was apparently demonstrated by its support of a permanent association with the United States, a nation that had embraced the fight against slavery and discrimination and for civil rights. However, as many Loízans clarified for me, the majority of Loíza's votes for the PNP over the decades have not automatically translated into a support for the pro-statehood status. In fact, I found the scene to be somewhat complicated when I learned that a few residents favored Puerto Rico's independence but voted for a PNP or a PPD candidate. Other residents indicated that they were from the left, but that they did not completely favor the pro-independence choice and the elite interests of the party's leaders. In these cases, being on the left was a way to critique broadly the Puerto Rican sociopolitical system. Many Loízans, like many Puerto Ricans today, made the distinction between ideals and pragmatism. In relation, some Loízans expressed their views along these lines: "Loízans, more than anybody, know very well the importance of this distinction." It was something Loízans learned the hard way because when they wanted their independence from Canóvanas decades ago they were unable to develop a plan about how to deal with the transition. Many Loízans believe they are still suffering the consequences of this development. Often I heard Loízans saying that this experience is an important lesson that should be applied to the situation of the country in general.

After the separation of Canóvanas and Loíza, Gabriel Santos, the first Loízan mayor from the PNP, fired a series of accusations against the PPD that charged party members with racism against his town.[7] The latest accusations came during a program of cultural revival sponsored by the PPD as one of the party's new strategies to combat the victory of the PNP in the early 1970s. This cultural revival brought about a dramatic increase in funding for cultural activities, although according Dávila (1997: 53–54) only a few of these actually promoted African and black themes. In addition, during Puerto Rico's preparation for the 1992 quincentennial of the "discovery" of Puerto Rico, the PPD administration and especially Governor Rafael Hernández Colón emphasized the Spanish tradition and the country's relationship with Spain through activities, exchanges, and highly publicized official visits to that country (Dávila 1997: 48–49). Could it be a coincidence that 1992 was the last year of the PPD in power?

Since the 1990s, Mayor Ferdín's PNP administration of Loíza has aggressively tried to promote the selling of Loízan folklore, taking advantage of an increased popularization and exotization of the Afro-Caribbean element on the island in its modern and folkloric forms. One of the big signs of the recognition of the modern Afro-Rican component of Puerto Rican culture is the declaration of March 23 as salsa day, with the sponsorship of the ICP. Salsa is officially recognized as having been influenced greatly by African elements. Other signs of recognition involve the advertising and publicity industries. Over the years (with ups and downs) more ads are including folk Afro-Rican elements, such as those of Budweiser, which have included symbols of the festival of Santiago Apóstol (Dávila 1997: 184). Another more recent case involves my meeting with Laura Meléndez, the director of Loíza's cultural center. The meeting came about through my cousin, who in 1997 was working for the advertising agency Corporate Communications, Inc. The company had been hired by San Patricio Plaza Mall in Guaynabo, a well-known town where many white middle- and upper-class Puerto Ricans live. The company was contracted to organize an exhibition of masks from African-themed parades representing different towns in Puerto Rico, including Loíza, to attract clients. This promoting of Loízan culture, I believe, is a departure from a previous administration's method of accusing the opposite party of racism in order to secure attention and funding. As the mayor told me once at his office while pointing with his eyes to a large picture of Governor Pedro Roselló of the PNP: "Loíza cannot continue playing the old victim role. It must move forward now that the PNP administration is back in power and is willing to help." The situation is more complex, however, because as racism has become more of a public issue and as the private sector has gotten more involved in the country's public affairs, owing in great part to the strong push toward privatization of the last PNP administration under Governor Pedro Roselló, Loíza's municipal government has become more willing to use accusations of discrimination and racism when convenient to combat the opposition against Loíza's development, including the opposition coming from its own party's government agencies and from the competitive businesses in the neighboring coastal regions (especially in the area of Isla Verde in Carolina, where the main airport is located).

Tomás, a resident of Las Cuevas who is in his forties, identified himself as pro-independence. A returnee from New York after living there for fifteen years, Tomás is a construction worker despite his degree in social work. He told me that there is no doubt that Loíza has been discriminated against in many ways, one of which is by giving more significance to the advancement of the town's culture than to supplying its basic needs. Many people think that advancing Loízan culture or preserving the town as a museum of African tradition serves to divert Loízans from class interests. To some extent Tomás applauded the fact that the municipal government has manipulated the use of racism to get different local and federal funding, but he also underlined the fact that these accusations help the municipal government to camouflage its poor administration and the way in which it favors a few Loízans from the PNP who are Protestants. Such favoritism occurred because the PNP has not always had a large majority of votes. While in town, every now and then I encountered a resident who criticized the administration's priorities.

Many Loízans claim that the people now in power clearly favor high-cost construction projects that serve tourists over low-cost projects that benefit needy longtime residents. These projects include expensive homes—some lived in year-round, some used as vacation homes—which most local residents cannot afford. The areas where these homes are located are now known by outsiders and Loízans as the good part of Loíza. (During my recent visit to Loíza in May of 2003, I saw three finished residential projects: Malibu Beach, Vistas del Océano, and Costa Mar.) For many Loízans, these new residents are "los riquitos" (a diminutive form of "rich" that is used sarcastically), who came from the outside. Even as these high-cost residential areas were being built, families I knew closely from Las Cuevas and other communities were living in extremely poor residential units. According to the supporters of the mayor's plan, however, the recent construction and restoration of low-cost residential areas (which I visited in May) confirm the administration's claim that revenue for the construction of low-cost residential facilities can be generated by increased tourism, which the advancement of Loízan culture helps to bring about. Accordingly, well-established tourism also improves the image of the town, bolsters the self-esteem of its residents, and fosters their commitment to keep the public facilities in good shape. Those skeptical of the plan, however, do not see the recent construction and restoration of low-cost residential areas in town as a direct effect of tourism but as the result of the initiative of the past PPD governor, Sila M. Calderón, the first female governor of Puerto Rico. This program is known as Comunidades Especiales (Special Communities); each community is identified with a big sign that includes the governor's name and receives extra funding from the government and other sources. Another related issue, which according to a sizeable number of Loízans probes the intention of developing the town at the expense of poor people, is the belief that the municipal government "no saca la cara" ("does not show its face," meaning that it does not confront outsiders) to defend its people against private interests. This attitude is evident in the government's relative lack of involvement in a highly publicized controversy: the extraction of sand on a rich person's property that has affected large natural ecosystems and residential areas. In Las Cuevas, residents also brought to my attention a situation I witnessed myself: the terrible odor coming from a plant to process waste from other municipalities, which was constructed without the residents' knowledge or consent.

The cultural center of Loíza vociferously claims to offer an alternate solution to the problems of Loíza and the government's development plan. This cultural center was created during the 1960s. It has its own facility downtown (next to the parish house), and like the festival of Santiago Apóstol it receives the financial and organizational support of the mayor's office, individuals, and organizations such as Frente Loiceño Unido or FLU, which has some non-Loízan resident members. One of the greatest accomplishments of the cultural center under director Laura Meléndez's term has been the program of "defending the culture," which she started with a group of children in the school where she was teaching. She called the group Niños Defensores de la Cultura. According to director Meléndez, tourism is the best card to play for Loíza's development. However, it would have to involve whole communities and families in order to benefit everybody. Tourism should not be imposed on Loízans. Instead, old town residents should be part of the planning, execution, and outcome of progress. The lack of people's involvement in the planning of development relates to the complaints of some of Loíza's local artists that buying culture or any other local product is growing more and more beyond people's budgets. These local artists blame an increased cheap global market that is competing with what is made in Puerto Rico, forcing the latter to become expensive or less accessible or even of poor quality. They also blame the state and the local governments, which prefer not to involve the people in order to avoid "trouble."

According to the cultural center's administration, Loízans' alienation can be resolved by educating children and parents about their historical and cultural traditions to develop a strong sense of self-esteem and identity and by providing knowledge of the town's social data in order for them to develop an interest in the town's problems. This is why the children from the program meet at the cultural center after school hours and on Saturdays to learn about Puerto Rican culture, Loíza's history and folklore, Loíza's geography and social data, and prominent Puerto Rican blacks and local figures. The vision here is that cultural pride is a necessary ingredient for upward mobility, as Dávila (2001: 239) has argued with respect to the Latino experience in the United States. However, the relationship between cultural pride and massive social involvement needs to be emphasized. This is why the program includes activities such as folk instrument lessons and training in crafts and other vocations in order to increase the opportunities for future jobs in and outside the area of tourism. When I visited the cultural center the children were learning to make *vejigante* masks and small souvenirs related to the festival of Santiago Apóstol, which as I have indicated earlier is one area of tourism in Loíza. The program also includes visiting neighborhoods and sites to know them better and serving these places by cleaning up the natural landscape and the public facilities to convince these kids that they can make a difference. According to Laura Meléndez, the cultural center has enjoyed relative freedom over the years because of the growth of the market of culture and the interest of the state and local governments in maintaining and selling Loíza's unique traditions. (On more than one occasion Laura expressed to me her vision to make Loíza's cultural center like Casa Pueblo, the cultural center of Adjuntas, which today operates as an independent cultural production company. One of its main products is Madre Isla coffee.) At the same time, this relative freedom has been a double-edged sword because it has enhanced the reputation of Loíza as unique and therefore a less integrated and more peripheral place. However, at this point it is important to ask: Is Loíza's experience only peripheral or is it becoming more transnational, and what are the implications?

Loíza in the Diaspora's Experience: More Identity Addictions and Contradictions

I discovered FLECHAS (Fiestas de Loíza en Connecticut en Honor al Apóstol Santiago, which means Festival of Loíza in Connecticut in Honor of the Apostle Santiago), with its main office in the barrio of Fair Haven, in New Haven, Connecticut, during the final stages of my research. During my field study, many Loízans were unfamiliar with FLECHAS. However, now people are becoming more familiar with FLECHAS because recently the mayor of Loíza and Loízan artists such as the musical bomba group Balet Folklórico de los Hermanos Ayala have participated in the festival sponsored by FLECHAS. Also, famous Loízan artists Samuel Lind and Evelyn Vázquez have participated as members of the board of FLECHAS. These artists have incorporated ideas from FLECHAS during the planning of the festival in Loíza.[8]

Today Connecticut has the sixth largest Puerto Rican population in the United States. However, it is the state in which Puerto Ricans comprise the largest percentage in relationship to the total number of inhabitants (5.7 percent). In 1960 there were 15,247 Puerto Ricans in the state and by 1990 the number had increased to 146,842. The total number in 2000 was 194,443 (5.7 percent of Connecticut's population). In New Haven County, the Puerto Rican population was 55,851 (6.8 percent of the county's population) and in the city of New Haven it was 17,683 (14.3 percent of the city's population).

Evidence exists of Puerto Rican migration since the early nineteenth century. However, many of the migrants came after World War II to do farming work: they were from the interior parts of the island (the towns of Caguas, Comerío, Cayey, and Coamo), had light skin, and a preferred the *jíbaro* traditions. Their migration was facilitated by the Department of Labor of Puerto Rico, which was created in 1947 to reduce high unemployment in Puerto Rico and decrease the labor shortage in the United States (1968 was the peak year of arrangements). However, the loss of contracts by farm workers during the 1970s forced many of these workers and their families to move to cities such as New Haven to look for other job opportunities (see Glasser 1997). It was during the 1970s that a number of Loízans migrated to these urban settings and established themselves. A group of these migrants came from the barrio Medianía Alta. Today, there are approximately fifteen hundred Loízans in New Haven, many of whom live in Kensington and Church Street South, two residential projects in downtown New Haven.

A majority of these Loízans, a sizeable number of them from the barrio Medianía Alta, began to leave for the United States at the end of the 1960s and the beginning of the 1970s, when, paradoxically, the number of Puerto Rican returnees began to surpass those leaving for the United States (Duany 2002: 211). Many Loízans traveled to the mainland during this time because of the high unemployment and poverty rates in Loíza when compared to other towns (Duany 2002: 224–25). The first person known to have migrated from Loíza to New Haven was Ezequiel López, who came from the Parcelas Suárez neighborhood in Medianía Alta and who later served as president of FLECHAS. Ezequiel was a soldier in the Korean War. After the war he returned to his hometown of Loíza. A few years later, he and his brothers moved to the United States to work as farm workers in the state of Maryland. The bad treatment and the difficult work conditions in Maryland forced them to continue searching for better jobs and living conditions until they settled in New Haven in 1960. A year later, Ezequiel asked his wife, Luz Selenia Osorio, to move to New Haven with him, and there they started a new family. They were followed by some of Luz Selenia's siblings, including her sister Menén Osorio Fuentes, who came as a teenager in 1973 to help baby-sit Luz Selenia's children. Menén particularly remembers that there were about five other black Puerto Rican families in the neighborhood and that other Puerto Ricans, who were mostly light-skinned, discriminated against them. At the same time, however, they were helped by a group of "white" families from the town of Utuado, in the interior part of Puerto Rico. Some of the Loízans who migrated to New Haven had plans to return to Puerto Rico in the hope that the separation between Loíza and Canóvanas would bring about positive results in the long term. However, some left the island with much uncertainty, anticipating that the separation would have long-term negative effects.

What about migration in general in Las Cuevas? At least thirty households in Las Cuevas had a former member who was living in the United States (mainly New York, Connecticut, and Massachusetts). A few of these absentees, especially mature adults and elders, come for short visits on a regular basis. Some individuals from these families complained about (but also tended to excuse) the fact that their family members living on the mainland (especially young adults) did not visit regularly. The reasons mainland family members gave their Las Cuevas relatives for infrequent visits included job commitments, lack of money, and fear of an increased crime rate in the area. The lack of employment opportunities (especially after the elimination of Section 936, which gave tax exemption to North American corporations on the island) has also reduced the interest of these migrants in returning to Loíza for good. Members of these families also indicated that as the years pass they lose contact with their relatives and receive fewer gifts. This is clearly consistent with Hamilton and Stoltz Chinchilla's (2001: 175) findings among Guatemalans and Salvadorans: remittances decline with length of stay in the United States.

Approximately sixty-six households had a former member of the household who was living outside Loíza but in another Puerto Rican town. A significant number of individuals (mostly elders) had lived in the United States or another town in Puerto Rico (for example, Río Grande, San Juan, and Carolina) for a long period of time and then moved back to Loíza for good. I did not find any residents who after settling back in Loíza made a long trip (of more than one month) to the United States, except a Dominican woman who married a Loízan while living in New York City and then moved with him to Loíza. She had made several long trips to work in the United States and to the Dominican Republic to visit her daughters. No doubt this data is consistent with Duany's (2002: 208–35) findings that Puerto Ricans like Dominicans are participants in a prolonged circular migration movement, their destinations being mostly New York (New York City and Buffalo), Pennsylvania (Philadelphia), and Connecticut (7.7 percent to New Haven and 3.1 percent to Hartford) (Duany 2002: 226). However, it is also true that circular migration happens internally as well, that it is not always consistent, and that it does not always happen with the same individuals.

The festival of Santiago, also known as the festival of Loíza, was first celebrated on the last day of the festival of San Juan in various Puerto Rican communities in the United States. But during the middle 1970s, the festival of Loíza became important in its own right, as the Loízan community and the support of the Loízan and non-Loízan communities from New York became more visible. In 1973, the organization Hermanos Fraternos de Loíza Aldea (Fraternal Brotherhood of Loíza Aldea) was legally incorporated in Manhattan with membership consisting of a large number of recent Loízan migrants. In 1977, FLECHAS was registered by the state of Connecticut. Menén Osorio Fuentes, whom I mentioned earlier, was one of the few people who worked hard to make the festival of Loíza a permanent event in New Haven, an effort that required much time and financial sacrifice. FLECHAS was legally registered as a not-for-profit 501(c) (3) cultural and educational organization in 1999.

Currently, the organization promotes awareness of the Spanish, Indian, and African legacies. (Next to the word FLECHAS the seal says "A Puerto Rican expression of three cultures.") However, its main goal is to document, preserve, and promote the significance of African elements in Puerto Rico's culture through history and the arts and by using classes, workshops, exhibitions, and performances in schools and for the general public, like those of its Folklorico Bohio Dance Troupe at Lincoln Center in New York, at Yale University in Connecticut, and in "The Puerto Rican Passage" (1995), a documentary about the Puerto Rican community in Connecticut that was directed by Frank Borres for Connecticut Public Television. The emphasis on the Afro-Puerto Rican heritage is also evident during the celebrations of the abolishment of slavery in Puerto Rico, the "discovery" of Puerto Rico, and Hispanic week. In addition, FLECHAS emphasizes the Loízan version of Puerto Rican African identity. While it has offered artists, crafts, and bomba performances from different towns in Puerto Rico, it has represented Loíza more often.

It is not hard to believe that FLECHAS, similar to Hermanos Fraternos de Loíza Aldea, came about because of a need to re-create and experience Puerto Rico. As Puerto Ricans were traveling back and forth, they also realized the significance of demonstrating Puerto Rican and Loízan identity outside of Puerto Rico. It was important for them to show their Puerto Rican identity and to firm up a critical perspective of the idea of national identity back home, which required residency on the island. Is it a coincidence that during the 1970s the Puerto Rican governor wanted to solidify the union of Puerto Ricans elsewhere and Puerto Rican researchers in New York began to question the island-centered discourse of Puerto Rican identity (Duany 2002: 167, 179)? Loízans in particular needed to affirm their Puerto Rican identity in relation to other Puerto Ricans living in Connecticut, who came from the interior part of Puerto Rico, where there has been a high concentration of light-skinned residents and a strong preference for the *jíbaro* traditions. Loízans in New York had the same need, but contrary to the Loízans of Connecticut, over the decades they have found other alternatives to Hermanos Fraternos (such as Rincón Criollo) to fulfill their need to experience and demonstrate Puerto Rican identity.

Loízans in Connecticut also needed to distinguish themselves from African-Americans, who became more visible in the area at the end of the 1970s while experiencing racial discrimination, and who like Puerto Ricans were competing for resources and social recognition. Today this distinction is considered an important issue because over the years more young Puerto Ricans have been identifying themselves with the African-American contemporary lifestyle while leaving behind their culture's original traditions, according to older generations. However, some young Puerto Ricans, such as those in New York, claim they are able to integrate Puerto Rican rhythms and lyrics with the "black" rhythms of r & b, hip-hop, rap, and jazz and to counter the idea of a static Puerto Rican identity. (One example is New York's hip-hop and rap group Latin Empire.) On the positive and optimistic side, many individuals in New Haven believe that the similarly difficult social and economic experiences of Puerto Ricans and African-Americans and a common cultural background have contributed to growing African-American support for the festival of Santiago and have helped create a unified search for a better socio-economic situation and a stronger affirmation of ethnic/racial identity for all minorities in New Haven. The preference of many young Puerto Ricans for modern Afro-Caribbean rhythms such as salsa and merengue over traditional Puerto Rican music is definitely an issue for Hermanos Fraternos in New York, although there, more so than in Connecticut, there is also a competition between salsa as representative of Puerto Rico and merengue as representative of the Dominican Republic, as more Dominicans are moving to New York and to Puerto Rico.

More significantly, Loízans in Connecticut have felt the responsibility to affirm both the African side of Puerto Rican culture, which has been marginalized, and their Loízan identity, for which they have been discriminated against both inside and outside Loíza. As a resident put it: "We are trying to do in Connecticut what we could not do in Loíza." This is even truer for the residents of Medianía Alta, where the festival of Santiago originated. As discussed earlier, the residents of Medianía Alta have been discriminated against by other Loízans because of their speech style, their superstitious mentality, and their "very black" color. Before these residents migrated to Connecticut, they experienced a subtle discrimination in Loíza during the foundation of the parish of Santiago Apóstol in 1971, which I will discuss in more detail in the fourth chapter. Many of these residents interpreted this event as something that would help to legitimate the festival in honor of Santiago and their Catholic practice in general and that would help their self-esteem and sense of community. At the same time, they believed this event concealed the old traditions of the festival, especially those associated with their African ancestry.

The important question now is this: Why has re-creating Puerto Rico using African-Loízan identity (and that of Medianía Alta) been successful in Connecticut? There are many reasons why Puerto Ricans such as Kevin Diáz, who were not originally from Loíza and who do not even pass as "black," have joined the efforts of FLECHAS to promote Puerto Rican culture with an emphasis on the African-Loízan component. The first possible explanation is that there has to be some "black" blood in Kevin's family. However, the issue is more complex than that. Kevin, a former member of the assembly of Fair Haven, has been a general coordinator for FLECHAS since 1990. Kevin was born in Manhattan and lived among different ethnic and racial groups, including white and black Puerto Ricans. His father, originally from the town of Juncos, in the interior part of Puerto Rico, worked in New York's factories for several years, as did Kevin's mother, also from Juncos. When Kevin was around six years old, his mother got very sick and the family moved back to Puerto Rico. They settled in Barrio Palmas in Cataño, an urban area on the coast of San Juan that offered more job opportunities. This area also had a long history of slaves, freed slaves, and interracial marriages. According to Kevin, music and musicians, including himself as a percussionist, were every-where. *Rumbones* (music improvisations with much percussion) happened any time in people's homes and in the streets. The music style was mainly Afro-Boricua; people played, danced, and sang bomba, plena, and salsa. After completing a B.A. in arts from the Interamerican UPR and working for the San Juan Mercantile, Kevin decided to move back to the United States to improve his English skills and his life in general. He settled in Connecticut in 1986–87 because of connections with a high school friend who helped him find a job in Bridgeport. From there, he was able to transfer to a similar job in New Haven. Once in New Haven, Kevin also began to study television media and to work for a local public television station covering cultural events and programs in the community. It was then that he learned about FLECHAS and joined it.

Right from the beginning, Kevin, like others with similar experiences, felt comfortable with the emphasis on the African-Loízan identity, which was familiar to him. He, like Blanca Irizarry, the executive director of Hermanos Fraternos and a non-Loízan Puerto Rican from Mayaguez, felt this emphasis was justified by a long history in Puerto Rico of the marginalization of the African element. Parenthetically, Kevin's familiar experience with Afro-Rican elements, like that of many other Puerto Ricans, explains in part the fact that only 5 percent of Puerto Ricans living in Connecticut classified themselves as white as opposed to 81 percent of Puerto Ricans on the island. However, Duany (in an e-mail communication) has argued that the categories "His-panic" and "Latino" are used by Hispanics in the United States as synonyms of "brown," that is neither black nor white. Neither Kevin's experience nor the fact that FLECHAS was the only significant Latino-Puerto Rican orga-nization in the community at that time explains why other Puerto Ricans from the interior parts of Puerto Rico, who do not share Kevin's experience, have joined FLECHAS. Contrary to the relative poor visibility of and participation in the carnival of Santiago sponsored by Hermanos Fraternos in Manhattan, in the recent years the festival of Santiago in New Haven has gained much momentum.

In 2002, the festival was declared in the media and by state officials the number one festival in New Haven as it was better organized and attended than even the Puerto Rican parade. The parade has been celebrated since 1964 thanks to the initiative of some residents and the local leaders of the Catholic Church. Today the parade has different chapters, representing the Puerto Rican communities of different towns. Earlier, in 1979, the festival received the First Connecticut Arts Award, among other recognitions. The success of the festival of Santiago has to do with the growing number of sponsors as well as the annual leadership award recognition dinner, which collects money. When it celebrated its twenty-fifth anniversary, the festival gathered around ten thousand people of different cultural and ethnic backgrounds, including Asians. The organizers spent approximately one hundred thousand dollars, including thirty thousand dollars from the city of New Haven and sponsors such as Telemundo (a Hispanic channel) and MTV español, which in collaboration with the Comcast cable company were in charge of the broadcast.

There are other factors that have encouraged the growing support of Puerto Ricans and other Latinos for the festival of Santiago. The support of Latinos, especially from South and Central America, is as significant in New Haven as it is in Manhattan because their numbers continue to grow. In 1990, the total Hispanic population in Connecticut was 213,116 and by 2000 it had increased to 320,323 (out of a total state population of 3,405,565), an increase of 50.3 percent (compared to a 3.6 percent growth in the total population). In the county of New Haven between 1990 and 2000, the Latino population increased 62.9 percent (83,131 of the county's total population of 824,008). Fair Haven, the headquarters of FLECHAS, has experienced a Hispanic population growth of 50 percent, mainly consisting of Puerto Rican residents. This is the opposite of what is happening in Manhattan, where many Puerto Ricans are going back to Puerto Rico or moving to other areas of New York and even other states.

In New Haven there is an established critical connection between cultural recognition and political power and there is a belief that the second comes through the first. Clearly, the situation here is more complex than that of the Mundang people in northern Cameroon, where the search for ethnic identity is motivated by self-esteem alone and not by competition for resources

(Schilder 1994), a case that challenges the usual understanding of ethnicity as the enhancement of collective political and economic interests. Loízan and non-Loízan Puerto Ricans and other Latino groups have to compete for access to resources. The support of the city's government (although often disputed) for the business community, other Latinos, and Puerto Ricans in New Haven shows a connection between self-esteem, which comes with cultural recognition, and political power. The leaders of FLECHAS take political power seriously: they see it as an essential step toward the economic stability of the whole community, especially when considering their position in the United States as "marginal" or as a "minority." This middle step between cultural recognition and economic stability is easily disregarded since it requires the leaders to consider the voice of the people. This is an area in which many Loízans in Loíza and the leaders of the town's cultural center claim their municipal government has fallen short. In Manhattan, the situation is particularly different in that Loízan and non-Loízan Puerto Ricans and other Hispanics have obtained public services with much less cultural activity and recognition from Hermanos Fraternos.

In Connecticut, such an association between cultural recognition, political power, and economic stability is also believed to encourage unity between generations, which according to Glasser (1997: 175–77) has become an important issue in Connecticut because of a growing gap between various Puerto Rican sectors for socioeconomic and geographical reasons. The leadership of FLECHAS has fought hand in hand with local residents and Hispanic elected officials for important causes in New Haven, such as Puerto Rican history and culture education and bilingual education (granted in 1977). Another important cause has been to increase the rate of property ownership for Hispanics. Likewise, in Manhattan Hermanos Fraternos today offers after-school tutoring, help in immigration matters, and general orientation to different Hispanic communities using federal, state, and city funding. However, these services do not have the same connection to the cultural activities sponsored by Hermanos Fraternos, which is contrary to the situation in New Haven with FLECHAS.

To accomplish its goals, FLECHAS has tried to involve the academic community in the state of Connecticut (Yale University and the University of Connecticut), including Puerto Ricans and other Hispanics.[9] Here it has been more successful than Hermanos Fraternos. In Connecticut FLECHAS has also tried to gain the recognition and support of the Puerto Rican government but with little success, although its success is still more than that of Hermanos Fraternos. It was not until June 17, 2002 that the PPD governor of Puerto Rico, Sila M. Calderón, proclaimed July 11 as the official day of the festival of Loíza in Connecticut. The leadership of FLECHAS wishes to establish solid economic and social relationships between New Haven and Loíza, similar to the relationship that is starting between the sister cities of Hartford, Connecticut and Carolina, Puerto Rico. Recently, the mayor of Hartford, Eddie Pérez, visited the mayor of Carolina, Luis A. Aponte, to solidify the effort. In this visit, Eddie Pérez was given a key to the municipality as a symbol of the ties between the two communities. Eddie Pérez is the first Puerto Rican mayor of a U.S. state capital.[10] In contrast, because of his many responsibilities as mayor of Loíza, Ferdín Carrasquillo has only agreed to visit the festival of Santiago in New Haven and has shown no interest in participating in the activities of Hermanos Fraternos. (The mayor's constant traveling is another issue of controversy in the town. He has defended himself by arguing that most of his traveling is to get funding for Loíza.) Recently, Mayor Ferdín carried the saint during the procession in New Haven. Ironically, FLECHAS has already recommended a limited role for Loíza's mayor, asking him to come "wearing only his cultural hat" and not to promote any personal political agendas.

Contrary to the Santiago Apóstol Carnival of Hermanos Fraternos, which is celebrated July 25–27, the festival in Connecticut begins on July 11 to avoid interfering with the festival in Loíza. Loízans and non-Loízans travel from Puerto Rico, New York, Boston, Chicago, Florida, and even Hawaii to participate in the festival. Some of them consider Connecticut's festival as a substitute for the Loízan event. For many people in New Haven, especially those who left Medianía Alta, the festival of Santiago of Loíza continues to be a good incentive for visiting their hometown. The festival in Connecticut is like its Loízan counterpart in that it includes a variety of activities; however, unlike the festival in Loíza, which lasts ten days, the festival in Connecticut lasts only three, despite yearly tempting offers by sponsors to extend the festival in order to attract the youth. FLECHAS is careful to safeguard the theme of the festival and also the Puerto Rican image and cause in general. This is especially so in light of the statistics concerning the generally disadvantageous socioeconomic situation of Puerto Ricans in the country and the prevalent negative stereotypes to which many recent, highly publicized events (such as the sex abuse of a group of men in New York's Puerto Rican parade and the controversy around a musical about a former Puerto Rican criminal, Salvador Agrón, in New York that was composed by the famous North American singer Paul Simon) have contributed. The fact that Hermanos Fraternos offers various social services on a regular basis to different Hispanic communities has disappointed Puerto Ricans in general and Loízans in particular: they see the organization as lacking a specific agenda in relation to their needs.

In Connecticut, the Puerto Rican image and cause are watched closely by various Latino groups that complain regularly about the priorities of FLECHAS. As in Loíza, some Puerto Ricans in Connecticut claim that the festival diverts attention from real issues and that the money could be used for solving many of their immediate problems. Some criticize the festival's African emphasis, and there have been attempts to create organizations that emphasize the Indian and the Spanish heritages, although these have had little success. In New Haven, some educated black and white Puerto Rican Pentecostal pastors have openly defended the Puerto Rican African heritage (including a Pentecostal pastor who collects *vejigante* masks). However, a large group of Pentecostals, including a sizeable number from Puerto Rico and Loíza, associate the African elements of the festival with evil forces and with the Puerto Ricans' slow progress. One positive effect is that their support of the *jíbaro* culture and their giving a low significance to cultural matters in general have reduced cultural competition between the African emphasis of FLECHAS and an emphasis on the other Puerto Rican cultural elements. Still, these Pentecostals have publicly attacked FLECHAS and politicians who have supported the organization, including Kevin Díaz and Raúl Ávila. The latter, originally a Pentecostal whose parents were from interior Puerto Rico's Utuado, has been a member of Fair Haven's municipal assembly. For several years he has been a strong advocate of FLECHAS. These accusations have been very personal and have used a religious premise. Regarding the latter, the leaders of FLECHAS and its political supporters have been publicly referred to as "piedras de tropiezo" (rocks in the middle of the road), and as pagans. This information has been used during the campaign season in public communications (for example, in the newspaper *La Voz Hispana de Connecticut*) to discredit both politicians who have supported FLECHAS and the projects that are supposed to benefit the Puerto Rican community in general.

Recently, during a festival procession, a Pentecostal publicly attacked the leaders of FLECHAS and the participants of the festival over loudspeakers.

The leader Menén Osorio Fuentes has been personally attacked with the argument that she is a witch and a Santera because of the way she dresses up (she often wears all black, white, or red), because of her hobby of making black dolls, and because of an alleged Santería altar she prepared in the office of FLECHAS, which was, in fact, a permanent exhibition of Afro-Puerto Rican arts and crafts. These attacks occur despite her known Catholic affiliation and her public denials of practicing Santería. The Pentecostal point of view is significant because of the steady growth of Hispanic Pentecostals in New Haven, making them a powerful group for politicians to please. Some of these Pentecostals, including a good number of Puerto Ricans, are politically active and also promote certain (Hispanic) political leaders and agendas (in some cases even during their meetings). In the last several years, FLECHAS has been involved in a legal case for permanent possession of the building facilities where its office is currently located. Residents in favor of FLECHAS claim that New Haven's government is not facilitating this acquisition in order to support many Pentecostal voters, especially the members of a Pentecostal church who have wanted the building for their permanent use and who have accused members of FLECHAS of paganism. Other Pentecostal and non-Pentecostal residents, though, prefer to stay neutral regarding the festival and FLECHAS in general as a sign of respect and support for the many things the organization has done for the community.

In New Haven, unlike in Miami where the Cubans' festival of Our Lady of Charity is primarily religious (although it carries a nationalistic tone as Tweed [1999] demonstrates), the festival of is considered more traditional than religious, or even mainly traditional. As is the case in Loíza, this view, which disassociates tradition from religion, justifies some Catholic and Protestant participation, as mentioned earlier. At the same time, those members or supporters of FLECHAS who are members of Saint Rose of Lima parish of Fair Haven encourage the official religious aspect of the festival. In Loíza, the existence of a parish in honor of Santiago does not eliminate the need for this encouragement. This is due to the common view that the parish is more the "real (spiritual) thing" than the festival, especially when considering that in the last several years the festival has increasingly adopted a "secular" character. To some Loízans the festival has a spiritual meaning because of the existence of a parish in honor of Santiago. This is true even if the individual does not participate regularly in the parish. In New Haven, as in Loíza, this promotion of the official religious aspect of the festival, through the celebration of a mass in Saint Rose of Lima parish, is also intended to give more credit and a more serious tone to the festival and to encourage further the participation of a group of people who otherwise would not relate to the festival, to Puerto Rican identity, and to the African/Loízan experience. However, the low attendance at the mass in New Haven may be a sign of the success of the concept of dissociating religion from tradition. It may also indicate that the official religious element is considered a private concern or that it is a part of the celebration but without a deep meaning (like a prayer at a graduation ceremony).

The Dialectics of Self-identity

Loízans' management of identities through daily interactions, through color/race classifications, and in their celebration of the festival of Santiago Apóstol in Loíza and New Haven reflects what Scherer (2001: 153) has called "strategic orientalism" or "self-orientalism" to describe the recent revitalization of Chinese-Cuban identity in Cuba. He explains this revitalization by using a model of a complex dialectic between Euro-American orientalist assumptions (represented by Cuba's state officials) and the use by first- and second-generation Chinese-Cubans of these assumptions with some alterations. These alterations, expressed in the arts, in literature, and in the devotion to the Chinese saint Sanfancón, are primarily molded by capitalist aspirations (such as an interest in developing a tourism industry) and also by Confucian religious ideas mixed with Cuban religiosity, particularly Santería. With this dialectic model, Scherer criticizes Edward Said's book *Orientalism* (1978), in which Orientalism is understood as a product of the West while presuming an essentialist view of both the East and the West (or the Orient and the Occident) and ignoring the voice of the Orientals themselves. Instead of repeating binaries such as colonizer/colonized, oppressor/oppressed, Scherer (2001: 160) locates "points of contact, encounter, even dialogue" in the process of self-identification. I, however, have avoided a model of a two-side contact, encounter, or dialogue between representations of Loízanness by non-Loízans and by Loízans themselves. Instead, I paid close attention to relations of power between different representations at and within the personal, community, town, national, and transnational levels. This explains my emphasis on a multisided dialectic model.

The analysis of Loízans' experience/identity from "here" and "there," similar to the work of Hamilton and Stolz Chinchilla (2001: 10–11), responds to the overemphasis on the newness of transnational links by stressing (in their own words) the active role of international immigrants in shaping their own experiences within transnational contexts and transforming both the receiving and sending societies in the process. Beyond this, I have questioned the existence of the links in the first place and their nature.

I have reacted to the common exclusion of the diaspora in studies or to notions of Puerto Rican experience/identity. This exclusion was recently pointed out by Duany (2002: 28–32). Nonetheless, I have also argued that transnationalism needs to be understood as something that manifests itself differently between communities and that works on at least three levels: (1) physical locality and ancestry, (2) sentiments and attitudes, and (3) social interactions. These distinctions are significant because, as this chapter has shown, Loízans in Connecticut experience Puerto Rico at the first two levels, while trying hard to establish real interactions with the island. Future research using a more comparative perspective may investigate more deeply which aspects of culture and/or identity are manifesting themselves transnationally (for example, modern pop culture, folklore, music, and food) and at which levels. Such research may also investigate the implications for the stability of the Puerto Ricans "here" (Puerto Rico or the United States) and "there" (the United States or Puerto Rico).

Regarding the stability of Puerto Ricans here and there, I am thinking specifically about Blanca Irizarry's assessment, based on her many years of experience working with Hermanos Fraternos in an area of Manhattan, that the slow socioeconomic development of Puerto Ricans in Manhattan has a lot to do with a mentality of living "con un pie en New York y otro en Puerto Rico" (with a foot in New York and the other in Puerto Rico). According to her, too much or too little Puerto Rican nationalism on the mainland can make Puerto Ricans feel a greater need to go back to Puerto Rico. Periodic traveling affects these Puerto Ricans' ability to save money and to progress in general. They are less willing to plan for the long term because they think that if things get bad on the mainland they have the alternative of going back to the island. The comparative perspective also relates to the situation described earlier, with the municipality of Loíza having the option of connecting with New Haven for cultural purposes. However, this connection has been limited economically and politically for many reasons, including Loíza's economic difficulties, while prompting a degree of competition between the people of Loíza and the Loízans of New Haven. The municipality of Carolina, in contrast, does not have a cultural connection with the city of Hartford through a specific cultural event such as the festival of Santiago Apóstol, but Carolina's economic situation, which is better than that of Loíza, makes more feasible an economic relationship with Hartford with possible social and political consequences.

The experience of Loízans reflects the complexity Burdick (1998: viii) has found in Brazil and about which he comments: "For every person who recounted stories of pain and suffering in connection with her color, another would declare that despite her color she had never suffered a moment's discrimination in her life. For every person I considered 'black' who spoke of her slave ancestry, another would matter-of-factly deny being the descendant of slaves." This complexity shows the processes by which color and cultural/ethnic heritage and culture/tradition and religion are strategically dissociated and reassociated. This is a significant research development in light of the fact that African and black identities are often the same thing in studies of Puerto Rican identity and in the popular understanding. Therefore, we should not be taken by surprise at the increasing popularity of the African elements on the island in the last few years and the fact that according to the 2000 census nearly 81 percent of the Puerto Rican population living in Puerto Rico classified themselves as white and only 8 percent as black. The same strategy of dissociation or differentiation between identities can have different purposes, meanings, and results over a period of time. In the situation I am studying, one reason to dissociate African cultural and color identities is to emphasize cultural identity while giving the false impression that cultural traditions and color have the same significance. Doing so helps to avoid dealing with or to cover up the issue of color, discrimination, and racism. At the same time, a lot of attention to African culture can make racism and discrimination more of an issue. The following chapters will gradually tie different identities to Loízans' religious experience to show more of the complexity involved in their management of identities. But first, it is necessary to have some general information about Puerto Rico's religious landscape.

The Restructuring of Religious Identity in Puerto Rico in the Last Few Centuries

Puerto Rico is traditionally Catholic, but the number of Protestants there has almost quadrupled since the 1960s, making it the country with the highest growth rate of Protestantism in Latin America and the Spanish-speaking Caribbean (Deiros 1997: 176). During my fieldwork when the population was about 3.8 million Puerto Ricans, the number of Catholics was estimated to be about 2 million and the number of evangelicals about 1 million.[1] As in the rest of Latin America, in Puerto Rico the majority of Protestants are Pentecostals. Only 14 percent of Catholics considered themselves to be active, while the majority of the evangelicals (about 80 percent) claimed to be active (*El Nuevo Día,* November 27, 1994, 16). However, during my fieldwork it was estimated that 20 percent of the Pentecostal membership (from different councils) have become passive or not actively involved in the church (Pérez Torres 1997: 69–70). The Catholic community is divided into 347 parishes, which are grouped into 5 dioceses beginning with the diocese of San Juan. The latter was created in 1511 (and elevated to archdiocese in 1960) and has the greatest number of parishes (around 150, which are divided into 6 *vicarias*). The Protestant community, in contrast, is mainly divided among 105 councils, without counting the Jehovah's Witnesses and the Latter-day Saints, or Mormons (*El Nuevo Día,* March 15, 1998, 7).

A recent estimate of the total number of individuals practicing Spiritism is 27,080 (Johnstone and Mandryk 2001: 531). Similar to Cuba in the last few decades (according to Arguelles Mederos and Hodge Limonta [1991: 190]), in Puerto Rico a sizeable number of individuals have begun to practice Spiritism openly and to mix it with, for example, Santería, astrology, psychic arts, neo-paganism, and new age practices. In an article in *El Mundo* more than three decades ago, the president of the federation of Spiritism argued that 80 percent of Puerto Ricans believed in "the Spiritist science" (*El Mundo,* August 26, 1970, 11C). A number of Spiritists I talked to from Loíza were convinced that Spiritist expressions continue among Catholics and even among Protestants, and that many of those who practice it hide or disguise it because of a long history of persecution of Spiritists and a strong criticism of Spiritism on the island, especially folk Spiritism.[2] In Las Cuevas it was proven that the numbers or percentages of Spiritists can be manipulated for many purposes: some Catholics have argued in a derogatory way that some Pentecostals are the same as Spiritists, Pentecostals have emphasized that some Catholics are really Spiritists, and Spiritists made similar claims.

In Puerto Rico Catholicism is still predominant in terms of nominal classifications and religious background. Here one has to keep in mind that decades earlier attending mass was less a requirement for Catholics than it is becoming today because of the changes the Catholic Church has been experiencing in the last few decades, which I will discuss in the following two chapters. The number of Protestants (most of them active members) and Protestant churches, meanwhile, continues to grow. Within this group there are individuals who classify themselves as Protestant but who barely attend church, despite the fact that church attendance and active participation are required by evangelicals.

This chapter and the following chapters will confirm a growth in active Catholic membership and a redefining of Catholicism, an increasing number of Protestant churches and a strong public presence, a constant church or denominational switching, the existence of passive Protestants, and a constant redefining of the Protestant practice at both the collective and individual levels as the dynamics of religious competition take place. A full account of the macrodynamics of religious establishment, dissemination, and continuity behind the restructuring of Puerto Rican institutional religion is beyond the scope of this study; however, my intention is to give credit to the reality of religious pluralism, which has a lot to do with churches' and members' management of identities. In accordance with Belanger (1992: 61), religious boundaries have become problematic but are still significant precisely because they are constantly redefined. As I will discuss in this chapter and the following chapters, national and town identities play a big role in religious practice and in redefining religious boundaries, while intersecting with significant political and economic agendas.

Establishments

As in other Latin American and Caribbean countries, (medieval) Roman Catholicism was established in Puerto Rico as the state religion under the Spanish regime near the beginning of colonization at the end of the fifteenth century. Constituting the Catholic Church was important because as Knight (1990: 71) indicates, "this was at the core of the Spanish expansion." This is why the first cathedral was built in Puerto Rico as early as 1509 and why the orders of Dominicans and Franciscans were established to begin evangelizing the Taíno Arawak population (Silva Gotay 1985: 53). The Taíno population at the time of the encounter was somewhat widespread and estimated to be thirty thousand. Theories have developed that their ancestors migrated to the Antilles over thousands of years from the Americas (see Kinsbruner 1996: 2). They had their own political government and belief system that included deities portrayed in wood, stone, and shell, and in carved stone figures known as *zemis*; they also had a religious specialist or leader (Rouse 1992: 118–19; Zaragoza 1995: 146). [3]

According to Silva Gotay (1985: 54), the Catholic Church became a state tool for giving an ideological justification for the domination and exploitation of the indigenous population during the conquest. Consistently, indigenous people were used as a labor force right from the beginning in mining work. A fast substantial decrease in the native population because of diseases brought by the Spaniards, the hard working conditions, and killings in confrontations caused the Spaniards to turn to African slaves for mining and other types of hard labor. Like the native Indians, these slaves, who had their own religious deities and beliefs, were forced to follow the Christian rules as their way of conduct (Scarano 1993: 150, 179; Díaz Soler 1965: 146, 167). [4] A revealing case of extreme oppression occurred in 1591 under the order of Archbishop Nicolás Ramos. It involved three African women slaves who were burned after they were forced to confess that they worshipped and had sex with the devil (Gutiérrez 1997: 12). Three years later, in a letter written by the same archbishop from the Dominican Republic to the king of Spain, black men and women slaves were accused of practicing witchcraft and of celebrating cults of the devil in the form of a goat (see Vidal 1989: xi). [5] It seems that an association between African religious traditions and witchcraft and devil worship was widespread, as in countries such as Brazil (Harding 2000: 23).

Nonetheless, direct or indirect resistance to the conditions prompted by Spanish colonial control of the island and to this type of Christianization led by the Catholic Church was evident early in the colonization. According to Quintero Rivera (1998: 52), though, not all resistance was against everything Spanish or even against colonialism; indeed, some resistance occurred against the subordinate position of those who resisted. Quintero Rivera describes this early resistance as an escaping type ("de huida" or "retraimiento"). In any case, a classic example of early resistance (at the end of the sixteenth century) has been studied by Zayas Micheli (1990: 26–33): the intensification of the devotion to the Virgin of Monserrate (or the Virgin of Hormigueros), after claims were made of her apparition on the livestock farm of a Spanish migrant family in the interior town of San Germán in the western rural zone of Puerto Rico (the second town founded after San Juan on the northeastern coast). Here, families descended from the Spanish, slave, and Indian communities became strong devotees of the Virgin. The first group had moved to the area to try to find better self-subsistence lifestyles and the last two groups arrived to escape from hard labor and harsh treatment and the controlling, urban-military societies in the coastal areas (Quintero Rivera 1998: 38–39). A group of elders from Las Cuevas indicated in their interviews that this development of popular Catholicism through the devotion to the Virgin became a reality on the coast. They admitted the possibility that it had been influenced by personal contacts with people from the interior zone, some of whom were freed slaves and whose descendants relocated in coastal areas such as Loíza. A similar form of resistance to official Catholicism and/or sociopolitical hegemony is alleged to have manifested in Mexico with the apparitions of the Virgin of Guadalupe in 1531 (Kanellos 1993: 371); and in Cuba with the apparition of the Virgin Our Lady of Charity at the beginning of the seventeenth century (Tweed 1999: 136). However, the development of popular Catholicism, as direct or indirect resistance to official Catholicism, also took other forms while implicating complex experiences in coastal areas of Puerto Rico, such as Loíza, during the following centuries.

The increasing scarcity of gold in Puerto Rico and other Caribbean islands during the first half of the seventeenth century caused the Spaniards to seek gold and other resources in the North and South Americas. In Puerto Rico, as in other Caribbean islands, Spaniards turn to the plantation system to produce sugarcane as the new main economic activity. This production, mainly active in the coastal areas, developed very slowly, making languid the economy of the island in the first three centuries of Spanish colonization. For this hard labor, the Spaniards continued using African slaves, establishing generations of slaves on the island, as well as freed and fugitive African slaves from neighboring islands, and free people of mixed color. These workers also raised livestock, labored in the production of small crops for subsistence, and did artisan and construction works (Mintz 1974: 97–98). This population's hard work paid off as production began to grow with the coming of the eighteenth century, but the beneficiaries were almost exclusively a small number of the population (Scarano 1993: 340, 346).

According to Zayas Micheli (1990), the strong devotion to the Virgin kept growing in the interior zone of Puerto Rico during the eighteenth century, related as it was to an ongoing sense of opposition to the Spanish colonial interests and official Catholicism, both of which were associated with severe socioeconomic inequality. For this and other geographically specific reasons, there were widespread complaints by priests (who were few in number) about their parishioners' lack of religious commitment and their devotion to folk religiosity.[6] This form of folk Catholicism mixed with native and Spanish folk traditional elements was probably also developing in the coastal areas, where *hacendados* in charge of the plantations cared less for Christianizing than for their economic interests (Romberg 2003: 40). Regarding this development, Schmidt (1996: 37) states that Afro-Caribbean religion did not develop as a coherent system in Puerto Rico during this period, as it did in other Caribbean countries such as Cuba and Haiti with the development of Santería and Vodou, respectively. However, as Díaz Soler (1965: 172) insists, one cannot completely deny the existence in Puerto Rico of Afro-Caribbean religion in a fluid form, especially after paying close attention to the popular religious development in Loíza, which manifested in the sudden apparition of Saint Santiago at the end of the nineteenth century.

Earlier in the nineteenth century, as Spain confronted the French military forces, political and religious loyalty was required of its colonies, including Puerto Rico. Thus, on April 29, 1809, the governor of Puerto Rico exhorted the five districts to strengthen the sacred bonds that united the island and other American domains with Spain and to keep the spirit of patriotism and loyalty to the motherland in such a critical moment (Cruz Monclova 1952: 11–12). Strengthening religion was meant to strengthen national ties, for which drastic measures were taken, such as limiting migration to Catholic Europeans and persecuting members of the clergy who held strong liberal ideas and opposed the Spanish regime.7 Measures such as tax exemptions for slave ownership were taken to improve the colonies' difficult socioeconomic situations and to guarantee their loyalty. These measures plus the relative drop in Haiti's production of sugar following the Haitian Revolution had a number of effects on Puerto Rico: exportation of sugar increased to the United States; the use of slaves (whose percentage of the population in 1848 was 14, the highest rate in the history of slavery) and of free laborers of different color (free people of color constituted the majority of the population) became more widespread; Puerto Rico became the second largest producer and exporter of sugar in the Caribbean; and the country was drawn into the world economy. This high production also prompted significant population and urban growth in the country and an increase in the number of officially established towns. One requirement of an officially established town was that it have a "decent" parish in the downtown area, in accordance with certain stipulations. It is not a coincidence, then, that the parish of Loíza, as it is today, was built during this period of national and local economic, population, and urban growth; in Loíza the beneficiaries were almost exclusively a small group of foreigners, although a group of *criollo* landowners, or Puerto Rican natives with Spanish ancestry, did benefit as well.

Nevertheless, during the second half of the nineteenth century, the production of sugar in the coastal areas of Puerto Rico slowed down. This situation caused the migration of a substantial number of laborers and landowners to the country's interior, where cattle breeding was developing as an important economic activity. These migrants came to stimulate the production of coffee in the area, causing the country to become the fourth largest producer in Latin America in 1880 (Scarano 1993: 466). According to Picó (1998: 153–55), during the nineteenth century migration to the interior zone of the island also came about in reaction to the development of communities at the margins of the hacienda economy (an economy based on sugar exports) on the coast. Shortly thereafter, however, the production of both crops began to suffer as the old hacienda or plantation system was giving way to foreign *centrales* and corporations that made less use of human laborers. These laborers also lost their access to cultivating land for their subsistence. This situation and the extreme measures the government was taking at the time to enforce labor for massive production and export became the fertile ground for the development of labor and nationalist or anti-Spain movements. In 1868, a good number of Puerto Ricans confronted Spain by military means for the country's independence. The events are referred to as Grito de Lares (literally, scream of Lares, the town in which the events were initiated). These movements further developed with the coming of the twentieth century, when political, judicial, infrastructural, and economic transformations were happening as the result of U.S. establishment on the island after its invasion in 1898.

The situation of the Catholic Church during the second half of the nineteenth century was increasingly difficult because of the continued scarcity of priests, who were described as ignorant and lacking seriousness, distant from the poor masses and close to the urban elite, and supporters of large property holdings and slavery (García Leduc 1994). In addition, the cost of the rituals was high and the liturgy continued to be in a foreign language and style. The Catholic Church tried to maintain its religious and political control by reinforcing existing measures and creating new ones that directed and organized people's ritual practices and everyday life experience (Romberg 2003: 42–50). Not surprisingly, after conducting a commissioned survey, Father Thomas Sherman, a Catholic priest in the U.S. army, concluded that Catholicism in Puerto Rico was dead (Silva Gotay 1997: 109). This survey was necessary because the governance of the Catholic Church in Puerto Rico was going to change: it would now be under Vatican jurisdiction and constitute a part of the North American Catholic Church instead of the Spanish Catholic Church because of the U.S. military occupation in 1898. The situation of the Puerto Rican Catholic Church made the case for urgent attention by U.S. Catholic hierarchies. The implementation of the U.S. political system and the principle of separation of state and church, highly influenced by an existing atmosphere of Euro-American liberal ideas (which in Spain prompted the creation in 1868 of a decree that allowed freedom of worship), caused the Catholic Church to lose its political privileges, its control over education, and many of its physical properties (Silva Gotay 1997: 168). All of this benefited the evangelizing interests of the North American Protestants, who were a majority in the United States.

Therefore, in addition to a weak Spanish colonial power, a weak economic system, a weak official Catholicism, and the development of folk religion at the margins of official Catholicism, there came the beginning of an intensive penetration of North American Protestantism and European Spiritism. About the last, González-Wippler (1995: 108) indicates the importance of tracing the origins of Spiritism back to the theosophy movement in the United States and understanding how the movement was deeply influenced by Indian philosophy. The fact that Spiritism presented itself more as a scientific and spiritual world perspective than a religion did not prevent many Puerto Ricans from seeing it in religious terms. Various reasons explain the great appeal of Spiritism on the island. Before the coming of Spiritism based on the ideas of the French philosopher Allan Kardec, the belief that (ancestor) spirits intervene in life had already been present since the time of the Taínos. In fact, according to Pérez y Mena (1995: 144), the Taíno belief system was organized around the worship of ancestor spirits, not gods or deities, despite the significance of the latter. Worship of and communication with ancestor spirits was also very significant in the religious traditions of the African slaves who were brought to the country. These beliefs were mixed with Catholicism and witchcraft.

The central ideas of Spiritism (folk and Kardecist), according to Loízan Spiritists, are the acknowledgement of a superior or ultimate reality or being, an understanding that communication between the spiritual and earthly worlds is possible, and various sequential existences for each human being that have a cumulative effect depending on each individual's behavior. To Nuñez Molina (1994: 54), Puerto Rican intellectuals were interested in Spiritism as a philosophical system that provided an alternate framework for social and moral development. They were also interested in its scientific orientation and emphasis on psychical research. This interest of the Puerto Rican elite was significant considering the political, economic, and Catholic Church-related events that were happening at the time. Those from the lower class embraced what Kardecist Spiritism had to offer in terms of fulfilling their immediate needs. What is clear is that in Puerto Rico, as in Cuba (and other Caribbean and Latin American countries), the coming of Kardecist Spiritism brought about the distinction between "official" and "folk" Spiritism (Koss 1976: 35).[8] (I will discuss later, though, the reasons why this distinction is not sufficient.)

It is worth noting, however, that the penetration of Protestantism goes back to the end of the sixteenth century, when Lutherans introduced Bibles to the island. This process was accelerated two centuries later by the development of the printing industry and the importation of Bibles from non-Spanish Caribbean countries, where Protestantism had been established since the seventeenth century under non-Spanish colonialism (Gutiérrez 1997: 9–13,

21–23). During the second half of the nineteenth century, Protestant meetings were held in different towns by a group called Los Bíblicos, most of whose members were migrants (Agosto Cintrón 1996: 45). In 1874, the first Protestant church was inaugurated in Ponce (Silva Gotay 1997: 8). Other Protestant meetings were held in San Juan and in the town of Mayagüez in the west, coinciding with Spiritist group meetings in the same cities.[9] In 1879, the first Spiritist center was officially founded in Mayagüez (Matos Salgado 1974: 7). In 1903, the Federación de Espiritistas de Puerto Rico (Federation of Spiritists of Puerto Rico) was founded and from this point onward annual assemblies took place.[10] The advancement of Spiritism continued with the first Spiritist congress in 1946 and the resolution to reconstruct the Spiritism headquarters building in 1954 (*El Mundo,* July 26, 1945, 10; September 9, 1954, 11). The Concilio Evangélico de Puerto Rico (Evangelical Council of Puerto Rico or CEPR) was founded two years after the foundation of the federation of Spiritists. This evangelical council became the umbrella organization for the Protestant churches commonly known as "historical churches" (also called "ecumenical" or "denominationalist") to differentiate them from the Pentecostal churches.[11]

Protestantism continued to grow with the development of the Pentecostalist variation, which had originated at the beginning of the twentieth century in the United States. Pentecostalism formally entered Puerto Rico in the second decade of the twentieth century through the Pentecostal Church of God. Today it is the largest Pentecostal denomination on the island. It did not take long for Puerto Rican preachers to spread the message to sister countries such as the Dominican Republic. However, it was not until the 1930s, a terrible decade in the economic history of Puerto Rico (and also of the United States), that Pentecostalism began to gain strength in the country, as it did in the Dominican Republic, Cuba, and Haiti (Álvarez Vega 1996: 101, 105; Pérez Torres 1997: 86–89). In Puerto Rico, Pentecostalism gathered momentum with the foundation of different Pentecostal churches in different towns on the island.[12] According to Deiros (1997: 29), the 1930s were a hard time for historical Protestantism in the Caribbean and Latin America, and also for official Spiritism, which according to Bram (1972: 374) was trying hard to gain legitimacy by distinguishing itself from folk Spiritism. Perhaps this came about in anticipation of what followed: a large campaign, headed by the Puerto Rican state apparatus, against Spiritism (especially folk Spiritism) in the name of social progress, although Spiritism (particularly folk Spiritism) was also seen as part of the Puerto Rican essence (Romberg 2003: 68–70).

Since the 1930s a number of local religious groups have developed. Although derived from established denominations, these groups have reinvented themselves as separate constituencies. One of these groups is Las Profetas (The Prophets), which was founded by a Korean War veteran. The distinguishing trademarks of this movement are the ceremonial wearing of veils by its female members and the central place given to prophesying and healing. One of the most significant religious groups is the Mita cult, which centers on the belief that Mita (originally a Pentecostal woman) is the incarnation of the Holy Ghost, that the Bible was sent by her, that she can change the Bible's message, and that she will take her followers to heaven after their deaths. Despite much persecution since its founding, today the number of Mita members reaches at least fifteen thousand, including a temple membership of seven thousand in Puerto Rico and several congregations in Caribbean and Latin American countries. Finally, there is the recently founded CFLW, which I introduced earlier and which I will examine closely in chapter 6.

Disseminations

The factors of migration and the distribution of literature were very significant for the spreading of Protestantism and Spiritism on the island.[13] However, systematic missionary work initiated by Protestantism had the greatest effect on Puerto Rico's twentieth-century religious landscape. To accomplish their missionary goals, Protestant denominations agreed to divide the island "like a piece of cake" (as is commonly said), as they did in Cuba, so that each denomination was able to select a geographical area in which to establish itself and expand.[14] (Over the decades, each has spread beyond the limits of its former selection.) In the case of Pentecostalism, the relative lack of this type of geographic limitation is believed to have opened greater possibilities for its expansion, especially during the 1930s. Pentecostalism came to the picture after this agreement between historical Protestant churches took place. Financial self-sufficiency was encouraged by Protestants since the beginning, but for some time their churches relied heavily upon the financial assistance of the churches in the United States (Silva Gotay 1997: 260–64). Pentecostal churches also depended upon their sponsors back home, but because many of them were founded independently of a denomination from the United

States they became self-sufficient. In fact, the relative independence of the Pentecostal churches since almost the beginning was regarded by old time Pentecostals in Loíza as a very positive element for the growth of Pentecostalism. This self-dependency gave these members a sense of ownership and pride (Agosto Cintrón 1996: 103).

Social action by historical Protestantism was related to its strong connection with the U.S. system. This new system was expected to bring positive changes in the areas of communication, transportation, recreation, sanitation, health, and education. Protestants were able to situate themselves in strategic administrative positions and to influence Puerto Rican social life, especially in the areas of health and education. Protestants founded hospitals and orphanages and were involved in many health services for the community; they were sometimes joined by Pentecostals. During the 1970s, my former Baptist church took the lead in organizing health clinics for prevention and basic treatment and also in sponsoring orientations about health, nutrition, and security. On their arrival, Spiritists also showed a strong commitment to the social welfare of the Puerto Rican poor. For example, between the 1880s and 1890s Spiritists built three hospitals and a shelter and collected money for the poor. Social commitment has continued until today, but mostly in the form of charities, donations, and community work by individuals (Rodríguez Escudero 1978: 44–50). In their early years on the island, Spiritists were also involved in educational programs; their main goal was to teach the Spiritist ideas in schools, something that does not exist today (Koss 1976: 31, 34).

Protestants also paid immediate attention to Puerto Ricans' education, as they did in other parts of Latin America, such as Guatemala (see Rose and Brouwer 1990). Education was thought to directly affect and transform a society of poorly educated people.[15] Their efforts to improve education resulted in specific programs and schools for technical and vocational training, such as the Instituto Politécnico, which was founded in 1921. (Today the school is called the Interamerican University of Puerto Rico.) Decades later, these educational efforts led to the use of church facilities for Head Start, the federal preschool program. This was the case at the First Baptist Church of Loíza and my former Baptist church in Carolina.[16] Private education has been very important to Protestants and today they have at least fifty-two private schools on the island.[17]

The professional religious education of the natives was another area of concern. Five years after the founding of the CEPR in 1905, the Seminario

Evangélico de Puerto Rico (Evangelical Seminary of Puerto Rico or SEPR) was founded; today it offers graduate studies in theology. Initially, the Pentecostal Church did not emphasize professional theological education, but some efforts did go forward. In 1937, it founded the Colegio Bíblico Pentecostal (Pentecostal Biblical College) of the Church of God from the Mission Board (recently it joined the Seminario Evangélico Pentecostal); today it is the most important of its agencies. The number of theological schools has increased over the decades as Pentecostal leaders have encountered highly trained professionals from the historical denominations and as the membership in general has become more educated. Also, a good number of the students at the Evangelical Seminary are Pentecostal. Still, the number of professionally educated Pentecostal pastors is small when considering the large number of Pentecostal leaders.

Within both Protestantism and Pentecostalism, the previously mentioned educational efforts far surpassed the efforts to organize biblical education within the churches through Sunday Bible schools (with courses for people of all ages), Bible studies during the week (in the church building or at homes), and summer (or vacation) Bible schools. The Baptist summer schools normally included Bible stories, missionary stories, collection of money for missionary work in foreign countries, training in arts and crafts, field trips, and a final presentation that was intended to show what the children learned and to evangelize the non-Christian parents.

A significant aspect of dissemination has been for denominations to legitimize themselves by discrediting the others (as Silva Gotay [1997: 149] puts it). A first case in point is the attacks upon the Spiritist movement in Puerto Rico by Protestant and Catholic churches and by individuals who claimed to speak in the name of science. According to former Spiritists in Loíza, they were denied the right to be baptized, married, and buried the Catholic way, and Spiritism was accused of being the cause of mental sickness. In 1920, an article in *El Mundo* (September 22, 1920, 8) indicated that Spiritism was a threat to future generations.[18] At least these attacks did not generally involve police raids as happened with Afro-Cuban religion in Cuba (Brown 1999: 206). In their 1941 assembly, the federation of Spiritists formally decided to respond to these public attacks with a strong campaign of public education about "authentic" Spiritism (that is, its moral and scientific basis) (Rodríguez Escudero 1978: 98). Since then, a campaign of information to the public about Spiritism has been conducted when possible through the newspapers

(*El Mundo,* October 7, 1945, 1, 12; August 18, 1980, 46; November 22, 1969, 12A). Conferences and seminars have continued to be organized in order to correct incorrect ideas about Spiritism and to distinguish it from folk Spiritism.[19] Also, Spiritists have developed a type of literature in which, as Spiritist leaders have stated, information takes precedence over proselytizing.[20]

Protestants have experienced strong verbal attacks from Catholics since the initial phase of the systematic penetration of Protestantism on the island. In the first decades of the twentieth century, in the Catholic journal *Ideal Católico,* Protestantism was described as the cause of liberalism, as an encourager of anarchism and socialism, and as a threat to (Spanish) nationalism and the unity of the people. Protestants responded mainly by disparaging Catholics for their lack of doctrinal truth, which they believed had a negative social and economic impact (Silva Gotay 1997: 169, 171, 240). Catholics are still criticized for promoting a doctrine that is not founded on biblical principles and for endorsing idolatry in the form of a strong devotion to the Virgin Mary and the saints. A signal example can be found in radio and television attacks by the Pentecostal preacher "Geñito" Rodríguez López that were known in Loíza: he referred to Catholics as the devil's children and called the Catholic Church a prostitute. He also attacked non-Pentecostal Protestants for distancing from the biblical truth. The reputation he gained for making these accusations made him popular in the country. In addition, he was the source of much satire in important television comedy and social critique programs, such as that of the famous comedian Sunshine Logroño. Before his death Geñito made a public apology to those he had offended. Nevertheless, the devotion to the Virgin Mary continues to be a hot issue between Catholics and Protestants in Puerto Rico; as in Latin America and the United States, it is considered a strong limiting factor for ecumenical efforts. One of the major complaints I heard from the priests from the two parishes of Loíza was that the Pentecostals used loud speakers in the main plaza downtown and other public areas to denounce the Catholic Church. Similarly to what I experienced in my neighborhood years ago, in Las Cuevas I witnessed Pentecostals attacking Catholics verbally and indirectly via loud speakers, although residents indicated attacks in general have declined.

Pentecostals have verbally attacked Protestants, including Baptists, for their liberal and too permissive attitude, especially in the area of women's behavior, and their solemn style of worship, indicating the absence of the Holy Spirit. In Loíza, great confrontations between Pentecostals and Baptists occurred for these reasons. It seems to me that Pentecostals refer to Baptists as cold or dead because the Pentecostals need to distinguish themselves from other Protestant groups who hold beliefs similar to Catholics. However, this Pentecostal attitude toward other Protestants has changed over time, especially toward those churches that have become *avivadas* (charismatic). In Loíza, as in my former community, a cross-denominational charismatic experience has encouraged the planning of common activities between Baptists and Pentecostals.

Many Las Cuevas residents agreed that Baptists have attacked Pentecostals, mainly through jokes that ridiculed Pentecostals as too literal, ignorant, crazy, emotional, and untalented. From a whole repertoire of jokes, I can remember one that ridiculed the Pentecostals' literal approach to the Bible. This joke, like many others, was very common in Las Cuevas: An individual asked God to speak to him through the Bible in order that he might obey Him. The first time he opened the Bible he read the passage that says, "Judas hung himself." The second time he opened the Bible he read the passage that says, "Go and do likewise." Another popular adage was that Pentecostal women have tongues as long as their hair. This is meant to criticize the Pentecostals' emphasis on external matters and their acceptance of women's gossiping. There are also two anecdotes (based on real events) used to ridicule Pentecostal ignorance and emphasis on the devil. In the first, a peasant, in order to make the point of how good the religious service was, used the expression, "The service was so good that we grabbed the devil by his balls and threw him to the floor." The second is a song that says something like "I have a sharpened machete to cut the cursed devil." Although these are examples of the ways in which Baptists have attacked Pentecostals, this attitude also exists toward "conservative" Pentecostals among more "moderate" Pentecostals.

Understanding dissemination and competition in church history requires the consideration of factors such as migration, distribution of literature, missionary work, establishment of churches, social involvement, and a dual process of legitimization and delegitimization through direct verbal confrontation and through indirect verbal means. However, this understanding also requires consideration of the internal characteristics that draw believers to these religious groups. These characteristics, when looked at carefully, are the direct and indirect ways that churches make statements about each other in a highly competitive environment. This explains why in many instances members describe their denomination's or church's ideology and practice in comparative terms. Most of interviewees from Las Cuevas talked about their denominations by narrating their personal experiences.

Many residents of Las Cuevas were attracted to Protestantism because of the clarity of the sermons and the Bible teaching, which emphasized the importance of each individual in God's eyes and in the church community of "brothers" and "sisters." Many were attracted by the music and the opportunities the church provided for developing leadership skills and artistic talents. According to César, who was in his early twenties when I met him at the end of my field study, one of the main reasons he joined the Pentecostal church Mission Board in Loíza was the variety of opportunities it provided for the youth to develop their talents. This explains why he has seen about five thousand young people in the national youth retreats of the Mission Board as opposed to a very low youth participation in the national youth retreats of the Universal Church of God. In his church César has had the opportunity to sing songs that he himself has written and also to play the trumpet, the keyboard, the guitar, the bass, the conga, and the kettle drums (the last was something he began to do when he was a member of a Pentecostal church in New York). This musical development allowed César to play "secular" nationalistic music on kettle drums in a televised competition and to win first place at the national level; he did so despite a bit of criticism from members of his church.

A great explanation for this conversion and church commitment pattern is the old tendency of Protestantism to give everyday life a sacred character (Silva Gotay 1997: 164) by bringing some selected "secular" activities of everyday life into the church and by involving the church in "secular" activities, which it then redefines or assigns a new significance. Three examples of this tendency are sponsored activities or events such as field trips, sports activities, and special artistic presentations at regular church meetings, holiday services, and other special events, some of which I was invited to participate in during my stay in Las Cuevas.

In Loíza sports have been significant as a source of social and economic mobility. Like music, sports have also been used by churches to attract new members. As the pastor of the Pentecostal Church of God in Las Cuevas indicated, "If I want to attract the youth, I have to play basketball with them." This action, according to him, might also bring the parents to the church and to the knowledge of God. In Las Cuevas, like in my barrio, sports have also been a way to establish relationships between different denominations.

Sometimes church teams in Loíza have been composed of church and non-church men from the community who have played against other churches of various nearby communities. This demonstrates what a few pastors in Loíza told me, that sport may be used as a means of social integration of competing religious interests. In Puerto Rico, sports, field trips, special artistic presentations, and also feasts, have helped compensate for the prohibitions of Protestants and Pentecostals against drinking, smoking, gambling, dancing, cockfighting, and horse racing, among other things.

Many Puerto Ricans would argue that Protestantism and Pentecostalism differ in theological principles, doctrinal codes, and ritual style. Some would argue that their differences are really a matter of emphasis or degree. In any case, differences need to be considered carefully for two reasons: Pentecostals comprise the majority of the Protestant community, and a growing percentage of Protestant churches are adopting Pentecostal doctrines and a charismatic worship style in Las Cuevas, Loíza and Puerto Rico at large. These factors have caused what I refer to as "neo-(historical) Protestantism." Many Pentecostal churches have become more liberal on issues such as clothing. They have also adopted contemporary worship styles and the latest technology. These churches can be referred to as neo-Pentecostal. Here one can include big churches that generally follow the Pentecostal doctrine but are nondenominational or interdenominational. The answers Las Cuevas's residents' gave to the question of what brought them to their Pentecostal church coincided with the usual characterizations of Pentecostalism: that it follows a "literal" interpretation of the Bible, that it emphasizes the manifestation of the Holy Spirit and an eschatological message. A common saying that characterizes Pentecostalism in a positive way is "In Pentecostalism, things are black and white, they are straight forward."

Pentecostal style, in the form of loud and informal praise, dancing, prophesying, speaking in tongues, and healing, provides an immediate and tangible emotional gratification that is so important for those who are not gratified socioeconomically. Here I must clarify the distinction between "immediate" and "tangible"; people may be gratified immediately at the level of emotion, but not necessarily tangibly in terms of the healing they may be expecting. Pentecostalism, like Spiritism and Santería, has a way to work the tangible aspect by providing visible signs to make people feel and believe that something concrete is happening or will happen (much like a placebo). When Pentecostals pray for an ill person, these visible signs may be anointing with oil, the laying on of hands, falling down on the floor, the scream of the congregation, gestures to take the illness or the spirit of illness away, stamping the feet, the beat of the congas, the strong sound of the music, and the like. Moreover, an informal and spontaneous worship style allows poor and uneducated members to become leaders while elevating their self-esteem.

Moreover, Pentecostalism made great sense, especially at the beginning of its insertion into the island, by emphasizing the message of the coming of Christ, who will save the poor and the marginalized from an unjust world. Strict codes of behavior, literally taken from the Bible, give structure to the individual's life and form a foundation from which to renounce a world from which the participants feel left out. In a context of highly religious competition, following strict codes of behavior is a visible way of demonstrating spiritual endurance and sacrifice and of holding a better position in God's eyes. Also, in a context of an increasingly generalized and relatively better socioeconomic situation like that of Puerto Rico, following strict codes can demonstrate God's support and approval.

Continuity in the Last Four Decades

Wuthnow's (1988) concept of restructuring to characterize religious changes in the last few decades in the United States will be useful in this section of the chapter. Wuthnow's (1992: 3) preference for this concept relates to his preference for the concept of "rediscovering" as opposed to that of "revival." He holds to this preference for restructuring because commitments to the sacred have been relatively constant overall, but have surfaced in different forms from one place and year to the next. He identifies a religious restructuring in the changes in the relationship of religion to politics and in the internal characteristics of religion.

With respect to the first dimension of restructuring, namely religion's relationship to politics, in Puerto Rico the political activism of the church since the 1970s has been more concerned with monitoring and legislating morality, which Wuthnow (1988: 199–207) argues has also been the case in the United States. Two recent examples are the legislative battle over a law endorsed by Protestant leaders that denies same sex couples the right to marry and the fight to combat an initiative that provides teens with contraceptives in schools without their parents' consent. (Another legal issue under serious consideration during my visit to Puerto Rico in May of 2003 was sodomy.) The church's latest political strategy—unlike its earlier campaign to influence public behavior and government policy mostly by converting or affiliating individuals—is a response to increased secularization, manifest in lower moral standards, higher crime rates, and more aggressive intellectual and popular criticism of religion, the church, and its political role. Explaining the tension between secularization and an increasing public influence in the church in Brazil, Rachel Harding (2000: 125–26) explains that it is precisely the official separation of church and state that drove the state to take over many of the church's former social responsibilities. The church, in turn, has been forced to develop ways to compensate for its loss of social role. In a public meeting in 1994, leaders from different councils produced social and spiritual suggestions about morality and also about political corruption, family disintegration, domestic violence, alcoholism, drugs, and crime. They recognized that the state alone is incapable of dealing with these problems (*El Nuevo Día,* December 18, 1994, 4–6). However, various religious leaders would agree with me that either these suggestions have not been developed or have not had a profound impact in terms of challenging governmental hierarchies and religious practice itself.

Similar to the situation in Brazil and Chile, where the alliance between Protestantism and politics can be seen through open endorsements by members of religious groups for a particular party and its political leaders (Freston 1993; Kamsteeg 1999), in Puerto Rico, well-known religious leaders such as Rodolfo Font (of the CFLW), Rafael Torres Ortega, and Jorge Raschke, to name a few, have publicly expressed their preference for certain candidate. This is one of the main reasons why politicians, especially from the PPD and the PNP, have been highly visible participants in major religious activities such as El Día de Clamor, a yearly national day of prayer celebrated in front of the capitol (or the Senate house) and originally initiated by the evangelist Jorge Raschke more than twenty years ago. A very recent example of this alliance, which was given much coverage by the media, involves Wanda Rolón, a pastor of a four-thousand-member church who publicly endorsed the reelection of ex-PNP governor Pedro Roselló. She reported his conversion from Catholicism to Protestantism a few weeks before the 2004 election and prophesied that he was going to be the first governor who would speak in tongues. She also criticized the PPD candidate Aníbal Acevedo Vilá (who ended up winning the election) for his stand against Protestantism (because of his Catholic faith) and his endorsement of homosexuality. This pastor's criticism is consistent with the public's general perception that Protestantism, especially Pentecostalism, is associated with the PNP (and its pro-statehood/American/Protestant ideology) and Catholicism with the PPD and PIP.

Other religious leaders have made public and precise statements regarding national identity and the country's status. This is because political status is seen as playing a significant role in developing the social and moral climate of the country. For example, at an interdenominational public meeting, Puerto Rico's lack of national identity was presented as one of the factors contributing to religious differences, lack of unity between the churches, and to the incapacity of the church to help resolve the difficult social and moral situation of Puerto Rico (*El Nuevo Día,* April, 5, 1996, 4). The centennial celebration in 1998 of Protestantism on the island brought together the Protestant community concerning efforts toward religious, social, and political unity. Statements of national affirmation were made throughout the centennial, like that of Bishop Juan Vera from the United Methodist Church at the time of its presidency of the CEPR: "We are confronted by a historical responsibility concerning the definition of our status and our definition as a nation. Silence is an accomplice. Each of our churches has affirmed that we are a nation, a Puerto Rican church" (*El Nuevo Día,* March 15, 1998, 6–7, my translation). The Reverend Jose Lebrón Velázquez, a well-known social activist and Protestant leader who was the coordinator of the centennial celebration, indicated publicly, in a more optimistic tone, that Puerto Rico is walking toward nationalism. Also, in the matter of national affirmation, while writing this book I learned that religious leaders from different denominations (including the executive associate minister of the Baptist churches of Puerto Rico) were arrested because of their involvement in the protests against the U.S. military presence in Vieques that finally resulted in the U.S. abandoning its base. These events took place after decades of military exercises covering two-thirds of the island had caused serious environmental and health hazards as well as damage to the island's economy. Some religious leaders used this opportunity to condemn the present political situation, while others characterized their involvement as more humanitarian or social than political. Here it is important to stress the fact that political involvement is seen by many Puerto Ricans as that which concerns the country's political status. Any religious involvement in social action (for example, to combat family disintegration, domestic violence, alcoholism, drug abuse, and crime, and to enhance the quality of life of communities) is seen as a spiritual affair (a response to God's call). This perspective coincides with the solution of transformation of life through conversion and social involvement through church activities, while dismissing or deemphasizing nonchurch avenues for social action.

The concept of disembedding serves to describe religion's restructuring in terms of internal characteristics in the last few decades in Puerto Rico. The term is used by Babb (1995: 4) in his study about the media in South Asia to refer to a change of pattern in which religion is not tightly interwoven with the social structures of kinship, neighborhood, and religious space (such as shrines, pilgrimage areas, and church buildings). To this list I add the social structures of geographical/national divisions and denominations, while emphasizing the latter. Disembedding in relation to denominational divisions is visible when similarities and differences (including those that may not be acknowledged) between churches in the areas of doctrine, teaching, evangelism, missions, social action, and liturgy are considered. Related to the latter, there is a noticeable decrease of the manifestation of the Holy Spirit in many Pentecostal churches. One example is the Pentecostal Church of God in Las Cuevas, which I will address in chapter 7.

At the same time, as I mentioned earlier, many historical churches in Puerto Rico have become charismatic, some of them including the physical manifestation of the Holy Spirit. For example, the two Baptist churches in Loíza, similar to my former church, adopted the charismatic style. More than two decades ago, Loízan Baptists did not clap their hands, and the music they sang was mainly from the hymnal book (translated from English to Spanish), which they sang with much solemnity. Today, folk instruments are allowed, as well as hand clapping, loud worship, repeated singing of *coritos* (short songs with simple lyrics), dancing in the spirit, speaking in tongues, and prophesying. During the late 1970s and early 1980s, supernatural healing and the practice of *liberación* (deliverance from demons or exorcism) became very popular in many Baptist churches, including those in Loíza. (The acts of deliverance in my church were mostly performed on black members or visitors and residents from the very inside parts of the "black" barrio my mother grew up.) In addition, many churches emphasized the second coming of Jesus Christ, which became central in Puerto Rico at large (of which the evangelist Yiye Ávila became the strongest emissary). During this time movies (translated from English) with an apocalyptic theme became very popular.[21]

Several forces have contributed to the disembedding of Puerto Rican religion. First among them is "special purpose groups" based on age, gender, career, charities, service, hobbies, missionary work, marital status, schooling, and a common work place. These can be religious or semi-religious, and as Wuthnow (1988: 100–31) indicates, they have been growing quickly in the United States in the past few decades. Examples of these groups are those developed at the UPR in which Loízan members participated. Members of these groups were encouraged to participate in conferences outside the country and to relate to Campus Crusade for Christ and other Christian university organizations and fellowships in the United States and Latin America.

The second force behind the restructuring of religious identity in the last four decades is the media, which in Puerto Rico, the United States, and Latin America has been a significant means of religious dissemination since the 1970s.[22] Today Puerto Rico is considered the country with the highest concentration of Christian media projects, and during my fieldwork it had about 12.5 million dollars invested in fourteen television stations and sixteen radio stations (*El Nuevo Día,* February 5, 1995, 4). Christian evangelical churches have about 56 percent of the television industry and 21 percent of the radio industry (*El Diario,* September 12, 1995, 4). For several years (from 1989 through 1992) I co-hosted my church's radio show "Rayos de Esperanza." During this time, I witnessed firsthand an interdenominational camaraderie between hosts and participants from different radio programs, although occasionally I sensed a degree of inter- and intradenominational competition. The fact that many churches produced radio programs at the same studio brought about a collaboration that extended to activities outside the studio. Christian media attracts people to the faith and facilitates the religious experience of those who are unable to attend church. However, many of the country's church leaders, including pastors in Loíza, complained that such media has become a substitute for church experience. In fact, over the years various programs sponsored by churches have followed the structure of a formal service (with a time for devotions followed by a sermon and an altar call or a prayer time for petitions called in over the phone). Christian media is also seen as a vehicle that can promote "false" doctrines and beliefs from other religious groups, confuse people, and cause them to switch religions easily.

In Las Cuevas, only 7 percent of the participants in my census indicated that they watched Christian television programs; however, this small percentage is due to the high concentration of churches in the area and great church participation, leaving television as a mostly information and entertainment alternative. Some individuals within this percentage and others outside this percentage acknowledged the positive and negative influences of Christian media. A higher percentage (12 percent) of participants listened to Christian radio programs, because they can do other activities while listening. The young Christian population continues to use the Christian media, but among those whom I interviewed in Las Cuevas, there has been a small decrease in usage. From their comments I determined that this decrease has to do with changes in the church service, such as incorporating more music and other artistic performances and the breaking of the "taboo" of a born-again Christian hearing "secular" music (as the Christian music style is becoming less distinguishable from the secular style).

In the last few decades, the number of Christian bookstores selling books and other religious items has also increased dramatically. During early 1980s I heard comments that indicated a Protestant effort to counter the *botánicas* (stores that sell religious paraphernalia: Catholic, Spiritist, and from Santera). In fact, according to Romberg (2003: 18), in the 1980s the influence of the global market on an increasing circulation of ritual goods and on what was available in *botánicas* was obvious. Sometimes bookstores are aligned with a Christian radio station and a church. This is the case of the Librería Evangélica de Carolina (Evangelical Bookstore of Carolina), which was founded in 1968 and is seen as one of the pioneers in the metropolitan area of Puerto Rico. Like Radio Vida, this bookstore was originally a project of the First Baptist Church of Carolina. The name of the bookstore was conceived to appeal to the non-Baptist community and, in fact, today this bookstore serves a significant number of clients from different denominations, a good number of whom are from Loíza. (I personally brought materials from the store to Pentecostal church members from Las Cuevas upon their request.)

Crusades or evangelical campaigns have become very important since the 1970s, although recently they have encountered great competition from Christian concerts, most of which draw audiences on a scale comparable to secular concerts.[23] As I mentioned earlier, many young church members from Las Cuevas told me that one of their churches' main attractions was the music ministry. The First Baptist Church of Loíza was remarked upon for its emphasis on music. Here, from 1979 through 1987, Rafael Osorio, one of the most popular Baptist pastors in Loíza, if not the most popular, pushed the music ministry forward, he himself being a musician and a band director. (Rafael Osorio had also been the pastor of the Second Baptist Church of Loíza from 1977 to 1979. It had been officially incorporated in 1961 under the pastorship of Luis A. Osorio, Rafael Osorio's father.) Music ministry has also promoted teenagers' attendance and participation in Christian concerts around the island and the integration and musical collaboration among members of different denominations. For this reason, many evangelists use Christian artists to attract people to their campaigns, particularly the youth. However, over the years tensions have grown between preachers and musicians in regular church meetings and evangelistic campaigns and concerts over which ministry is more important and deserves a longer period of participation.

Both the Christian music industry and individual or group Christian ministries are enjoying growing and widespread support across denominational lines. One such group is 33 D.C. (in Latin the abbreviation is A.D.), which tours Latin America and the United States. This group, like many music and preaching ministries, is helping to connect Puerto Ricans and to create a transnational religious experience. During my one-month visit to Springfield, Massachusetts in August of 1992, I witnessed the great popularity of 33 D.C. among members of a Hispanic Baptist church in the city. The pastor was Rafael Osorio, the pastor of the two Baptist churches of Loíza who had greatly encouraged the music ministry in these two churches. As the Hispanic population continues to grow in the United States and as more church members in Puerto Rico are becoming pastors and missionaries, an increasing number of native-born Puerto Rican pastors, like Rafael Osorio, are being transferred to Hispanic churches in the United States. Other retired pastors use their experience to keep Hispanic churches in the United States. Regarding these transfers, it is important to further investigate how Puerto Rico is becoming less an importer of missionaries and more an exporter. (During my latest trip to Puerto Rico, I learned about an increasing number of members from my former Baptist church who had become pastors of the church's missions. Others were studying to become pastors [they did not have a formal education in any other profession], and still others considered themselves to be missionaries after one or two trips overseas.)

Returning to Christian music ministries, their widespread popularity relates to the fact that the number of local Christian artists who have contracts or are managed by "secular" and "international" agencies or individuals keeps growing. This growth has caused changes in the groups' styles in accordance with sales and global connections.[24] The group 33 D.C. started playing mostly *jíbaro* or *nueva trova* music. Recently, it has incorporated hip-hop, soft rock, pop, flamenco, and other international music styles, which it has recorded overseas. The group has also been involved in transnational music projects, such as that with the famous Spanish Christian singer Marcos Vidal.

The widespread popularity of different Christian music ministries also has much to do with another subdued sign of religious restructuring on the island and among the Puerto Rican diaspora's religion: an increasing number of nondenominational churches founded or redefined in reference to a music ministry. (Some of these ministries have developed after the conversion of "secular" music artists, whose number continues to grow.) An illustrative case is the home church of 33 D.C. Members of the group are church leaders or have blood ties to the church's main leaders. The church's name is Asociación de Misioneros y Evangelistas Cristianos (Association of Christian Missionaries and Evangelists), but recently it has been known as Casa de Alabanza (Worship House). The church is also known by the name of the pastor (a well-known composer himself) or as the church of 33 D.C. The positions of worship leaders and worship pastors have become significant in churches such as Casa de Alabanza, which continues to grow at a rapid rate. In fact, in recent years it was joined by a group of families from my former Baptist church, many of whom had been involved for several years in the music ministry in my former church and in the Christian community in general. Another example involves the ministry of Richie Ray and Bobby Cruz, two Puerto Ricans who made salsa very popular internationally. They are also considered to be among the group of pioneers of secular and Christian salsa. Today, their ministry includes about seventy churches spread throughout different countries.

The preaching/evangelistic type of individual ministry using crusades, evangelical campaigns, and music performances continues to be significant, especially among the Pentecostal community (see Pérez Torres 1997: 50–64). Two of the most popular ministries within the Protestant community have been those of Yiye Ávila and Jorge Raschke, the latter having been surrounded by much controversy lately. Both originated in Puerto Rico during the 1970s and were much influenced by North American evangelism. Neither is strictly tied to a specific council. They are well known in Latin America and among the Hispanic community in the United States thanks to television and radio. Centro de Ayuda Social (Center of Social Help) is another such ministry. It was founded in 1967 by the Reverend Aurea Martínez Vilar, who was ordained by the Assemblies of God Church, although the ministry is not strictly affiliated with the Assemblies of God council. The Centro de Ayuda

Social focuses on social ministry and offers its services to needy children, the homeless, AIDS patients, and the needy community in general. It depends upon donations from the Christian community, including Catholics, who are recruited through Martínez Vilar's radio program on Sundays. Martínez Vilar's ministry has helped communities in Loíza, including Las Cuevas, during various emergencies, especially after hurricanes. In the future, it will be worth researching the extent to which the success of this social-oriented type of Christian ministry has to do with Martínez Vilar's gender or motherly role.

Somewhat related to individual ministries is the continuing growth in the number of individuals who can be considered passive Protestants and who follow what I call a personal religion. (In the past Protestants were considered active by default.) These individuals normally do not classify themselves within a religious denomination or church; instead, they claim to follow religion or God in "their own way." However, in Las Cuevas I found a number of residents who do classify themselves under a denominational or church category, but who do not attend church regularly. Firth's (1996) idea of religious personal adjustment elaborates on religious experience in its many dimensions and possibilities for variation and transformation.

Let me start with Carlos, with whom I became very close. Carlos, who is in his late sixties, lives in a comfortable house he inherited in Las Cuevas. He married a Pentecostal woman with whom he had three children, two of whom work as teachers. The importance of education was something he made sure to pass on to his children. He himself was not able to become an engineer because he did not have the money to go to school. Carlos told me many times that this was his greatest frustration in life. However, thanks to his uncle, who moved to Santurce in the San Juan area, Carlos received a better middle and high school education than he would have received in Loíza because its bad economic situation. He became a clarinet player and a refrigeration technician. In Loíza, for several years he directed an evangelistic band with musicians from different churches and directed the music ministry in his local church.

When I asked Carlos about his religious affiliation, he immediately answered, "Pentecostal, since childhood." Carlos told me that his sister was one of the founders of the Pentecostal Church of God in Las Cuevas, close to his house. When I asked him why he was Pentecostal, he told me its doctrine was the closest to the Bible. With jokes and funny anecdotes, Carlos explained why he did not prefer other religions or "philosophies." For example, he told me that it was common knowledge that drunk people had carried the images in the Catholic processions in the past and that the only words Catholics knew in Latin were those in the benediction because they were happy to leave mass. In a humorous way, Carlos also told me that in the past, during the season of *tiempo muerto* (literally dead season, referring to the end of the growing season), people thought witches and spirits were doing harm everywhere. They did not realize that their situation was bad because there was no work to provide income.

Carlos strongly defended his Pentecostal affiliation, but clarified to me that he, unlike his wife, was not a Pentecostal "de clavo pasao" (meaning he was not a fanatic and did not strictly follow the Pentecostal doctrine). He described his Pentecostal lifestyle as "elástica" (elastic, meaning flexible). Carlos made this clarification with a defensive attitude, clearly evident in his face and gestures, because people, including some "inteligencia" (meaning scholars), think that Pentecostals in Loíza are a bunch of ignorants, and that Pentecostalism is another form Spiritism. To explain why he is not a fanatic Pentecostal, Carlos narrated, in his usual humorous way, something that happened to him when he began to work at the beer company. He laughed throughout his narration, laughing it seemed at the joke and at the kind of person he was before.

> One day, Maribrás [a well-known and powerful socialist leader in Puerto Rico] came to the beer company to give a talk. He was a great speaker, who made everybody excited. After something he said, everybody clapped their hands and I said, "Praise the Lord." I felt very embarrassed and looked around to see if someone was laughing at me. How could I say that? I just said that automatically, without meaning. Then I realized what was happening in my life and to many Pentecostals. You cannot fool God. You have to do things using your mind and not by being a hypocrite. Damn the hypocrites! That what I hate the most, hypocrites!

Carlos does not see the point of going to church all the time, because it becomes something you do routinely without meaning. He says that you can communicate with God anywhere and anytime. To Carlos, reading the Bible is as important as knowing what is going on in the world and learning other "philosophies." Also, there are many things he dislikes about the Pentecostal doctrine and attitude, some of which he learns from the radio. One of the main things is the concept of "sin," which he calls "imperfection." Also, you cannot judge people "a la raja tabla" (a Puerto Rican expression meaning strictly). Carlos has learned to coexist and respect other "philosophies" beginning with the experience of living for many years in Santurce with his uncle, who was a staunch Catholic. (Carlos and his wife were taking care of his uncle, who was sick and in a wheelchair.)

Carlos's "philosophy" of life is to believe in God, to be honest with God, yourself, and others, and to take responsibility for your actions. This is why Carlos does not care for people who criticize him because he does not always go to church, works in a beer company, plays the lottery, make jokes all the time, and says many "bad words." Carlos's emphasis on sincerity is closely related to his emphasis on practicality. This manifested itself in the way he often brought up the issue of political preference and defended his affiliation with the PNP and his position in favor of the pro-statehood alternative for Puerto Rico as the most practical solution for Puerto Rico's situation.

Last but not less revealing is the experience of Manuel, whom I met while doing the census. Manuel, who is thirty, was raised by his mother along with his five siblings. Manuel's father, who was originally from Cuba, abandoned them to go back to Cuba, where he formed another family. Manuel thinks his mother found a good refuge in the Baptist church, as the Pentecostal church was too hyper-emotional for her and the Catholic church did not provide enough spirituality. Manuel converted to the Baptist faith when he was about thirteen years old and participated actively in the areas of church administration, youth ministry, teaching, and music. However, as Manuel got older and busier, he gradually quit attending church.

When I asked Manuel about his religious preference, at first he did not want to use any classification. "I think it is not a matter of religion but a matter of believing in the Creator. Well, I grew up Baptist [he laughed]. Let me say I prefer the Baptist doctrine. Put me down as a Baptist then. Yes, put me down as a Baptist, although I do not have any problem visiting another church. Some churches have good things that other churches do not have."

Manuel's mother and uncles always encouraged him to excel academically as they realized he was an intelligent child. Thanks to the Pell Grant, Manuel graduated magna cum laude with a bachelor of science degree in accounting from the UPR. The fact that he was accepted at the University of Louisiana, where he began a master's program in public administration, connected us and engaged us in long and deep conversations. His studies abroad and his Loízan identity were frequently mentioned as sources of pride because of misconceptions about Loízans. While in the United States, Manuel did not attend church that often, but in his mind and heart he kept close to God, a pattern that more or less has continued since his return. Manuel was not able to finish his degree because of financial and health problems. Since his return to the island he has worked in accounting.

Manuel emphasized repeatedly the fact that living in the United States opened a new world to him in terms of possible lifestyles and religious perspectives. He explained to me that in the United States you are not pressured and can survive by constantly crossing religious borders or by becoming rigidly attached to a religious doctrine. He said that he did not have any problem adding to his "spiritual journey" practices from Zen Buddhism, for example yoga and meditation. Manuel also talked about how living in the United States greatly helped him to overcome stereotypes. Manuel mentioned to me that some people think he is homosexual because he has a male roommate, a South American student he met in the United States, who came to study as an exchange student in Puerto Rico. Manuel admits that he does not possess a typical macho personality and that he is gentle in behavior and mannerisms, and he recognizes that these facts have contributed to people's opinions about him. This situation has supported his belief that people's stereotypes can have a serious negative impact on others and limit their progress.

According to Manuel, stereotypes are one of the greatest obstacles for the church in Puerto Rico. Stereotypical thinking also leads to a lack of honesty and a distraction from real issues and actions. Manuel disdained the recent involvement of religious leaders in opposition to the state's sanctioning of marriage between individuals of the same gender. Although he contends that it should not be the case, he believes that church attendance contributes to the formation of stereotypes. He nurtures his spirit by reading spiritual material, including the Bible, and listening to music with a positive message, including "some" Christian music. Manuel also told me that Christians spend too much time going to church and do not have time to share and witness God's love for others. He referred to the example of Jesus, who spent a lot of time with the socially and spiritually marginalized. "If you really believe deep inside, you have to commit," he told me. Manuel has been socially active since his return to Puerto Rico. He has been a member of the municipal assembly (at one point he considered running for mayor), helped organize civic activities, participated in protests, given free financial advice, and helped people with their taxes. Although he has voted for the pro-independence party, deep in his heart Manuel believes pro-statehood is the best solution for Puerto Rico. Manuel said that he will have to learn to overcome his concern about the criticism that will come from his pro-independence friends when he makes his real political preference known.

The cases at hand present noticeable problems for Rappaport's (1999: 119–24) argument that "acceptance" as a public act is what is required for ritual participation, rather than "belief" as a private state. In the personal experiences of Carlos and Manuel, it is precisely the requirement or the high standard of sincere belief for ritual participation that leads to lack of church involvement. These cases also present problems for Rodríguez Toulis's (1997: 30–31) observation that in Rastafarianism the older generation tends to be fundamentalist, passive, and uncritical, while the younger generation is open, proactive, and critical. Both of these cases speak about the way macro social and religious processes intersect with the community and personal dynamics involved in religious identity formation. The experience of Manuel touches upon an issue on which I am not able to elaborate appropriately: the role of the migration experience in the formation of religious identity. (However, this role is addressed somewhat in the experience of two pastors from the CC and the CFDC of Las Cuevas; both pastors participated in the military and lived in the United States and became pastors after coming back to Puerto Rico.)

I would finally like to point out the tensions Manuel found himself facing on a personal level: tensions among secularization (with the church-state separation), a growing religious pluralism, and the public's increasing influence on the church. As the next chapter will show, the Catholic Church's response to the reality of church-and-state separation is complex in the sense that its strategy has not always been clear and consistent (to substitute, to antagonize, to cooperate?), although it has not been impossible to identify.

4

From State to National
to Loízan Catholicism

Based on the experience of Loíza, in this chapter I analyze the movement of the Catholic Church away from being the state religion, a move that was forced by the implementation of the U.S. policy of separation between state and church at the beginning of the twentieth century. The fact that the people in political power in the United States were mostly Protestant helped Protestantism become the cultural and social standard in the island as well as the Catholic church's greatest competitor. Consequently, by the 1940s the Catholic Church was moving strategically toward being the "national" religion, which I use to refer to the religion that best represents whatever is identified as authentically Puerto Rican. The timing of the Catholic Church's movement was appropriate because, as I mentioned earlier, Puerto Rico was also moving quickly toward development with U.S. support and control, making critical the need to affirm national identity. As the religious competition intensified and dramatic social and economic changes occurred during the 1960s and 1970s, so grew the need for the Catholic Church to move strategically toward becoming the Loízans' religion. These movements were reflected in church life and ritual experience and, more specifically, in the idea of the role of the church in relation to the rest of society. I certainly agree with Picó (1998: 154) that addressing the issue of identity was not the only strategy the Catholic Church adopted to reinforce itself and cope with the great social changes and strong religious competition that began with the twentieth century. However, I argue that the strategy was significant, especially when combined with others.

The fact that I explore the movement toward Loízan Catholicism in the parish in Loíza as manifested in the ritual context has required me to look at the ways ritual has been approached. Many of these approaches have moved from emphasizing ritual's expressive or symbolic properties to what it actually does to people. More in the line of emphasizing the "doings" (using Zuesse's words [1975: 518]) of ritual or of a certain element of ritual, a sizeable number of cross-cultural works have focused or privileged one "doing" over the others. I classify these works into the following main "doings," each having many possibilities for the participants: 1) management of power, 2) alteration of reality, and 3) transcendence.[1] These three main doings of ritual are evident in the experiences of the parishioners of the Catholic Church in Loíza.

The data demonstrates that the Catholic church's march toward becoming the national and the Loízan religion were believed to be necessary. However, they became challenging and difficult because of a lack of consensus about national and town identity and because of the influence of conflicting socio-political agendas and competing religious and community groups.

Finally in this chapter I discuss the movement toward a more meaningful religious experience with the coming of the influence of the charismatic movement, which will be the focus of the following chapter.

Coming to Terms with Loízan Religion

During the Spanish colonial period, the establishment of the Catholic religion through the foundation of parishes was related in a supportive way to economic, urban, and population growth and the case of Loíza clearly exemplifies this relationship. During early colonization, an area in Loíza close to the river became an important gold mining zone (the first substantial economic activity on the island) mainly with the use of Indians. By the second half of the seventeenth century, three of the eleven sugar mills in Puerto Rico were located in the area of Loíza. Each mill had a chapel, but there was only a single chaplain, who exercised the duties of rural priest three months a year and who was sustained financially by the owners of the sugar mills.[2] By 1670, there was a significant concentration of population around the chapel, which was located near the river. The chapel was named after Saint Patrick after he was successfully petitioned to stop a huge ant plague that was destroying the *yuca* harvest in Loíza. (*Yuca* is a root that was also cultivated by the natives.) An Irish settlement controlling most of the hacienda production in the area of Canóvanas at the end of the eighteenth century assured the endurance of the name. The growth and concentration of residents in the area was such that in 1692 the governor asked permission of the Spanish monarchy to create the village of Loíza. Two years later, Loíza became a *partido* or *ayuntamiento* (a territorial division under the Spanish military colonial regime).

The eighteenth century began a new phase in Loíza's history. In 1719, Loíza was declared a town, becoming the seventh founded in Puerto Rico. Ten years later, a baptism in Loíza appeared on record for the first time. There is evidence that at this point the parish was named after the Holy Spirit, which is why the parish's full name today is Parish Holy Spirit and Saint Patrick. In 1821, the parish, of neoclassic design, was described for the first time as it is today.[3] By the same year, the parish had a priest, an assistant priest, a sacristan, two altar boys, and a manager or superintendent. Ten years later, the parish was described as financially prosperous. The town's economic growth, which placed Loíza among the most important sugar milling areas on the island, continued over the nineteenth century in great part thanks to the hard work of slaves, who in the middle of this century reached a significant number, and also to the work of free laborers, who are better referred to as *agregados*.[4] As the example of my grandfather revealed, these were small peasant farmers who were allowed to live on and work for subsistence a piece of the landowner's property in exchange for major labor.

During the second half of the nineteenth century, as Loíza's population continued to grow, the production of sugar in Loíza, as in the rest of Puerto Rico, began to slow down. This was due to a large extent to the elimination of European markets because of the production of sugar from sugar beets there, an increasing production of raw sugar in Cuba and Louisiana, and later the abolition of slavery in 1873. Despite the slow down, Loíza maintained a higher production than other towns, again thanks to the hard work of slaves, some of whom also had other jobs such as cattle breeding and domestic work. In 1876, Loíza ranked second in the total number of slaves working in town (Crespo 1974: 4–6) even though slavery had been abolished three years earlier. This means that the abolition of slavery took years to accomplish. Wage laborers, who were referred to as *jornaleros,* also contributed to the economic production of the town. These workers, as opposed to the *agregados,* were systematically regulated by the state; some slaves were considered *jornaleros* because they were rented out by slave owners to work on the plantations (Zaragoza 1995: 29–33). The end of the nineteenth century was also a difficult period for Loíza because of the change of economic structure from the hacienda system to *centrales* or mills. The latter had more advanced techniques to mill the cane and were mostly controlled by sugar firms in the United States. In the area of Loíza, La central de Canóvanas and the Fajardo Sugar Company gave jobs to a sizeable number of Loízans and residents from Las Cuevas.

Loíza's difficult situation at the end of the nineteenth century caused a group of landowners and important individuals (including foreigners established in the area) to seek to transfer the administrative center from what began to be called "Loíza Aldea" (the urban center of the town of Loíza today) to the barrio of Canóvanas (about eight kilometers from Loíza Aldea and far from the coast).[5] Canóvanas was enjoying economic prosperity with a small group of white residents of Spanish and Irish ancestry controlling the economy. Framing these efforts was the belief that the isolated location of the administrative center from the big market at Canóvanas and nearby urban centers contributed greatly to the town's general socioeconomic problems and served as an obstacle to economic plans for future prosperity. The timing of these efforts corresponded with the establishment of the new policies endorsed by the United States toward the improvement of the social and economic situation of Puerto Rico. Under the initiative of Don Alfredo Soeggard, a merchant and the president of the municipal council, and Major Luis (Lico) Hernaiz Veronne, the transfer of the administrative center and of the parish seat officially took place in 1910, although an unofficial transfer had already occurred in 1908. From then on, the area of Canóvanas continued to enjoy economic prosperity while the rest of Loíza continued to decline.

The transfer of the administrative center involved the transfer of the parish seat, and those who could financially support the restoration of the church therefore lost their interest in it. In 1867, an earthquake damaged the church structure and nine years later a strong hurricane left the structure cracked and weakened, which led to the eventual destruction of the sacristy. From 1876 onward, the church was utilized less and less for liturgical purposes, although it was not until after 1924, when the choir loft of the church finally collapsed, that all the liturgical items were removed from the church and "put into a box" (the way Loízans describe it). As a section of Stevens's (1902: 2) poem says, "It was unsafe, so the people said. The roof might fall at any time." After the transfer, priests from Canóvanas, Carolina, Humacao, and municipalities outside the ecclesiastical district were expected to help by celebrating mass and administering the sacraments in Loíza Aldea, since it no longer had its own priest. However, according to elders from Las Cuevas, in many instances the priests did not show up, or came with a negative attitude, and even refused to baptize children, sometimes because they were black. This situation created an ambiguous attitude toward the clergy similar to what Taylor (1995: 102–66) has found in small villages in Ireland. In Las Cuevas this attitude manifested itself in sarcastic remarks about the church and the clergy and also in jokes about priests, most of which were inspired by actual events and involved ridiculing the priests' Spanish or North American English accents, drinking habits, laziness, and feminine mannerisms.

The lack of access to clergy and to doctors or health facilities in Loíza promoted the development of religious specialists such as *curanderos* (healers) and *santigueros* (specialists in healing through massaging and ritualistic anointing). Some of these specialists depended on the guidance of the spirits. As a resident of Las Cuevas explained, "If it weren't for the 'witches' many people would have died. There were no doctors around here and the doctors in Canóvanas did not want to come here." The lack of access to the parish seat in Canóvanas and the decrepit structure of the parish building in Loíza Aldea led to the conversion of homes into places for confession, baptism, and altars for saints. Furthermore, according to the elderly people with whom I spoke, during the time I just described the devotion to Santiago Apóstol became significant, although the saint's importance had grown steadily since the second half of the nineteenth century after a group of Loízans claimed to have seen the image of Santiago Apóstol appear at the beach and then shortly after inside the parish. Another version of the story says that after the image moved to the parish in Mediania Alta, it miraculously moved back to a tree at the beach to establish that Santiago was with his people in Loíza. This pattern is similar to that of the apparition of the Virgin of Our Lady of Charity that floated off the eastern coast of the island of Cuba in the beginning of the seventeenth century (Tweed 1999: 136). The representation of Santiago as a warrior and the fact that he was the most important saint in Spain meant that Loízans gave him greater importance than Saint Patrick during a difficult and crucial time in their history.

It was at this moment of Loíza's history—characterized by the weak presence of the Catholic Church, a steadily growing popular Catholicism through the devotion to Santiago Apóstol, and a significant practice of witchcraft and/or folk Spiritism mixed with locally developed African traditions—that the first Protestant denomination came to Loíza. (Loíza corresponded to one of the areas selected by the Baptists to evangelize.) Contrary to the usual pattern of founding the first Baptist church downtown and close to the main plaza, the First Baptist Church of Loíza was founded in 1902 in the barrio of Mediania Alta, where the festival of Santiago Apóstol originated. There are two reasons for this unusual pattern in Loíza. First, the downtown area was in bad shape. Second, the first person who became a Baptist was a resident of Medianía Alta. He had connections with missionaries from Carolina and allowed Baptist meetings at his house.

Initially the Baptist church (or "the Protestant church" as it was known in the town then) did not attract many Loízans in Medianía Alta or in the downtown area. Still today this fact is considered one of the reasons why Loíza has developed more slowly socioeconomically than Canóvanas, where Protestantism was initially more successful. (We already encountered this view in the JP report regarding the separation.) During a phone interview with Pastor Rafael Osorio (on October 8, 2002), the pastor of the First and the Second Baptist Churches in Loíza, he indicated that the area of Medianía Alta has always been challenging for the gospel because of the superstitious and "party" mentality, social problems, low-self esteem, and conformist attitude of the people. He added that this has been so even from the official Catholic point of view.

The situation was a little bit different for Pentecostalism in Loíza, which as is the case in most of the rest of Puerto Rico, entered the area in the 1930s with greater success than the Baptist Church, although the fact that the Baptist Church had already opened the field for evangelistic work in various communities, including the downtown area, must be taken into account. Today there are two congregations of the Pentecostal Church of God in Loíza, one of which is in Las Cuevas and was founded about thirty years ago. Given the characteristics of Pentecostalism discussed in the previous chapter, there is no doubt that Loízans felt attracted to Pentecostalism because it offered something that popular Catholicism, witchcraft, Spiritism, and even the Baptist Church could not offer: a unique combination of old elements (such as open leadership, supernatural manifestation, and immediate gratification) and new elements (such as a strong centrality on the Bible and clear-cut codes of behavior).

However, this new religious alternative did not stop a sizeable number of Loízans from fighting for the transfer of the administrative center from the barrio of Canóvanas back to Loíza Aldea in order to help their personal lives and the town's social stability and progress. According to elderly Loízans, the idea of fighting to get the administrative center back had been in the Loízans' minds since the center had been transferred away in 1910. [6] During the transfer there were many protests, especially by people from the barrios of Medianía Alta and Medianía Baja. However, it was not until the 1940s, when the country was moving with a concrete plan to help the progress of the island, that many Loízans were inspired to come up with a definite plan to help Loíza Aldea. After decades of failure in this endeavor, in the 1960s Loízans endorsed the separation of Loíza and Canóvanas as a way to start over as a municipality. In 1965, they founded a committee to help their new cause, the Comité Cívico Pro-restauración del Municipio de Loíza (Aldea). At this point it was established that the 1910 transfer was illegal. Members of this committee and their supporters brought to the public attention the fact that the leaders of the elite involved in the transfer in 1910 had worked hard to improve the new city's services and facilities in barrio Canóvanas. In fact, only eight years after the transfer, the service and facilities in town were as good as those in other municipalities (Alonso 1922: 5). The area of Loíza Aldea in contrast, was left with the city hall building, the plaza, the cemetery, and the parish building, all of which were in bad shape. Loíza Aldea did not have a meat market, a slaughterhouse, a jail, or local offices to provide public services to a population, mostly colored, illiterate, and unemployed, that continued to grow faster than the population in the area of Canóvanas (U.S. Census 1930, 128, 147, 161). Loízans made public reference to the fact that still in the 1960s they did not have enough public services and facilities in the areas of health and education.[7] They lacked residential areas, had problems with utilities, and suffered high unemployment and underemployment rates.[8] The high rates were exacerbated in the 1960s by the closings of La central de Canóvanas and of a very important leather factory. Loízans also made public their lack of sufficient recreational facilities, which was a significant problem given that sports (especially softball and baseball) were very important to Loízans, as demonstrated by their active involvement in sports over the decades.[9]

As Pérez (1994) has demonstrated to be the case in Cuba, sports have been an instrument of sociopolitical order and also of identity, integration, and social mobility. During my fieldwork, the lack of sport or recreational facilities was a common topic of conversation. Many adult residents from Las Cuevas told me that they would like their children to be more involved in sports to avoid the dangers of the streets. Some children and teenagers who gathered in the streets told me how much they wished to become famous athletes in order to be "somebody" and have enough money. For a few of them, becoming a famous and wealthy athlete was more important that getting a formal education and having a professional career. (This was also the point of view of the parents of two young adults who at the time of my research were earning incomes in the United States through professional sports.)

Loízans' efforts paid off. With the coming of the worst economic crisis in the history of Puerto Rico since the Depression came the separation of Loíza from Canóvanas in 1971, along with the simultaneous creation of the municipalities of Loíza and Canóvanas. However, the event had serious consequences for Loízans, which were already discussed in chapter 2.

Building Bridges between Official and Popular Catholicism

The Loízans' movement to regain status as a municipality, to improve their social and economic situation, and to affirm their identity as a *pueblo* (town or a unified group of people) with respect to Canóvanas and Puerto Rico happened during a critical time of larger competitive social, political, and religious agendas. The country's competitive religious landscape, which was discussed in chapter 3, had the element of a weak Catholic Church confronting popular Catholicism, which included popular eschatological movements such as Hermana Elena (Sister Elena) and Hermanos Cheo (the Cheo Brothers). These popular movements developed in order to manage the dramatic changes that the establishment of the U.S. system brought to the social and religious landscape. In Loíza, popular Catholicism manifested itself in many ways, but especially in a strong devotion to Santiago Apóstol that integrated elements from Spiritism, witchcraft, and later from Santería. Also as I mentioned earlier, after the U.S. occupation the Catholic Church began to function under the jurisdiction of the U.S. Catholic Church, forcing a fast restructuring of the church and requiring a solid plan to compete with the fast penetration of Protestantism. One of the most significant strategies of this plan was to propel the idea that Catholicism was the national religion and therefore the religion of the *pueblo* (people), although in the situation of Loíza these two were at times strategically distinguished. But first, the Catholic Church needed to reconstitute itself spiritually, socially, and materially in most parts of the island.

In Loíza, strengthening Catholicism needed to begin with restoring the parish downtown. The systematic efforts for this restoration began in the 1940s under the initiative of Father Roberto Angel (who was in charge of the parishes of Canóvanas, Loíza, and Carolina) and his assistant Salvador Salinas. They led Loízans' concrete initial attempts to transfer the administrative center back to its original place in Loíza Aldea. Indeed, these two efforts are closely related: as far back as the era of Spanish colonialism a downtown parish was a prerequisite for a town. These efforts to restore Catholicism also responded to the successful growth of Pentecostalism. In 1960, the parish seat was officially regained, after having been lost during the transfer of the administrative center from Loíza Aldea to Canóvanas in 1910. Another significant event, which happened in 1976, was the registration of the parish building in the National Registry of Historical Monuments. Part of the commonwealth's agenda to advance Puerto Rican culture was to preserve historical sites and monuments, such as that of the parish building of Loíza, which was built in a European style and contained an exhibition of Indian archaeological material found in the town.

Those interested in the restoration formed various groups such as the Committee of Saint Patrick's Church Restoration and the Honorary Committee in San Juan, both with Loízan and non-Loízan residents as members. Thirty thousand dollars were even collected with the help of the Irish Catholic community and members of Saint Patrick's Cathedral in New York City (*El Mundo*, July 31, 1949, 1). Here I would like to point out that during the time of the donation (late 1940s), this Irish Catholic community in New York was experiencing a change of perspective from Irish-American nationalism to extending progress beyond the Irish community (Díaz-Stevens 1993b: 81–83). This experience clearly points to the use of both nationalism and ethnic identity for the purpose of expanding Catholicism and reaching out to the general population and particularly to ethnic minorities or socioeconomically marginal groups. For instance, in the United States, a committee of bishops representing Spanish-speaking communities was created in 1945 to establish social and pastoral programs in Texas, California, Colorado, and New Mexico and to fight against prejudice and discrimination against Hispanics in the church (Kanellos 1993: 378). This occurred in a moment of intense Protestant outreach to migrant workers (Privett 1988: 110). In Guatemala, the Catholic Church also made manifest its support of indigenous people, who had been previously ignored and damaged by national developmental policies and by the Catholic Church itself (Belanger 1992).

Nevertheless, the unequal valorization of national identity by Catholic leaders and the various versions of what was considered to be authentic Puerto Rican presented challenges to the Catholic Church's efforts to solidify its image as the national religion of the country. A case in point, which occurred decades after the reforms of Vatican II to transform the church in order to reach out to the masses, is the 1960s controversy surrounding the inclusion of Puerto Rico in the mission of Consejo Espiscopal Latinoamericano (Latin American Episcopalian Council or CELAM). This organization was founded in 1955 with the purpose of theologically defending indigenous Catholicism in Latin America. For some Catholics, the inclusion of Puerto Rico in CELAM represented a break with the Spanish traditions that had come from centuries of Spanish colonial power and also a break with North American traditions (although the North American Catholic leadership initially adopted the Spanish style to differentiate itself from Protestantism). For these Catholics, inclusion in CELAM was a necessary step for the indigenization of the church in Puerto Rico. Opponents, however, were wary of any threat against the North American values already implemented on the island as part of a "new" national identity associated with the United States. Not surprisingly, a few years later the Partido Acción Cristiana (Christian Action Party or PAC) was founded to oppose liberal public policies, such as those regarding public education (while defending Catholic education), those that were against Catholic principles, and those that served primarily the interests of the United States. PAC's membership was composed of former members of different political parties, but mainly the pro-independence party.

The events in the town of Comerío, in the interior part of the island, also reveal the challenges the Catholic Church was facing at the time. In this parish, a controversy exploded in 1971 because of the incorporation in the mass of folk or *jíbaro* music with an allegedly subversive or anti-Spanish and anti-American message. The events resulted in the excommunication of the Dominicans in charge of the parish and the closing of the church (Díaz-Stevens 1993a). I suggest that behind the risky experiment (from the point of view of the church) of allowing *jíbaro* music in the Catholic liturgy lay the need to move ahead of the Protestant churches, some of which were already trying to use the nationalist discourse to attract people and with this to counteract the view of Protestantism as an urban middle-class religion that also largely identified itself with North American culture (Agosto Cintrón 1996: 101). As I mentioned earlier, *jíbaro* music became popular in the late 1970s in the Baptist community in general. In fact, during the 1980s, the Baptist pastor Luis A. Ortíz who had become popular for preaching as "Don Crédulo Bautista," a *jíbaro* from the mountain, was invited by many Baptist churches to be a guest speaker. Years later, in 1995, Pastor Ortíz became the pastor of the Baptist church of Medianía Alta. He recently retired and moved to the United

States. (The Web site of the Baptist Churches of Puerto Rico, as of June 15, 2005, features a photo of Pastor Ortíz pretending to play drums in front of a large painting of *vejigantes*.)

Establishing Catholicism as both the national and the people's religion was particularly challenging in Loíza because of the need to safeguard official Catholicism while building bridges to a strong popular Catholicism that had some connections to African traditions that had been marginalized and also while competing with a proselytizing Protestant program that involved discrediting the Catholic Church. Father Antonio Hernández, the Trinitarian priest who had been the pastor of the downtown parish the longest, since 1973, was a strong defender of the "true" Catholic faith in Loíza. For him, Catholicism was authentically Puerto Rican by default. This he substantiated with the Catholic Church's long history on the island as opposed to that of Protestantism, which came centuries later. To support his point even further, he constantly mentioned that Protestantism was the most threatening development for the unity of the people of Puerto Rico. As I mentioned earlier, Loízan Catholics have gotten used to public attacks against the Catholic Church. These attacks, according to Father Antonio and many parishioners, usually happen with the mayor's consent because he and many of his employees are Protestant. However, Father Antonio also admitted that there have been public town events and funerals in which Protestant and Catholic leaders have participated in harmony.

According to Father Antonio, attacking Protestantism, as the Catholic Church did in the past, was not the best way to reform or revive Catholicism in Loíza or anywhere else. Father Antonio began his plan of revival by "ridding" the church of witchcraft, Spiritism, and especially Santería, which to many Loízans has been promoted by the festival of Santiago (because of the festival's substitution of Santiago with the deities of Changó and Ogun from Santería). The folklorization of Puerto Rican culture that began in the 1970s also helped these practices to be accepted more openly in the country. As explained by Father Antonio, ridding the church of these pagan beliefs eliminated one Protestant rationale for criticizing the Catholic Church. At the same time, some of his comments seemed to suggest that the individualist mentality, which came along with Protestant ideology and with industrialism, had something to do with people adhering to religious concepts because they thought doing so was personally good for them, even if these concepts did not represent truth. This perception coincides with Romberg's (2003:

19) statement that the Protestant individualist ethos unwittingly promoted a relative, laissez-faire orientation and a value for free choice while opening more space for the practice of marginalized religions in different types of combination or forms.

Father Antonio's plan also involved reminding people that the "real" town's patron since the seventeenth century had been Saint Patrick, and not Santiago Apóstol, who became the central figure in Loíza's coat of arms later on. Therefore, the festivities in Saint Patrick's honor were the "real" patron saint festivities. Like the efforts of the leaders of the Cuban Catholic Church of Miami to distinguish between the worship of Our Lady of Charity and Ochún, the Yoruba goddess of Santería (Tweed 1999: 142), Father Antonio drew a distinction between the festival of Saint Patrick as a "religious" celebration and the festival of Santiago Apóstol as a "traditional" celebration. (I have to confess that I got tired of Catholics telling me about this distinction.) Father Antonio and his parishioners fought to have the festival of Saint Patrick publicly recognized and in 1980 the festival was first observed with the sponsorship of the Instituto de Cultura Puertorriqueña, the Cultural Center of Loíza, and the mayor's office, which saw this celebration as another public relations opportunity. Father Antonio believed that Catholicism represented Puerto Rican national identity, that the celebration in honor of Saint Patrick was Loíza's "real" patron saint festival, and that it was a religious festival, and he intended to change Loízan society accordingly. This change was even more urgent as the patron saint festivities became more secular and indecent. Father Antonio insisted that the Saint Patrick's celebration include "decent" presentations. This meant an emphasis on the Spanish classical and *jíbaro* traditions. Here I argue that the existence of the festival of Santiago, which over the years has included more secular activities, has helped the festival of Saint Patrick to preserve its "religious" and "decent" character.

Father Antonio was also very interested in doing further restorations to the parish structure to make it look more like its original European style, a connection he celebrated. (In the summer of 2000 restorations were reinitiated, but sadly, Father Antonio had died and was not there to see them.) During my field study, the Saint Patrick's celebration enjoyed the participation of Archbishop Luis Cardenal Aponte Martínez, various parishes, including the parish of Santiago Apóstol, and government and cultural groups and organizations, such as the choir of the UPR.

Similarly to Father Antonio's request of local artist Samuel Lind that he paint a dark Saint Patrick to put inside the church and close to the altar (the image of Santiago used in the festival continues to be a white saint), Father Antonio's distinction between a "religious" and a "traditional" celebration was a critical way of building bridges between official and popular Catholicism without compromising the former or ignoring the latter. A similar tactic has been used by the Indonesian government in order to deal with the demands of recognition by so many ethnic groups. According to Kipp (1996: 118), the Indonesian government has promoted a distinction between *agama*, an officially sanctioned religion, and *kepercayaan*, an ethnic religion that often connotes something like superstition, allowing the latter to survive "under the umbrella of culture."

Another step involved Father Antonio's approval of placing the image of Santiago inside the church during the festival. However, he did not allow the placement of Santiago de las mujeres (Santiago of the women) and Santiaguito or Santiago de los niños (little Santiago or Santiago of the children), which he regarded as "inventions" of the people. He allowed these concessions in spite of his strong sentiments about many elements of the festival of Santiago. In fact, he considered the festival to be an opportunity for criminals, gays, and transvestites to challenge openly the authorities, traditional values, the church, and himself. The pressure on Father Antonio to make a few but significant concessions regarding the festival had much to do with the fact that the guardians or "mantenedores" of Santiago's image had become faithful members of the Catholic Church. It also had much to do with a presumed association of the festival with the parish of Santiago Apóstol, although that is still disputed. This parish was founded in 1971 (the same year of the closing of the parish of Comerío, as I mentioned earlier) under the pastorship of Father José Ramón Fernández, and in the barrio of Medianía Alta, where the saint's image first appeared on the beach in the nineteenth century.

According to some founding members of the parish of Santiago Apóstol, they used to meet in a small and rustic chapel but had to travel about five kilometers to meet at the parish or with its members downtown. A priest came specifically to them every once in a while to help with mass. Nuns helped with catechism under an almond tree at the beach. This became the favorite gathering area after the devastation of Hurricane San Ciprián in 1932, which destroyed the existing rustic chapel. At the end of the 1940s, when the efforts to restore the parish downtown were on their way, Santiago Osorio Santos, a merchant from the area, donated a piece of property so that parish members could construct a more adequate chapel of their own. Residents collected money by going house to house. The bishop of San Juan, Jaime Pedro Davis, made a special donation. Feeling disadvantaged compared to the parishioners of the parish of the Holy Spirit and Saint Patrick (whose efforts had the commitment of local, national, and international groups) and because of the very poor situation of the region, the residents of Medianía Alta supported the idea of extending the celebration of Santiago Apóstol to ten days in order to collect more money for the construction of a permanent chapel. The construction of a new cement chapel was completed at the end of the 1950s and underwent a major expansion at the end of the 1980s because at that time attendance at mass was so great that some people had to watch mass through the window from outside.

I argue that the Catholic Church's decision to approve the foundation of the parish of Santiago Apóstol showed that it was moving ahead of the PNP in reaching out to people: by helping the people of Medianía Alta in particular, the church appeared to be siding with the most marginalized. With this move, the Catholic Church was able to counter allegations that it gave preference to the downtown Catholic community during the 1940s, when both parishes were trying to have a permanent parish building. As a longtime member of the parish of Santiago Apóstol put it: "We appreciated the cardinal and the bishop for helping us to have our own parish. We did not want to be left behind." The Catholic Church's point of departure was to recognize the significance of the devotion of Santiago Apóstol in Medianía Alta and then to provide the people of Medianía Alta with the opportunity to legitimize their Catholic practice by making the devotion to Santiago more in line with official Catholicism. This put the Catholic Church in a better position to compete with the Baptist and Pentecostal churches, which at the time were gathering momentum in the area. According to various longtime members, pursuing this common goal strengthened the unity of the community while helping self-esteem and a sense of identity. However, some degree of separation among residents occurred because the founding of the parish required some distancing from the most unofficial elements of popular Catholicism. Also, as I mentioned in chapter 2, the founding of the parish of Santiago Apóstol was thought by some residents, including those who migrated to Connecticut, to be a way to silence their old ethnic traditions (which is the reason why some Baptist members supported the founding of the parish), to control the religious situation, and to conceal deep social and economic concerns during a crucial historic time in Loíza because of the separation.

The efforts of the Catholic Church to become the national and the local religion had two side effects. One the one hand, they helped the revival of Catholicism. On the other hand, they encouraged a group of people to realize their need for something else: something larger than national or ethnic identity or something outside the Catholic Church, such as Pentecostalism, which could help them deal with their identity as poor people. As the atmosphere of religious competition (including the competition between the two Catholic parishes in Loíza) and the competition between sociopolitical agendas and communities became more intense over the decades, Loízans began to search for different solutions. As I mentioned earlier, one of these solutions was to fight for the town's socioeconomic stability. Pentecostalism (and the historical Protestant churches) continued to grow while providing (consciously or not) some space for national and Loízan identity in the liturgy, with a simple peasant style and national and local rhythms, and helping Loízans to resolve socioeconomic concerns. The latter was also a technique used by the Catholic Church with some good results, although not as many as had been gained by the Pentecostal churches. It is not a coincidence that during this time members of the Catholic Church began to search for what they described as "more meaningful" or "more spiritual" religious experience through an emphasis on the Holy Spirit's work while purposively leaving behind the issue of identity. One of the most critical steps in this search was the adoption of the charismatic style, already highly characteristic of Pentecostalism. As I indicated in chapter 3, in the 1970s in Puerto Rico many historical Protestant churches adopted the charismatic style because it was becoming a great attraction and a source of spiritual legitimacy.

The Coming of the Charismatic Experience

The charismatic movement, which emphasized the Holy Spirit's supernatural manifestations, began in the Catholic Church in the United States at the end of the 1960s and spread rapidly all over the world (Boudewijnse 1998: 99; Stoll 1990: 50). Marcelino, a deacon from the parish in downtown Loíza at the time of my field study, was one of the first members to attend charismatic retreats in the towns of Caguas and Aguas Buenas and to celebrate prayer meetings at homes in the 1970s. He became a deacon with diocesan priest Father Lozano, the first priest after the official reopening of the downtown parish in 1960. According to Marcelino and other parishioners, with Father Lozano immediate transformations occurred in the parishioners' financial commitments, in the teaching, in the liturgy, and in the leadership. Father Lozano was particularly concerned about recruiting men, and on one occasion he organized a special procession with approximately four hundred Catholic men from the town of Cidras. He also made home visits and sent a group of men, including Marcelino, to take *cursillos de cristiandad* (small courses on the faith) in Río Piedras, which according to Marcelino and contrary to Díaz-Stevens (1993a: 148) did not have anything to do with any political agenda, such as supporting or preventing liberation theology. To Marcelino, the *cursillos* did not have to do with identity either but with the work of the Holy Spirit. The open attitude of Father Lozano and the parish laity to the charismatic experience, I suggest, prevented in Loíza that which happened in other towns in Puerto Rico, Adjuntas for example, where the charismatic movement in the 1980s resulted in the formation of a separate charismatic church.

Adopting the charismatic style was a way for Catholicism in Loíza to legitimize itself as authentic religious practice, especially considering the tensions between Catholics and Protestants and the subtle differences between the parish of the Holy Spirit and Saint Patrick and the parish of Santiago Apóstol.[10] At the same time, it was also a way for Catholics from the parish downtown to defend their version of Loízan authenticity, although as I will discuss in the next chapter, a sizeable number of parishioners still insist on disregarding the issues of religious competition and identity in relation to the charismatic style and other climatic changes. Here I cannot ignore a large push by the Catholic hierarchy for a discourse on more spirituality in the Catholic Church, which the charismatic movement served directly or indirectly. As Hurbon (2001: 121) observes, in Haiti, for instance, this pushing by the Catholic hierarchy, which also opposed the government of Aristide after the collapse in the 1980s of a long-established dictatorship, was intended as a break with the growing success of liberation theology (or its fundamental principles) in Latin American churches. (I remember Aristide's visit to the UPR for a major presentation when I was a student there and the great controversies it brought about.) From the point of view of the popular masses, the charismatic movement in Haiti constituted a new way for Haitians to interpret the country's social and political problems in the midst of confusion, through emphasizing an inner spiritual change.

In sum, the movement of the Catholic Church from a state to a national to a people's or Loízan religion was not linear, because the movements often intersected. It was gradual, cumulative, and specific to Loíza and its various communities, such as Medianía Alta, and it was also greatly influenced by the forces of religious and social competition and identity. Certainly, this effort of the Catholic Church to become a Loízan religion was proven to be necessary but insufficient. Understanding how and why it was not enough for Loízans is the purpose of the next chapter.

Figure 1. *Vejigantes*: Santiago Apóstol festival.

Figure 2. Mass celebrated during the festival in honor of Loíza's patron saint, St. Patrick, attended by Archbishop of San Juan, Luis Cardenal Aponte Martínez. The dark skin portrait of St. Patrick by the Loízan artist Samuel Lind is on the left.

Figure 3. Parish of Santiago Apóstol in barrio Medianía Alta.

Figure 4. The Catholic church of downtown Loíza evangelizing in neighborhoods during Easter. This high crime neighborhood is considered very dangerous.

Figure 5. Authentic Loízan Catholic tribute.

Figure 6. Church of Christ of Las Cuevas. This church was recently relocated away from homes because of complaints about the noise during church activities.

Figure 7. Church of the Faithful Disciples of Christ of Las Cuevas in a residential area.

Figure 8. "Lydia": A proud Christian and *jabá* Loízan with messy hair.

Figure 9. "Bartolo," keeping his knees calloused until the Lord comes for him.

"No more Latin"

Toward a More Meaningful Loízan Catholic Experience

The purpose of this chapter is twofold. Here I examine closely the movement of the Catholic Church in downtown Loíza toward furnishing a more meaningful religious experience through changes in the last thirty years in the teaching and liturgy and regarding the "doings" of ritual, discussed in the previous chapter. I analyze how this movement also responded to issues of identity and the dynamics of religious competition, without ignoring a deep motivation to experience God openly and personally and the Holy Spirit's guidance for spiritual and social action. In fact, the parishioners claim that the Holy Spirit is the most important motivation behind these changes. However, I insist that the parishioners' hierarchical model of explanation translates into a way of managing identity, into a way to affirm and experience authentic spirituality and simultaneously Loízan Catholic identity and therefore to downplay stereotypes that Loízan religion is based on folk religion and resistance. This is significant when considering that Protestants have viewed Catholic identity within the cultural and not the spiritual domain, although other social forces are also significant.

Transformations in the Parish of Loíza

I would like to begin locating the transformations in Loíza's downtown parish by providing a brief description of the experience of the Catholic Church in Puerto Rico in the last few decades. At the public level, the organization of large events has greatly helped the visibility of the Catholic Church on the island in the last few decades and in the midst of a very strong Protestant presence. One of the events remembered by Puerto Ricans of all denominations was covered heavily by the media: the visit of the pope in 1984. Thousands of people participated in the pope's visit, including leaders of Protestant denominations. Ten years later, as I mentioned earlier, the archbishop of Puerto Rico appeared with leaders from other councils in a public meeting, also covered heavily by the media, to discuss ways to help the Puerto Rican social and moral situation. The Catholic Church's role as a moral guard was strengthened recently, during my field study, when it raised its voice, together with Protestant leaders, against contraception, homosexual marriage, and the banning of the sodomy law. The Catholic Church also participated heavily with the Protestant community in protesting against the U.S. military presence in Vieques.

In the area of social ministry, the Catholic Church's efforts are extensive. It has hundreds of ministries such as hospitals, nursing homes, prisons, orphanages, shelters, and homes for unwed mothers. It has chapels in hospitals, police stations, prisons, nursing homes, and at the main airport in Carolina. During my field study, in the area of education, the Catholic Church was administering about 138 private schools, 6 university chapels, 1 interdiocesan seminary (with 2 campuses), and another small seminary. It also owns 2 radio stations, several radio programs, its main newspaper, *El Visitante*, and 3 popular magazines. The acquisition of television's Channel 13 in 1995, which covers the island and boasts of a large number of Protestant viewers, including many from Loíza, has improved the visibility of the Catholic Church in the country.[1]

Important changes have encouraged active participation in the Catholic Church. Here I can point out the nine sanctuaries spread throughout the island and especially the nineteen spiritual retreat centers that place a strong emphasis on developing a personal relationship with God. The significance of spiritual retreats relates to changes in the teaching and in the liturgy associated with the adoption of the charismatic style and an emphasis on the leading of the Holy Spirit. Even today, Loízan Catholics use the expression "no more Latin" to summarize the movement toward a more meaningful experience through an emphasis on the Holy Spirit's work. Beside the literal view of the word "Latin" there is a symbolic use of the word to refer to "the unknown," "the far distant," "the superficial," "the inauthentic," the nonspiritual or less spiritual, and the meaningless or less meaningful. More specifically, this phrase is normally used by Catholics in Loíza to distinguish Catholicism in the present from Catholicism in the past. It is also used by Protestants to justify their dissatisfaction with the Catholic Church and their conversion to Protestantism.

As I discussed in chapters 2 and 4, the 1970s marked a new era in the history of Loíza as it became a municipality and in the history of its religion with the growth of Pentecostalism, the founding of the parish of Santiago Apóstol, and the coming of the Trinitarians, who gradually welcomed the charismatic experience, to the parish downtown. The first Trinitarian who came to the Parish Holy Spirit and Saint Patrick in downtown Loíza (or Loíza Aldea) in 1971 was Father Martin VanTrieste. Like Father Lozano, the first priest after the reopening in 1960, Father Martin is remembered for encouraging leadership, particularly through the Eucharist ministry to the sick and disabled. Father Martin was followed by Father Antonio Hernández in 1973, who as stated earlier has stayed in Loíza the longest and therefore has had the greatest impact.

Father Antonio encouraged the financial commitment of the members, which for him was an important step in the church's revival. Under his pastorship, a system of voluntary tithing of 10 percent was established (and continues today). Like his predecessors, Father Antonio strongly encouraged laity leadership to the point of seriously confronting the Catholic hierarchy. One night he called a meeting of Loíza's parish administrative committee. After invoking the Holy Spirit, he wrote down the names of all the members of the committee and randomly chose three deacons who would help him with the liturgy, teaching, and leading of the chapels in different sectors of Loíza, an idea he supported with reservations because he did not want the chapels to replace the mother church downtown. Father Antonio also sent the deacons to take special biblical courses outside Loíza and in 1981 the first three deacons, including Marcelino (whom I mentioned in the preceding chapter), were officially ordained.

Even more important than ridding the church of folk and false religions and encouraging elements of national and Loízan identities was Father Antonio's desire to revive Catholicism by allowing the presence and guidance of the Holy Spirit and encouraging an open and personal relationship with God. This is why many parishioners described his sermons as tied to the Bible, practical, and relatively informal (although he told me he always used a guideline prepared by himself in case somebody went to the cardinal complaining about something he did not actually say). Father Antonio emphasized the reading and study of the Bible instead of its use as an amulet. He also encouraged spontaneity and less formality in the liturgy and wanted people to understand the purpose of coming to the church. He bought an organ, introduced new songs with a clear, simple, and reality-based message, and also encouraged people to express themselves more freely in worship and in prayer.

The program of re-evangelization, which was already established in other countries such as the Dominican Republic and which seemed to offer a "more spiritual" alternative than liberation theology, was introduced during Father Antonio's pastorship "under the Holy Spirit's guidance," according to parishioners. The program's main goal has been to enable people to understand God's teaching and to recommit to God. It involves house visits to invite people to rejoin the church. Usually the participants start by attending seven conferences to affirm their biblical understanding and knowledge of Catholic doctrine and a three-day retreat for personal spiritual nourishment. Those who have not fulfilled the holy sacraments are encouraged to do so. By the time of my field study, four hundred people had been re-evangelized since the program started and a sizable group of people had been baptized and gotten married in the church. Significantly, the program has also created a consciousness about community work, about the need to survey spiritual and social needs and to bring these needs to open discussion and solution. Father Antonio and the parishioners saw these activities as very necessary considering the situation of Loíza.

Father Antonio's ministry can be summarized with an expression he used to say: "We do not come to count cows. We come here to worship the Lord, to feel His presence, and to learn His word." (Here the expression "counting cows," like "counting butterflies," refers to being spiritually lazy.) This phrase, well remembered by the parishioners, reflects the content of his message and his straightforward attitude. Before the second stage of my field study in Loíza, Father Antonio had left on a missionary trip to Colombia after finishing his term in Loíza. During the third stage I heard he had died of a heart attack. The news surprised me because he seemed physically strong and healthy, although when I interacted with him he seemed, as many people said, to take things too seriously and personally. A large and well-attended funeral was celebrated during the time I was not in the field. Among the attendees were individuals who had resented Father Antonio, but who acknowledged his work in Loíza. In fact, a common expression after he died was "Father Antonio put us on the right path."

Father Marco Antonio Sánchez, the priest who succeeded Father Antonio, was appointed in August of 1997, but he was kept in Mexico for several months because of problems with his visa. During this time, an appointed temporary assistant, a Trinitarian missionary originally from Chicago, helped in the church full-time. The priest from Canóvanas, who like Father Marco Antonio was originally from Mexico, was helping out in the celebration of the mass. Father Marco Antonio had worked in Los Angeles, California and for two years before coming to Loíza he had been the assistant priest of one of the parishes in Canóvanas. Just by looking at him, I confirmed opinions that he was very different from Father Antonio. To begin, Father Marco Antonio was only thirty-four years old and a little dark skinned. He walked among the people while wearing shorts and sandals and did not have any problem with dancing, drinking a beer in a bar, attending cultural events, and also relating to and visiting non-Catholics, including Spiritists. According to Father Marco Antonio himself, these characteristics were the reason why the people from Canóvanas did not want him to leave their parish.

Father Marco Antonio was very supportive of lay leadership in the church, including women, youth, and those who did not have an official position. In Loíza, the leadership has become more complex throughout the years as new positions have been created. Currently, working under the priest are the deacons, who help him in the liturgy, in counseling, and who are also in charge of the chapels. The ministers of the Eucharist visit the sick and disabled and give them communion. Also working under the priest are the treasurer, the teacher of catechism, chapel coordinators, and members of different committees. In tandem with his support, Father Marco Antonio admitted that he needed to keep his authority over the strong lay leadership that had developed during the time the church had no priest.

The financial situation of the church continued improving thanks to the system of voluntary tithing, the increase in attendance and contributions, and the $3,500 the church had been receiving monthly from the Trinitarian headquarters. During the field study, the sanctuary, which accommodates about 125 people, was regularly full on Sundays and Saturdays. The goals of Father Marco Antonio were to have two thousand families visited and registered in the following year, to target the youth, and to be more present socially in the community. Regarding the latter, Father Marco Antonio told me that personal religious experience cannot be at the expense of community action and that this was clearly understood by most of the leaders.

During Easter, I participated in the Good Friday procession in Villa Cañona. (The word *cañona* in Puerto Rico refers to getting something by rude insistence or aggressive means.) This neighborhood is considered to be one of the most dangerous in Loíza, which is why many parishioners, mostly elderly and adult women, and I were a little bit tense during the event. The procession was intended to make a call to people to seek or return to God. We made thirteen stops at thirteen stations in front of residences. At each station a church member, using a microphone, read something inspired by the Bible, another individual said a prayer, and we all sang songs. Everybody thought the event was a success despite the fact that at the end some individuals in the area were driving motorcycles and cars very fast while making a lot of noise to show their discontent. I even had to calm down some elderly women from Las Cuevas. In addition to activities like this, the church was increasing its counseling program and donations (for example, for food for the poor, for programs such as Hogar Crea to stop the use of drugs, and Centro Providencia to treat AIDS patients). In the last few years, the church has tried to share more with other Catholic communities, including the parish of Santiago Apóstol and the parish of Canóvanas.

Under Father Marco Antonio's pastorship, the liturgy followed the guidance of *Misal 1998: Para todos los domingos y fiestas del año*, published by Obra Nacional de la Buena Prensa, A. C. in Mexico. At the same time, changes in the liturgy continued. Although the organ was used during services, it was also alternated with an electronic keyboard, guitars, and folk instruments such as congas, *bongó, panderetas* (tambourines), *güiro,* and maracas. Many of the songs that were played and sung during mass were very popular within the Protestant community. In addition, parishioners clapped their hands and praised God loudly. Father Marco Antonio preached in a very down-to-earth way, used analogies to make the message clear, and constantly asked questions to encourage the congregation to participate as he walked down the aisle and among the people. During Easter, Father Marco Antonio did two things for the first time in the history of the parish: he changed the way the seats were located, putting them in a semicircle, and took the Eucharist out of the holiest place and placed it over a huge dried tree he had found nearby. Some members considered these moves to be controversial, especially given the fact that the Eucharist was placed in a room very close to the archaeological exhibition.

According to Father Marco Antonio, liturgical changes encapsulate the very "nature" of Loízans, whom he described as sensitive, spontaneous, happy, and faithful to their traditions. He has found these traits to be very characteristic of blacks or "people of color," whom he finds very exciting to work with. For Father Marco Antonio, an authentic worship and lifestyle is extremely important for meaningful religion. By this he means a worship and a lifestyle that correspond to the way individuals are "naturally." Therefore God, who created different people, is really behind these different forms. This is why Father Marco Antonio had some reservations regarding the program of re-evangelization when it tries too much to change people's identity as a *pueblo*. According to him, the role of the church should be sharing the message of salvation through Jesus Christ without imposing any particular lifestyle, of which he thinks leaders in his parish need to be constantly reminded. By the time I started writing this book, Father Marco Antonio was leaving the church, according to my informants, because he got tired of gossip and rivalries among members of the congregation and because of disagreements regarding the degree of change he wanted to happen, including more promotion of Loízans' authentic identity or some re-Africanization of their Catholic experience (as has happened to an extreme in other countries such as Brazil [Jensen 1999]), a distinction parishioners have manipulated for different purposes. Many of them thought Father Marco Antonio had gone too far while reversing the efforts of Father Antonio to separate Catholicism from pagan Afro-religions, thus giving more opportunities for Protestants to criticize them. Some young and more educated Catholics, including church leaders, appreciated Father Antonio's work; at the same time they felt gratitude for Father Marco Antonio's efforts to bring about Loízan/black/African consciousness, even as a means to nurture the faith and not as an end in and of itself. Here Duany's (1998: 165, 168) recent description of popular (Catholic) religion in Latin America and Puerto Rico as something that gives less significance to the official sacred and liturgical rituals of the church and that is distant from the church hierarchy becomes a little problematic. However, it confirms Wuthnow's (1995: 9) statement that the religious hierarchy may be more deeply implicated in popular religion than we like to think. The example of Loízan Catholicism suggests a more fluid concept of popular religion, which can be applied to Protestantism as well.

This attitude of Catholics in the parish downtown, which the next sections will show in more detail, contrasts somewhat with a recent direct emphasis on the theme of Loízan identity in the parish of Santiago Apóstol, according to Father Francisco Conkle, the current priest of this parish. Here, a sense of pride about being Loízan has become a critical aspect of religious experience, especially to the young sector, most of whom are college students. Loízan identity has also become a significant part of religion for white parishioners, who recently moved to the new high-cost residences in the areas nearby, and to Dominican parishioners, whose number continues to grow in Loíza; both groups are making an effort to become insiders. The different experiences of the Catholics from downtown and from Medianía Alta, briefly discussed in chapter 2, explain a greater acceptance of Father Francisco's approach than of Father Marco Antonio's. Also, Father Marco Antonio's arrival in Loíza after Father Antonio's long stay in the town made Father Marco Antonio a better case for comparison.

Issues of Las Cuevas's Religious Classifications

In Las Cuevas, there is only one Catholic chapel and it belongs to the mother church downtown. The church downtown, like the parish of Santiago Após-tol, belongs to the *vicaria* of Río Grande and to the archdiocese of San Juan. Also in Las Cuevas are the Church of Christ or CC, the Pentecostal Church of God (International Movement) or PCG, the Heavenly Doors Evangelical Church (from the Christian Assemblies) or HDEC, and one independent church called the Church of the Faithful Disciples of Christ or CFDC, which was originally associated with the Church of God, Incorporated, and was best known as the church where women wear veils. However, the distribution be-tween Catholics and Protestants in Las Cuevas is relatively even. Participants used the following classifications: Catholic 205 times (49.5 percent); Pente-costal 150 times (36.2 percent); Baptist 18 times (4.3 percent); CC 10 times (2.4 percent); CFLW 10 times (2.4 percent); no specific religion 8 times (1.9 percent); evangelical 6 times (1.4 percent); Jehovah's Witnesses 4 times (.96 percent); Catholic-Spiritist or Spiritist-Catholic 2 times (.48 percent); and Adventist one time (.24 percent). Similar to what Chatters and Taylor (1994: 203–5) have found among African-Americans in the United States, a greater number of the residents in Las Cuevas identified themselves with a denomi-nation with less hesitation than when they had to answer questions of politi-cal affiliation, financial situation, and color.[2] Among these respondents, some were ambivalent and rejected the term "religion" because they considered it to represent ritual observance without meaning or understanding. Among Protestants, this approach was often used to distinguish themselves from Catholics; among Catholics, it was used to distinguish themselves from old Catholicism and from Protestantism. Those who placed themselves under the category "no specific religion" did so mostly because they did not attend church or did not fulfill all the requirements of a true Christian; similar to what Chatters and Taylor found, a substantial number of these individuals told me they believed in and communicated with God frequently. Only three individuals refused to classify themselves religiously because they resented God or did not believe in anything. (When I approached them, they did not want to talk about the issue further. I sensed some embarrassment in their hesitation.)

Two residents of Las Cuevas were classified as Spiritists or Spiritist-Catholic (called witches by residents) and there was no Santero.[3] Santería, which has been mentioned throughout this book, is more properly understood as a mix of Catholicism and beliefs and practices that came from Africa, particularly those of the Yoruba people, who are mostly found in Nigeria. Pérez y Mena (1995: 85) indicates that in Santería "syncretism occurred in two directions: the assimilation of local Yoruba divinities and other African gods by the generic Yoruba orishas; and also, the identification of the latter with Catholic saints." Santería originated in Cuba at the end of the eighteenth century and expanded to Puerto Rico after the 1960s with the migration of Cubans to the island (Schmidt 1996: 37; Clark 1998). Many of these Cubans who practiced Santería were not fully trained and lacked sound knowledge of the rituals and dogma (Pérez y Mena 1995: 93). It is possible that there were Santeros in Las Cuevas who kept their practice secret: the element of secrecy is still an important aspect of the practice of Santería because of its long history of marginalization in Cuba and Puerto Rico; at the same time, in Puerto Rico in general and in Loíza in particular the marginalization of Santería is twofold because it is seen as more negative than Spiritism, which has also been marginalized. This helps to explain Pérez y Mena's (1995: 139) and Schmidt's (1996: 39) arguments that Spiritism and Santería have been more distinct in Puerto Rico than in the United States, although as Romberg's (2003) study shows, various interrelated forces have prompted the open practice of these religions (she refers to this as a "spiritual laissez-faire") and their mixing with Asian, Indian, Native American traditions, and so forth since the 1980s.[4] This again brings to mind the rebuilding of Puerto Rican culture in the 1970s and the economic crisis at the time that helped the marketing of folklore, including Afro-Puerto Rican folk traditions. An important part of this openness to popular religions is the process of globalization, particularly the roles of the media, migration, and transnationalism, discussed in chapter 2. In the United

States, Santería has gained popularity among Latinos and among American blacks as a source of ethnic/racial identity (Pérez y Mena 1995: 95). Nevertheless, asking about Santería and spiritism offended many Loízans, including those who have migrated back home and especially Las Cuevas's residents, making research about it challenging. Many people laughed sarcastically when I asked the question, as though they were saying "Here it comes again. . . ." In this situation I decided not to ask directly about Santería or spiritism and to wait for people to bring it up (as in the cases of two women I will discuss in chapter 8).

San Antonio Chapel of Las Cuevas

San Antonio Chapel of Las Cuevas is one of the six chapels of the mother church that are located in different barrios or sectors of Loíza. The parish of Santiago Apóstol, however, has only four functioning chapels with an overall average attendance of 350. All of these chapels began to function officially with the purpose of bringing the Catholic Church closer to or integrating it with the community. However, each chapel has its own saint, its history of ups and downs after it started to function officially, and a trajectory before it started to function officially. The exact origin of the devotion of San Antonio in Las Cuevas is unknown. However, according to some residents, at the beginning of the twentieth century in the central area of Las Cuevas a family built a small chapel in honor of San Antonio, after having ordered the image from Spain. Hurricane San Felipe destroyed the chapel in 1928 and years later, after the head of the family had died, the family donated the image to a church. People from Las Cuevas and other communities continued celebrating the festival of San Antonio using an image they bought with money they collected under the initiative of a family who became the image's guardians.

The festival of San Antonio was celebrated around June 13, the liturgical feast day of Saint Anthony of Padua. Sometimes those in charge of the celebration had to move it to another day and they would chose the day closest to pay day to be able to cover the expenses of ornaments and refreshments, although they also counted on the contributions of landowners. The festival usually began with nights of chanting and reciting, mainly coordinated and directed by a group of designated women. One of the chants began like this, "Oh divine San Antonio intercede for the sinners. . . ." The festival also included a large procession led by local religious leaders or the priest. The image of San Antonio was carried from Las Cuevas to the church downtown where it stayed until the next day, when it was taken back to Las Cuevas. (A popular story describes how once one of the men carrying San Antonio was so drunk that he almost caused the image to fall over.) A *cantaleta* (noisy party) occurred on the last night of the festival. The festival sometimes incorporated special activities, for example a raffle of a calf usually donated by landowners, a performance of a band, and a special dance. It has gone from nine to three days as its importance has decreased over the years, coinciding with the growing popularity of the festival of Santiago Apóstol, the official founding of the chapel of San Antonio in Las Cuevas, and the Catholic Church's spiritual revival in Loíza, which began in the 1970s.

In addition to the yearly celebration of San Antonio, the people of Las Cuevas as a community have celebrated *promesas* (chants at homes as vows) in exchange for some favor from San Antonio and also from other saints such as the Virgin Carmen. They, like the people in the other communities in Loíza, have also participated in holidays such as the fiesta de la Cruz, the fiesta de la Candelaria, and the festival in honor of the Virgin Pilar, the patron virgin of Canóvanas.

Having a chapel in honor of San Antonio in Las Cuevas has also provided a sense of community and local identity to the people of Las Cuevas, although the influence has also worked the other way around: an existing sense of community has helped to form a stable Catholic community relationship. (I will explore this further in chapter 7). I experienced vividly this sense of community and local identity during different activities, including the procession in Villa Cañona mentioned earlier, where members of the chapel of Las Cuevas gathered in a circle to express their disappointment because nobody from Las Cuevas had been called on to participate in leading the readings and the prayers, and, thus, to represent Las Cuevas. I felt a little concerned when they almost forced me to join them in their circle. I wanted to show my solidarity, but I also did not want others to see me siding exclusively with them as this could affect my interaction with other parishioners. My strategy was to join them while showing with facial expressions and gestures an attitude of ambiguity and objectivity.

The first time I saw the chapel of San Antonio, I thought it was an abandoned structure because it was in bad shape. The chapel borders street #951, is next door to a house, and does not have a parking lot. The property had belonged to the Febres family, who first rented it to the owner of a store.

Then they rented it to a cooperative financial agency, which went bankrupt. Finally, the people of Las Cuevas collected the money to buy the property, a structure with a capacity of about forty people. The transaction was facilitated by a Catholic parishioner who worked at the agency for several years and who is the husband of a member of the Tapia family, and is therefore a relative of Rosa, one of the leaders of the chapel whom I will talk more about in the following section. Those who led the collecting of the money for buying the image of San Antonio felt they had rights over decisions regarding the chapel. Tensions mounted when it was determined that the deacons would be in charge of the chapels; however, over the course of years these tensions have necessarily disappeared.

One Night in the San Antonio Chapel

It was March 24, 1998. On the altar were the communion table in the center and two podiums at each side. An image of Jesus on the cross hung above the altar. An image of the Virgin Mary with flowers on its side and a big image of San Antonio were located in the far right corner. Pictures of scenes from the Bible adorned the walls. Attendance, usually around twenty-five (counting the two subgroups that belong to the chapel, each with two female coordinators, who are highly educated and financially stable), was twenty-three, consisting of nineteen women and four men, including my father and me. All of the participants were over twenty-five years old, *trigueño* or black, and originally from Las Cuevas (a small number were not living in Las Cuevas). The group was relatively equally divided between employees, housekeepers, and retirees, and the average monthly family income was between one thousand and three thousand dollars.

Almost everybody was on time (about 7:30 p.m.). Before starting we greeted each other enthusiastically, as these meetings are considered a significant opportunity for expressing God's love to one another. Then, we positioned the chairs to form a close circle, so that we could see each other face to face. Everybody was asked to sign their names in a notebook that Rosa, one of the coordinators, brought. Carmen, who was Rosa's co-coordinator, was in charge of the meeting. She began by saying that the purpose of having the two groups meet together was so that I would know everybody and could distribute the questionnaires.

The meeting began with a *corito* from the song book, which included many of the *coritos* I knew from the Protestant repertoire; many of them talked about the Holy Spirit. Also included were songs from the repertoire of what has lately been referred to as *música de adoración* (worship music), a slowly paced style of music that came from the United States and Mexico. Its lyrics evoked a loving, personal, and informal relationship with God. We clapped our hands while singing the first *corito,* and Carmen and another member played the tambourines. The lyrics of the *corito* are as follows (my translation):

> Pass around here Lord, pass around here. Oh Lord, pass around here.
> Holy Spirit, pass around here. Oh Lord, pass around here.
> Fill us with you Lord, fill us with you. Oh Lord, fill us with you.
> We are one people and one is the Lord. Oh Lord, fill us with you.

After the *corito*, Rosa prayed, inviting the Holy Spirit to be among us. In the prayer, Rosa also invited us to worship the Lord. While praying, Rosa moved her hands, increased the volume of her voice, and rubbed her arms as though she were cold or were feeling goose bumps. During her prayer, several people (mainly the coordinators Carmen and Crucita) said "amen" and praised God loudly. The second prayer, by Carmen, was a confession directly to "Papito Dios" (diminiutive for "Father God"), which was the way she mainly referred to God during the service and during the various conversations I had with her at her house. This way of addressing God is considered by many Catholics to be indicative of a less formal relationship with God that has come about in the last few decades.

After the second prayer, Carmen read John 5:1–3 and 5–16, which talked about Jesus healing a man who could not walk. Carmen encouraged us to follow the reading closely and invited those who brought their Bibles to share them with those who did not. Having a Bible and bringing it to the meetings was something leaders were encouraging members to do. In fact, during mass at the mother church, Father Marco Antonio and other leaders constantly advertised Bibles for sale. After reading the verses, Carmen began to explain the passage. The important thing about the miracle was not the pool where Jesus sent the man to be healed, but the power of Jesus. She talked about how many religions focus on the power of things such as amulets, rosaries, images of saints, prayers, and leaders, instead of focusing on Jesus himself. Carmen also brought some applications to the passage regarding the celebration of Lent. She argued that during Lent and Easter many Christians follow the traditions and do not think about their real meaning, which is to love Christ with all their hearts, minds, and souls.

Carmen contrasted the "traditional" or "religious" experience of the Catholic Church in the past with the close relationship with Jesus that the Catholic Church now encourages. In fact, most of the members of Las Cuevas were raised as Catholics and at some point in their lives quit attending church. Then, as many described it, they had a personal encounter with Jesus Christ. Carmen clarified that Catholics in the past did not relate to Jesus closely because they did not know much about the Bible. As she told me, "Mass was in Latin," an expression Catholics themselves often laugh about. As she spoke, members reaffirmed what she was saying with gestures and soft comments. Carmen insisted that rituals and practices do not have meaning in themselves unless one gives a personal significance to them, although God can do whatever he wants independently of our attitude and thoughts. She mentioned different Judaic and Catholic practices, such as the Catholic practice of not eating meat during Holy Week, and indicated that their main purpose is to remind people to avoid being contaminated by the things of the world. Participants commented that this was something emphasized by Father Antonio.

After Carmen's biblical presentation the group moved to an open discussion about the importance of relating to God through their relationships to others. Individuals began to participate more and to speak more loudly. They began criticizing divisions among Christian churches. A member brought up the issue of lack of unity among family members because of religious differences, although members concluded that in Las Cuevas religion was not as strong a reason for conflicts as politics and socioeconomic status. At the same time, they acknowledged the role of religion in strengthening family relationships, as was happening with members of the Tapia family who belong to different churches. A participant indicated that religion does not make people fight with one another; however, it makes people do things separately so that there is not much time to share. Another participant observed that while many Catholics had visited a Protestant church or participated in a Protestant activity, Protestants had not yet visited them. I experienced this my entire life, for example when I distributed invitations to special programs at my church. A Catholic visiting a Baptist church was expected because of the belief among Baptists that Catholics needed to repent and be saved, but a Baptist visiting a Catholic church was not even imagined.

Participants at this service also talked about the individualistic mentality that has increased in Puerto Rico and insisted that they could not tolerate this in the Catholic Church of Loíza. Awilda, the fourth coordinator who at the time was getting her master's in education at the UPR, talked about a new program of cooperative education that was developing in answer to the highly individualistic and competitive atmosphere in education. Everyone agreed that the Catholic Church has to be united and cannot ignore serving the community while tolerating different political, social, and religious perspectives.

After about fifteen to twenty minutes of talking about social problems such as lack of discipline, distance between elders and youth, family disintegration, early sex, early pregnancy, lack of education and employment, conformist and victim attitudes, laziness, crime, and drugs, Carmen clapped her hands to quiet the crowd. She said that they would continue talking about these problems in the future and more importantly about ways to help resolve them. Then Carmen asked me to explain how to fill out the questionnaire I had brought and to distribute the copies. Carmen finally announced the activity of spiritual reflection on the coming Thursday in the sanctuary and encouraged people to attend the activities related to the Lent and Easter celebrations. After the meeting of an hour and a half ended, some members stayed to talk while others went to their homes. After attending his first Catholic service, my father said: "Catholics have really changed."

Rosa's Life with a Living Christ

I was impressed the first time I met Rosa during my very first days in Loíza. Her house was next door to Eunice's house, where I stayed in Las Cuevas. Immediately, I noticed her kindness, willingness to teach someone something new, and critical but positive outlook on life. These qualities made me love being around her (she always called me "Miss"), sitting on her balcony and walking with her on the street as we went to church and to visit people. Rosa's energy and physical appearance made me think she was younger than her sixty-nine years. Rosa usually dresses nicely but casually: stretched jeans, nice shirt, high heels, quite a bit of makeup, and a nice hairdo, because as she explained, her religious identity relies heavily on her physical appearance. As she indicated on more than one occasion, her concern was to present a good image of Loízans as people with education who were *de caché* (sophisticated). She demonstrated her concern, among other ways, by speaking the language properly (she corrected me on a few occasions) and by keeping her house clean. About her physical appearance Rosa told me:

> I dress nicely because I like to inspire others positively. I try to show the way I am, what I believe, not the way I feel . . . sometimes I feel [she laughed] the years on me. I like to look good to feel good about myself . . . to help others. Do you understand me, Miss? I do not care that some people think I am old to dress like this or that Christians should not dress like the world does. I do not believe that. The other day, I was talking to Luis and his wife downtown. They told me they like to hear my taconeo [the sound of my high heels] walking down the street because they know they will encounter a big smile. I am a happy person [she took a deep breath]. I like to greet everybody so that they feel God's love. I tell you, even with a nice greeting you can bring people to Christ. [She laughed while imitating her exciting and high volume personality]. You have to be free. Here we [Loízans] are free, spontaneous, and happy people by nature, although it is Christ who really makes us free.

Rosa belongs to the Tapia family and lives in a modest cement house built with her and her husband's money on a piece of property that she inherited from her father. Her house is very close to the chapel of San Antonio, bordering street #951. In 1952, Rosa married a quiet and reserved man, whom I always found reading the newspaper. He is a veteran and a retiree of the General Electric Company. They have three adult daughters, one of them living in New Orleans and the other two in other barrios of Loíza.

Rosa is a retired elementary school teacher who enjoys taking care of her grandchild. She began to work as a teacher in 1949 for a monthly salary of $105, all of which she gave to her mother. She thinks God gifted her with the ability to teach. When she was in her early teens, Rosa gathered the kids of the neighborhood to teach them what she learned in school. Rosa's mother always encouraged her and her twelve older siblings to study and have a career, something Rosa also did with her daughters. For Rosa as for other Loízans, education has been a vehicle for upward mobility. Rosa's mother, who is in her eighties, finished high school with honors. Rosa's father, who died when she was in college, worked hard to pay for transportation to the high school in Canóvanas. He and Rosa's oldest sibling, who had to quit school because of financial problems, helped her rent a car to take her to the university. Rosa has a sister who was a nurse, a brother who worked in social services for many years, and another brother with his own store in Las Cuevas (which became one of my favorite stops for a drink), two houses from her house. In 1946 she began studying to be a teacher at the UPR. She said it was difficult because she was discriminated against. The two experiences Rosa remembers the most are when she was accused of robbery by a white student and when she was denied proper service during registration. When the latter happened, Rosa complained to the dean and to the president of the UPR, Dr. Jaime Benítez of the PPD, who finally helped her to finish her registration.

After twenty-five years and six months of teaching, Rosa quit her job because of problems with her voice. During her teaching years, she helped many young teachers and was recognized for excellent work. I saw various certificates and plaques on the walls of her house. During the fifteen years she was not teaching, she worked with an attorney (who later became the interim director of the Asociación de Empleados del ELA [Association of Commonwealth Employees]) and as a receptionist in the Congress under the leadership of Senator Miguel Hernández Agosto of the PPD.

Rosa's desire to keep active and to help others inspired her to run for mayor of Loíza for the PPD in 1988. In the election, in which she competed against Gabriel Santos of the PNP, the incumbent mayor, she lost by only eight hundred votes. Rosa attributes the loss to the lack of money for her campaign and to people's sense of loyalty to the PNP, the party that helped Loíza separate from Canóvanas. However, Rosa does not regret the experience because of all she learned about injustice, envy, corruption, and favoritism. She is also thankful for the opportunity it gave her to feel her supporters' care and love and to help "her people." For example, she helped the community of Vacía Talega get water and power, the community of Vieques to get property titles, the health center to have twenty-four-hour access to doctors, and young fathers to get jobs. Also, the experience helped Rosa to realize that there is only so much one can do in politics and that the real problems Puerto Rico has are lack of education and moral and spiritual decay. In 1990, she went back to teach for five more years in order to complete thirty years of work and to receive full retirement.

Rosa has always been Catholic. She and her family did the sacraments and participated in collective religious events. Her parents carefully taught her morals and values. But she always asked herself why her mother was a strong devotee. Her own search for something deeper and the changes in the Catholic Church with Father Antonio greatly contributed to her "encounter with a living Christ." The classes Father Antonio encouraged Rosa to take helped her to understand God's purpose for her life and to feel his presence inside her. Rosa explained this further and talked about her religious experience as follows:

I became a different woman. I was a nice person but controversial. I did not accept people telling me what to do. I learned to surrender to God and to accept what others had to say. I cultivate my spiritual life by reading the Bible, praying, and by sharing His word. I meditate on Him. I enjoy helping others. I think I got this from my mother. When I do these things I am honoring her. I send money to a child I sponsor from Ethiopia through World Vision. I like to talk to teenagers. I enjoy teaching at church. People call me to pray for them, especially those who are sick. God speaks to me through prayer and the Bible. He also speaks to me subconsciously. He speaks to me through dreams. Sometimes I have nightmares and I wake up screaming and with heart palpitations, but I pray. I know God in some way is telling me something, to pray for something or somebody. Then I get calm. I find serenity and smile at God. I know it is God. I encourage my relatives to break with the routine and to experience a living Christ. They inspired me when I was distanced from the church. I also tell my daughters to seek God first and then move on. I want to be an example to them and my grandchildren. My daughters' husbands belong to Protestant families. I do not care as long as they believe in God. I do not have a problem hearing the pastors around here preaching, except when they say something negative about the mother of our Lord Jesus Christ. Sometimes I go to my brother's store and listen to a radio program of a Pentecostal church. My brother is Pentecostal. I respect all religions, but I have read and know that the Catholic Church has been the true church since the time of Christ. For me it is very important to believe in a living Christ. The Holy Spirit helps me. I do not fear anymore. I was afraid to take an airplane and now I visit my daughter in New Orleans. I am preparing myself to see my Lord. It is not religion but to believe in a living Christ, to communicate with him, to relate to Him personally, day by day. In the past we Catholics served a dead Christ, but now we serve a living Christ. [While saying these last sentences she began to raise her voice gradually and to touch my arms.]

Rosa is aware of the different circumstances that led her to get closer to God. She sees herself as the result of these circumstances and the changes in the Catholic Church and as part of the cause of these changes. But she believes God or the Holy Spirit is behind these circumstances as He has been behind changes in the Catholic Church.

Contingent Loízan Catholicism

Rappaport's (1999) model of the hierarchical dimension of liturgical orders is applicable here. There are three types of liturgical orders: one involving ultimate sacred postulates; the second, cosmological axioms; and the third, specific rules that transform cosmology into conduct. While the first liturgical order lies on the fundamental end of the hierarchy and the third liturgical order on the contingent end, the relationship between the two can change. This model underlies the change in the parishioners' ritual experience and in their understanding of that experience, where the Holy Spirit's function to lead people toward personal relationship with God ranks highest among explanations of the changes in the Catholic Church, while the Holy Spirit's function simply to lead is emphasized together with tolerance and the church's community activity. The motivations of religious competition and social identity are secondary or denied, which reminds me of the reactions of members of Seattle's Japanese Presbyterian Church, studied by Duntley (1999: 296), where ethnicity is not given more significance than spiritual family and "faith roots."

Following the three classifications of the "doings" of ritual, transcendence is put by most parishioners at a higher position than management of power and alteration of reality. However, there are different opinions and experiences regarding the significance of the social identity and forces of religious competition to deal with power and, therefore, to transform their reality. This is quite evident when considering the voices of local priests, leaders, and regular parishioners, and more specifically, different versions of national and local identity (as discussed in the previous chapter). Relatedly, Lawson and McCauley (1993: 121) argue the following: "A theory of religious ritual systems should also be able to systematically account for a range of participants' judgments about various features of those actions that it faithfully represents."

But what reality explains this hierarchical model I have proposed? The Catholic Church in Puerto Rico has been greatly valued for its cultural and nationalist role. However, this cultural role has been transformed by the Protestant ideology into a less significant function as compared to the spiritual one. However, I would point out the fact the Protestants have not ignored the issue of identity and the cultural role; some have even openly recognized it, especially in the last few years. (Another example in addition to the CFLW, which I mentioned earlier and will discuss again in the next chapter, is that of the United Methodist Church in Puerto Rico, which recently agreed to eliminate all the translated hymns with war themes to avoid promoting a military mentality as it is believed to be associated with the ideology of U.S. imperialism.)

The fact that the Catholic Church in Puerto Rico has been seeing as relying heavily on culture or tradition is especially true in Loíza, which has been regarded as the town that best represents the African tradition in its most folklorist version. For the same reason Loízan Catholics have had many opportunities to express their identity outside ritual, opportunities that have been more available to them than, for example, the Baptist side of my family, which was not allowed a space outside the ritual context to express national identity. I believe this to be the reason why *jíbaro* identity was so emphasized inside the ritual context of my Baptist church, to the point of doing Christian music presentations dressed up like a *jíbaro*.

I insist that the hierarchical model claimed by Loízan Catholics points to a greater significance of the integration of issues of identity and religious competition than they want to admit. I propose that this model is a way to respond to their "ethnicization" by those who have interpreted their religious actions as simple acts of resistance, while assuming that they are devoid of their African cultural ancestry. In a context where black identity is somewhat forced and exploited, the parishioners seem to be responding as well to the idea of Afro-religion as the requirement for authentic identity and religious experience. However, the large collection of Puerto Rican and Loízan art in Carmen's home and Rosa's insistence that I try traditional Loízan dishes and her desire to confirm that in Loíza there are people *de caché* all speak to the fact that Loízan identity in particular is not completely disregarded. Instead, town identity is legitimized as it is placed within a larger spiritual framework.

Also, the significance of a personal relationship with God, without sacrificing community action and tolerance, brings about the issues of Loízan identity and religious competition, as community action is something some Loízan Catholics believe Loízans in general should not lose because it is very characteristic of their identity. These Catholics also believe that community action is something Protestant churches and certain Catholic churches (those moving toward more spirituality) are lacking and something they need to preserve and even increase in order to move forward. The emphasis on a meaningful or spiritual Catholic experience through community action is particularly strong among Loízan Catholics, who recognize both general and individual socioeconomic progress but are greatly concerned about the enormous socioeconomic challenges Loíza continues to face.

Moreover, the evidence I have presented demonstrates that people's hierarchical order is not a simple semantic game. For example, Catholic respondents to my questionnaire refused to be defined as religious people if "religion" meant following rules and participating in rituals without purpose or meaning. My experiences in the chapel of San Antonio and with Rosa show that the motivation for a personal relationship with God guided by the Holy Spirit is more than a cognitive model because it involves people's emotional and physical experiences, including body practices. Also, Rosa is convinced that she experiences her closeness to God even in her subconscious, as when God speaks to her through her dreams. These examples lead to the question that Rosa and other Catholics have asked me: How can all this be anything other than "spiritual" or anything other than the Holy Spirit's work? Here I would like to mention again Duntley's (1999) study of the religious experience in the Presbyterian Japanese Church in Seattle, where she finds evidence of motivations that point to something beyond cultural similarities and ethnic categories: a transcendental experience in worship.

"We are the King's children!"

Creating a New Consciousness in Loíza

Rompamos toda cadena que tenga la humanidad.
No importa el color que tengas Jesús te da libertad.
Deja toda diferencia, unidos más fuerza hay.
Te ofrezco a tí mis manos, ven lucha tu libertad.

When I first heard them as a student at the UPR, these lyrics encouraged me to investigate the relative silence of the Protestant church regarding the issue of color.

Let us brake every chain that humanity has.
Your color does not matter because Jesus gives you freedom.
Leave any difference behind; in unity there is more strength.
I offer you my hands; come and fight for your liberty. (My translation)

Entitled "Cadenas" (Chains) and written by Alejandro Andino, a *trigueño* singer with the Christian group 33 D.C., it begins with African-style drumming and stands as an exception in the Christian music repertoire. Intrigued by its exceptionality, I began to ask myself why the issue of color had only been vaguely addressed during my years of membership in the Baptist Church despite the fact that there were white, mixed, and black members. My church founded a mission in the black barrio where my mother grew up and which was believed to be deeply influenced by witchcraft and Spiritism. There I witnessed racism. A group of church members, including me, went to an area of this barrio every Sunday afternoon to hold Sunday school. Initially students of this Sunday school participated in our regular meetings from the church's back seats and years later they became a semi-independent mission of the church, which is currently pastored by a white old-time church leader. Also, the issue of color was almost completely ignored during my visits as a member of various Christian music groups to many churches of different denominations all over the island.

According to Reverend Margarita Sánchez de León, in the last several years there has been a greater awareness of the issue of color in the Puerto

Rican religious sector. Margarita is not an authority on this topic, but being herself a black woman, a graduate from the Evangelical Seminary of Puerto Rico, and a known religious leader, she has followed closely its development. Currently, she is the general coordinator of Movimiento Ecuménico Nacional (National Ecumenical Movement) and the director of the Puerto Rican branch of Amnesty International. The first organization is an independent religious entity that derived from the Episcopal Church. It was founded in 1968 with the purpose of proclaiming the gospel to the marginal sectors of society, particularly the gay community. The second organization fights for citizens' civil rights and was founded forty-five years ago in London and about ten years ago in Puerto Rico. In recent years, several religious leaders have brought up more openly the issue of discrimination based on skin color. Some of them admit and I agree that this is occurring in great part because of the influence of a secular anti-racist movement on the island that has been greatly influenced by coordinated international efforts.

The anti-racist movement in Puerto Rico has manifested itself in the first congress of discrimination celebrated in Puerto Rico with the endorsement of the Board of Lawyers of Puerto Rico and the Civil Rights Commission. Various municipalities have their own organizations. For example, my home-town of Carolina recently created the Comisión Especial para la Educación en Derechos Humanos (Special Commission for the Education in Human Rights) to address all kinds of discrimination and especially discrimination based on skin color.[1]

Other national organizations, recently founded, directly address the issue of racism in the country. These are Alianza Anti-Racista Puertorriqueña (Anti-racist Puerto Rican Alliance), Concilio Puertorriqueño Contra el Racismo (Puerto Rican Council against Racism), Instituto de Identidad y Raza de la Universidad de Puerto Rico (Institute of Identity and Race of the UPR), and Unión de Mujeres Puertorriqueñas Negras (Union of Black Puerto Rican Women). The first organization, with a few members from the religious sector, focuses on community awareness through activities such as the Jornada Anti-Racista (Anti-racist Journey), which is normally celebrated from October 12 to November 19 (the day of the celebration of the discovery of Puerto Rico). This activity involves different stops at different stations in urban public areas where various participants recreate the hardships the slaves experienced in order to encourage deep reflection. During its third annual celebration, the group held a conference at the Evangelical Seminary of Puerto Rico entitled "Theology and Racism." The second organization focuses on issues of discrimination from a legal perspective, such as police profiling. The third organization has more access to the official structures of the state and focuses on academic research and public information. The fourth organization was officially established by a group of female scholars who worked on the topic of gender and race in Puerto Rico for the conference entitled "Encuentro de Mujeres Negras de Latinoamérica y el Caribe" (Encounter of Black Women of Latin America and the Caribbean), which was held in the Dominican Republic. The organization has some male members and focuses on Puerto Rican black women's experiences in relation to various issues in the communities.

Additional groups deal with other types of discrimination, such as that against the gay and lesbian community, and also with environmental injustice. The strong protests in the last few years against the U.S. military presence in Vieques, in which various religious groups participated, also has played a significant role in gathering momentum while helping to overcome *partidismo* (a separation based on political party membership). The latter has been considered a big obstacle for the success of various initiatives for social justice in the country (for example, the feminist movement and the fight for low-income property ownership).

There are a few signs of a growing awareness of the issue of color in the Protestant community. Recently, the Evangelical Seminary of Puerto Rico co-sponsored a conference on theology and racism in collaboration with Alianza Anti-Racista Puertorriqueña. Also recently, the Reverend Moisés A. Rosa, who was dark skinned, created the Martin Luther King Jr. Award while serving as the executive secretary of the Evangelical Council of Puerto Rico. The award is granted to any religious institution that helps the cause against racism and for social equality. After Rosa's recent death, many people agreed that bringing up the issue of color was one of his main contributions as a Protestant leader.

However, many religious leaders agree that this award, like the issue of racism in general, is seen by Puerto Ricans as similar to Presidents' Day: something that has some value but is still far from the Puerto Rican experience. (Kinsbruner [1996: 5] recently observed the indifference of many Puerto Ricans to the visit of Martin Luther King, Jr. to the island.) Some pastors, like many other Puerto Ricans, prefer to believe that a lack of open discussion about the topic is a sign that is not a real issue, instead of considering that lack to be a part of the problem. In many Puerto Rican Protestant and Catholic churches discrimination on the basis of color continues to be less significant than discrimination based on socioeconomic status or social class, and there is little deep questioning about a possible connection between them. Even more problematic is the presumption that racism has already been addressed or resolved by the Christian message of love and brotherhood. Some church leaders have addressed the issue of color in specific situations, for example when trying to attract predominantly black communities or neighborhoods, but their approach is not part of a specific, large anti-racist agenda against discrimination. This, I argue, is the case of the Church of the Fountain of the Living Water (CFLW) in Loíza, even though some credit can be conferred upon this church's leaders, who raise some sort of awareness of the issue.

The first thing I heard about the CFLW, more than fifteen years ago, was that its members believe that because God's people are the king's children they should live like royalty. I also learned about their emphasis on faith, which they thought was the key element for a prosperous life. Accordingly, when an individual is not prospering physically and financially it is because he or she does not have enough faith or is sinning. Looking back, I could picture members of my Baptist church adopting this emphasis on faith, which manifested itself in their answer, "In Victory!" to the question, "Brother, how are you doing?" The CFLW's emphasis on healing and material prosperity explains why a sizeable number of popular figures (including actors) have joined the CFLW and why initially the church was mostly associated with people with money. I also experienced the emphasis on material prosperity in my Baptist church, but more subtly, especially through the participation of Pentecostal guest preachers and singers (most of whom drove expensive cars, wore nice clothes, and were eager to sell their sermons and music on audiotapes). I finally asked myself: What is it about this message (or that larger thing that it comes from or is part of) that has led many Puerto Ricans and some Loízans to embrace it?

The Church of the Fountain of the Living Water

The CFLW was founded in the early 1980s in Puerto Rico because of Pastor Rodolfo Font's vision.[2] He was born in Loíza's neighboring town of Río Grande, received Christ when he was eight years old, and spent his years as a teenager in the United States, where he attended different Pentecostal churches. Back in Puerto Rico he became a member of the Assembly of

Christian Churches and studied in his denomination's seminary. At the age of twenty-five, while working as the manager of a shoe store, Pastor Font received a special visitation from God, in which he saw a beam of light cross the roof and touch his forehead. He heard God's voice telling him, "Rodolfo, levántate y date prisa, no pierdas mucho tiempo" (Rodolfo, wake up and hurry up, do not lose more time). He also saw these words written in big letters. Pastor Font immediately understood that he was called to preach the different message that God was putting in his heart.

The CFLW is a Christian and specifically Protestant derivation. Its message is different because of its strong emphasis on God's will for humans to prosper in all spheres. In one of the booklets for public distribution, the CFLW presents itself in opposition to the "formalism," "extremism," "fanaticism," "obscurantism," "traditionalism," and "corruption" of the contemporary Christian church. The booklet states, "No more churches full of fanaticism and doctrines that promote low self-esteem, leading people to frustration and religious slavery" (my translation)." The CFLW claims its interpretation is the most representative of God's will and the most adequate for modern society. Its mission or purpose is not to modify behavior, but "to create a new consciousness" about individual maximum potential in modern times, spiritually, physically, and materially.

As stated earlier, the CFLW has been strongly attacked by the Protestant community for various reasons, but principally for its emphasis on material prosperity. Recently, there was a controversy with one of the pastors of a CFLW church who wanted to separate from the council. The pastor counted on the support of the congregation, who also wanted to stay with their investments and assets. The church has also been criticized because of Pastor Font's statements in support of the pro-statehood party (the governor who endorsed pro-statehood status has visited and addressed the congregation) and his statements that the Armageddon had already passed in the 1970s and that Christians have to focus on continuing to spread the message of prosperity to accelerate the establishment of the church's kingdom. In a recent interview, the pastor Font defended his emphasis on prosperity by contending that the CFLW follows the example of Jesus, who was not a carpenter but a cabinetmaker, who was not really poor, and who came to this world to teach people how to escape from poverty. To those who criticized Pastor Font for wearing a flashy cape while preaching on television, he responded by arguing that it was only a strategy to attract people's attention, something that Jesus usually did and for which he was considered crazy (*El Nuevo Día,* February 28, 1998, n.p.). To those who have criticized his emphasis on the divine potential of humans as very much influenced by new age ideas, he responded by saying that the church's message is a call to wake up, to take action, and to elevate the spirit to the work of God.[3]

The CFLW has a four-member administrative council, including the founder, who is in charge of the mother church and deals with other ministries, such as the television program. The CFLW has two legal and financial assessors. The leadership claims that the organization is theocratic (not democratic) because God is really in charge. The ministers or "apostles" are ordained to be in charge of a church or a specific ministry at the level of the council. This happens after they have received some biblical training, demonstrated that they can be role models of good behavior, and have spent a year garnering experience as leaders under the supervision of an ordained apostle. The administrative committee makes the final decision for appointing the apostles. Most, if not all, of the apostles once had or currently have a professional job.

The mother church is located in my hometown of Carolina and has one service on Sunday morning and another service on Sunday night. These two services and the ones celebrated on Mondays and Thursdays at 7:00 p.m., are quite similar in that they follow an informal style and include various dance, drama, and music presentations. These services also include the sermon, testimonies, singing, prayers, and offerings. On Tuesdays classes are offered for beginners; on Wednesdays classes on theology are held at the institute, and on Fridays the youth meeting is held. All of these services and meetings also begin at 7:00 p.m.

The CFLW has special events and activities such as the convention to celebrate the twelfth anniversary of the CFLW council, which was held March 15–17, 1998. The activity had more than twenty thousand people in attendance. The Reverend Randy White, the pastor of Without Walls, one of the greatest ministries in Florida, was the visiting preacher. The theme of the celebration was the conscientious offering. The CFLW has offered other major activities using ministers from the United States, including the Reverend Benny Hinn and the Reverend Frederick Price, and ministers from other countries, including the famous Latin American evangelist Alberto Motessi from Argentina. These actions clearly indicate that although the CFLW was born in Puerto Rico it is part of a broad phenomenon in the United States and has expanded to other parts of the world.

The CFLW also has special activities to attract nonbelievers and believers, for example the concert of Yuri, a popular Mexican singer who recently converted. Six thousand people attended the concert on March 14, 1998; it was sponsored by secular companies, including the newspaper *El Nuevo Día*, which dedicated several pages to the activity. In December of 1999, the CFLW held the Christian Music Awards for Christian singers who had recorded albums between January of 1998 and October of 1999; soloists and groups from different denominations participated. More recently (in the summer of 2003), it organized a contest of the same type as *American Idol* in the United States, which was covered heavily by the media. In this show, two hundred aspiring singers were to choose thirty semifinalists who would then compete by doing television performances for an entire month. The finalist would be chosen during the last major event, which would be open to the general public for a cost of ten dollars per person. The finalist would be awarded the opportunity to record a CD and a month of publicity for the CD. Another church event that was held during my fieldwork in Loíza was the Congress of Sexual Abstinence for Youth, which was advertised heavily in the church of Las Cuevas. This event was organized by the Ministerio de Jóvenes Generación Xcelencia (Ministry of the Excellent Youth Generation) and also coordinated by the international project Real Love Waits. The event had the direct support of five legislators. The latter is another example of the public and official support of politicians and social leaders for the CFLW.

The CFLW is the most prosperous church in Puerto Rico and the one with the fastest growth rate, which is regularly reported in the media. The temple called Pabellón de la Fe (Pavilion of Faith) of the mother church accommodates about six thousand people, but the church has twelve thousand contributors. The CFLW has thirty churches in Puerto Rico with a total membership of twenty thousand, as well as churches in the United States, Japan, Argentina, Peru, El Salvador, and Costa Rica. On the side of the temple, written in big letters, resembling those of a movie marquee, is the word "Blessed," and the names of Pastor Font and his wife. The word "blessed" is used instead of "God bless you" because of the doctrinal principle that God has already done His part and the rest is our responsibility or a matter of faith. During the early 1980s, this substitution was made by some of the members of my former Baptist church, but this lasted only until the response became directly associated with the CFLW.

The temple, the best equipped on the island, is part of a whole complex resembling a mall, with libraries, coffee shops, a beauty salon, museums, and so forth. It has a huge sound and light system, central air conditioning, padded seats on a raked floor, which improves the audience's view, and a huge platform with flowers, seats, and banners with different symbols. "Jesus Christ is the Lord" is written on the top part of the wall of the altar. There is no cross, but a structure at the top of the stage resembles the crown from the Statue of Liberty. The symbol of the CFLW is also present, a brown, black, and white eagle with extended wings, similar to the U.S. eagle. The construction of a huge building called the Torre de Oración (Tower of Prayer), a project costing millions of dollars, was expected to be finished during my fieldwork. The tower is located next to the church building and is close to the island's main airport. To support the cost of the construction, the CFLW has been advertising the Torre de Oración Master Card.

To disseminate its message, the CFLW has three television channels, different radio programs, and a free newsletter entitled *Nueva conciencia: Un periódico positivo* (New consciousness: A positive newsletter), which publishes eleven hundred copies every month and which uses many business advertisements. The newsletter includes accounts of the CFLW's activities, details about future events, and information about different churches around the country and around the world. It contains articles about special topics such as physical and emotional health, woman's image, family life, financial success, and controversial issues such as homosexuality. The articles are written by leaders of the congregation, including the editor, who is Pastor Font's niece. In the March 1998 issue, the governor's wife wrote an article about women entitled "Mujer sabia" (Wise woman) in honor of the women's week celebration. Two of the books written by Pastor Font are *Programa de libertad financiera* (Program of financial freedom) and *Creando una nueva consciencia* (Creating a new consciousness). Pastor Font's wife wrote *Mujer feliz ¿Quién la hallará?* (Happy woman, who may find her?) and *Aprendí a tener fe* (I learned to have faith). Other books written by different members of the administrative committee include the following: *Los principios de la fe cristiana* (The principles of Christian faith), *Es cosa de sabios aprovechar bien el tiempo* (It is for wise people to take advantage of time), *Nueva criatura* (New creature), and *Willy Bobo se murió* (Willy Dummy died). ("Bobo" is the last name of a famous story character who represents the ignorant Puerto Rican peasant. As I will discuss later, the concepts of intelligence and consciousness are very significant in the message of the CFLW.)

Special events and activities for believers and nonbelievers, including concerts, try to combine evangelism, education, and entertainment. One of these celebratory activities has been the International Carnival of the Caribbean, with tents representing different countries and with a cultural display. The church organizes trips, for example, to Israel and Europe with Pastor Font and his wife. It also offers special children's activities with clowns, sports teams, and recreational attractions such as "Power Rock," for young people to climb, and "GX House," a place for young people to hang out. In all of these special activities as in its worship service and in its advertising literature, the CFLW exploits the arts. For example, to advertise its activities, in one of its booklets the four chief apostles are dressed up like musketeers, simulating an advertisement for a movie. Here they are called "the musketeers of faith." The CFLW has also increased its involvement in social ministry. For example, in the concert by Yuri, which I mentioned earlier, the church collected $20,000 from ticket sales to give to the ministry for the homeless and drug addicts called La Fondita Fuente de Vida. It holds community campaigns for health promotion, vaccination, and blood donation, as well as money collections such as the collection it held for the Red Cross during Hurricane George.

A Sunday Morning at the CFLW Mission in Las Cuevas

I visited the CFLW mission in Las Cuevas on five Sunday mornings. The church also holds another worship service on Wednesdays and a prayer service on Tuesdays, both at 7:00 p.m. However, these services are not as well attended as the Sunday morning service. Saturdays are for personal evangelism, wherein members make home visits to share the message. Like the mother church, the mission in Las Cuevas does not have Sunday Bible school or a Bible study that allows open discussion. It does have special services and activities in the temple for sharing among members, for example a meal or a birthday party. For the mission in Las Cuevas, it is important to show its support for the mother and founder church and to participate in that church's activities, for which transportation is provided. There is much freedom regarding social entertainment, although the mother church tries to provide it itself.

The church building looks nicer than the other churches in Las Cuevas. It also has an air conditioner. This is due to its larger budget in comparison to other churches in Las Cuevas, which is the result of the contributions of the majority of the members with relatively privileged backgrounds, especially the Correa family, which constitutes a little more than half of the congregation, which has an average attendance of forty. (During the time I visited the mission, there was only one poor family from Las Cuevas in attendance.) There is no cross on the altar and the words "sanctity" and "prosperity" are written on top of the altar wall. At the center of the altar and on the wall there is a picture of the eagle, the symbol of the CFLW council. There is also a figure of the eagle on the glass podium. During my visits, the altar had flowers at each side of the podium and Christmas lights. There was a keyboard at the left side of the altar. At the right corner and close to the altar, there was a sketch of a large and beautiful temple, which members were expecting to build in the near future because they were sure that the number of members would continue to grow and also because they believe that God deserves the best.

When I entered the temple on the morning of October 26, 1997, the congregation was playing *música de adoración* using good sound equipment. Neither the pastor nor many other people were there at 10:00 a.m., when the service was supposed to start. Luisa Correa, the co-pastor and sister of the founding pastor, once commented to me that although punctuality is expected, freedom is also encouraged. Luisa, who was already expecting me, and her sister welcomed me nicely. They kissed me and said, "Bendecida" ("Blessed"). Both were dressed up. They wore makeup, pants, nice hairdos, and exuded the sweet and soft smell of perfume. I met their humbly dressed mother, who also hugged and kissed me warmly. The rest of the congregation, most of them dark-skinned like Luisa, her sister, and mother (except members of one household and the wife of the founding pastor of the mission), greeted me as they came in, saying "Bendecida."

Attendance the morning of October 26 was thirty-seven. According to Luisa, attendance is difficult to increase because when people decide to come they are discouraged by other Christians. This is so because the majority of the CFLW members are former members of Protestant churches. The first part of the service, which Luisa led, was for praising, singing, prayers, reading of the Bible, and testimonies following an informal style. Luisa testified that right before she came to church, while she was praying with the Reverend Marilú Dones on her television program, God had healed her knee. Dones is a well-known female pastor of one of the largest Baptist churches in Puerto Rico, which was one of the first Protestant churches to make an open transition to a charismatic style and is one of the best representatives of individual ministries.

During the devotions Luisa constantly encouraged us to worship loudly and to keep a thankful and victorious attitude. She said, "Brothers, how beautiful it is to see you here. What a blessing, seeing here my brothers and sisters and my blood brothers and sisters. God is so powerful really. We need to preach this message and declare the salvation of our relatives." Then she asked a young woman to be in charge of the singing, and we sang three *coritos* about five times each, accompanied by a young man on the keyboard. While singing, the majority of the congregation praised God loudly, raised their hands, clapped their hands, and danced a little bit (but not in ecstasies). Some people played the tambourines. Then we read Rev. 3:14–21, a message to the church of Laodicea in which God calls His people to do right, to change their hearts, and to open the doors of their hearts so that God can enter. Luisa used this passage as a biblical foundation for the idea that what happens in our lives depends on us, on what we do with our lives, how we approach God, and the amount of faith we have.

The first part of the service was followed by a sermon preached by Pastor Correa, Luisa's brother. Pastor Correa, as I mentioned in the introduction, is the founding pastor of the mission. He is a tall black man with firm posture and strong eye contact. Unlike other pastors in Las Cuevas, he dressed elegantly, wearing expensive-looking clothes. Before starting to preach, Pastor Correa asked us to keep our Bibles open and encouraged us to take notes and to participate actively by answering questions and reading some passages with him and for him. He wanted us to see that what he was preaching was "completely based on the Scriptures" and not something he was simply inventing. (The emphasis on supporting the CFLW's twenty creeds with verses from the Bible is evident in its booklet of information about the CFLW.) Pastor Correa also indicated that we had to exercise our reasoning capacities because the message he was going to preach deserved serious and careful consideration.

Pastor Correa began his sermon by talking about an article he had read in the newspaper about the Mormons in Puerto Rico. According to Pastor Correa, the real motive behind the Mormons' interest in converting people to their religion is matrimony because they cannot marry individuals outside their religion. As I indicated in the introduction, Pastor Correa said he could not understand how any Loízans could listen to the Mormons, who believe that being black is a punishment from God. According to the pastor, this belief is an indicator that Mormonism does not follow the Bible. Pastor Correa then read a verse from Revelation that warned about adding or taking anything away from the Bible. He said that racists are not smart and that any black who accepts Mormonism deserves to be hung. The congregation laughed because they knew he really didn't mean it, although they knew he was trying to make a point. Using himself as an example, he contrasted the Mormons' belief with the CFLW emphasis on lifting up the individual and treating everybody equally.

Then, Pastor Correa talked about an article in the same newspaper about the preparation in Cuba for the visit of the pope. He said, "Shaking incense to bless people is a stupid thing. People believe and do things that do not make sense. This act does not have any power. It does not make people rich. The Catholic Church is the only church allowed in Cuba because it supports the Communist system. Brothers, the Virgin Mary can bleed or cry because the devil has power, but that does not mean that she has real power." Pastor Correa asked us to open our Bibles to Matt. 12:46–50, where Jesus indicates that his mother and brothers are those who do the things that God wants them to do. "Mary is a person like us, therefore Jesus is the only one who deserves our worship," Pastor Correa said. He covered this during most of my visits to the church. On one occasion he talked about the theme of the Virgin Mary so much that he said, "Brothers, I do not know why I am talking so much about it, but God knows."

Within the theme of idolatry, Pastor Correa added that the Catholic saints are the same gods of Spiritism and Santería and that none of them but God alone can transform our lives positively. He said, "It is stupid to think that God wishes us bad." As I wrote in the introduction, Pastor Correa strongly criticized Christians with conformist and pessimistic attitudes, and he used facial gestures to ridicule these kinds of attitude, about which the congregation laughed. Then he narrated the following: "You know what a woman told me the other day? She told me that God allows bad things to happen to test us. Brothers, I laughed. I suggested she visit our church and watch Channel 58" (58 is the channel of the CFLW). Pastor Correa indicated that he finds this poor attitude among Christians who visit the court where he works as a police sergeant. He said that this attitude did not make sense to him and he argued that both the Catholic and the Protestant churches have been largely responsible for this attitude because of their emphasis on guilt, punishment, sacrifice, and a strict doctrine. Pastor Correa continued: "The lady mentioned to me the experience of Job, who lost everything. Brothers, she forgot all the things that God gave Job back." He asked us to read John 8:31–32, where Jesus tells the Jews that if they obey God's teaching, they will know the truth and that the truth will make them free. "I cannot serve a god who is not capable of saving me and my family," said Pastor Correa. "I need a strong and powerful god. I do not need a god whom I have to carry or dress up. (He started to laugh loudly.) If a god wants to be my God he has to carry me and I will serve him. Our God does not need us to carry Him. He carries us."

Then, as a joke, Pastor Correa commented that in the festival of Santiago Apóstol the images are carried by drunk people. The congregation laughed and he said, "You laugh, but that was the way many of us believed in the past. We had false beliefs because we were ignorant, but not because we were bad people." Then Pastor Correa stood up straight and firm and said loudly, almost screaming, "Loíza urgently needs another message, a message that makes sense, a message that takes the town away from poverty and its backwardness. The usual Christian message is of 'don't,' but the CFLW's message is of 'do.' The issue is not if God can do something. We are the problem. It is the way we look at things. It is a matter of consciousness, of responsibility, of faith and obedience."

Pastor Correa then explained that some Catholics will be saved without fully enjoying God's perfect plan for them. The gospel is not only a matter of salvation, but also a matter of fulfilling God's desire for his children to prosper in all ways. He recited John 15:7, where Jesus says that we must ask for anything we need. To explain better the distinction he made between being saved (he believes Pentecostals and Catholics are saved) and fulfilling God's desire, Pastor Correa used the example of the division between the holy place and the holiest place in the Jewish temple in the Old Testament. Crossing the veil that divides one place from the other is a matter of consciousness. Sacrifices, traditionalism, rituals, a conformist attitude, pessimism, a fanatic attitude, and extremism represent the outside area of the temple. However, prosperity at all levels represents the holiest place, the closest place to God. This is why the mission of the CFLW is to tear away the veil, creating a new consciousness. Getting to the holiest place is not easy because the place is dark, and it seems even darker when one is so used to the light, to what has been established. According to Pastor Correa, this is the reason why the holy place is a more comfortable position than the holiest place. The holiest place may seem uncomfortable and risky at the beginning, but it is the place of direct and free connection with God, the place of victory.

Pastor Correa finished the sermon by affirming that Loízans, in particular, must believe in God's power. Christians, according to the pastor, can touch people and exercise God's power. Pastor Correa himself has touched people and they have started to cry. "We have to dream with faith," he said. "We have to expect that all our relatives serve the Lord. We have to dream to have a good house, a good job, and to have a daughter *bien casada*." (This means a daughter who is a virgin when she marries.) Then he told us that we must ask God to provide good husbands to the girls in the congregation. People laughed, especially young people from the church. He said that he was already seeing this happening and seeing young people graduating and becoming professionals (people were praising God louder and louder at this). He said, "See your son graduating. See it." The sermon lasted more than two hours, which is not uncommon. I have heard sermons by visiting preachers in my former Baptist church that were more than three hours long. After the sermon, Pastor Correa invited people to accept or recommit to the message of the CFLW.

As on all the occasions I visited the CFLW mission, Pastor Correa's style turned very conversational and more direct at this point. On Sunday, October 26, for example, he requested that those who were not baptized raise their hands and he asked them why they had not been. Pastor Correa also asked each one of us to indicate the reason why we follow Jesus. After I answered, "because he saved me," Pastor Correa corrected me, indicating that I must not speak in the past tense and that I have to emphasize the present tense. (This is the same reason why members of the congregation say "Blessed" instead of "God bless you.") He raised his voice while telling me this, telling me also that I needed to speak louder as a sign of my strong conviction. I felt Pastor Correa trying strongly to pull me into his religious community. On another occasion he asked each one of us if we were going to a special activity they were having at the mother church. To those of us who indicated that we could not go, he asked the reason why, in front of everybody. Here I must note the strong emphasis by the religious leaders on the need for members to connect with the main church and the great pressure I was constantly under to visit the mother church to experience fully the effectiveness of the message of the

CFLW. On Sunday, October 26, after asking those who were not baptized the reason why, Pastor Correa prayed for the perseverance and faith of those who had raised their hands and for everybody else because, he insisted, everybody should have raised their hands because we always need prayer. As usual, this section was followed by various testimonies, singing, the collection of offerings, and the benediction.

Strategies and Substrategies of Legitimacy

One can identify several strategies of presentation in Pastor Correa's sermon, all of which are closely associated with the beliefs of the CFLW. However, I argue that the most important strategy for legitimizing the CFLW's message is to highlight Loíza's black identity and its social and economic backwardness while demonstrating the urgent need for a different message in the town such as that presented by the CFLW: a message of freedom, victory, control over one's life, and prosperity. This message is expressed in one of the editions of the booklet of information about each CFWL church, where Loíza is described as a community that needs "a message of faith and prosperity to affect the economic and civil life."

This approach also relies heavily upon support by political leaders, systems, and elements that endorse or facilitate the model of prosperous society proposed by the CFLW. This support is not necessarily expressed in the sermons, but examples of this support come from Pastor Font's statements endorsing the pro-statehood government, the church's direct support of or attack on political leaders in its newsletter, and from Pastor Correa's statements during the sermon against Communism in Cuba, which he indicated is endorsed by the Catholic Church there. The previous governor, Pedro Roselló from the PNP, and his wife have visited the CFLW to address the congregation. The CFLW has also had other politicians as speakers, such as the president of the PPD and the mayor of Carolina, who is also from the PPD. An article in the November 1999 issue of the newsletter indicates which leaders the CFLW wanted its members to support.

Pastor Correa's approach also relies heavily upon a characterization of the existing Christian message (Catholic and Protestant) as ineffective. Contrast is frequently used in this way by various religious groups to qualify themselves and this technique is also clearly evident in the CFLW informational booklet. Extending the qualification of "tradition" (commonly associated with Catholicism) to the message of other Protestant churches is both an exercise of contrasting and self-legitimacy and a reaction to the downplaying of religion or Christian faith as tradition. The lack of traditional religious paraphernalia such as the cross and a communion table and the intention of making the temple look more like a modern nonreligious building are indications of this position. At the same time, the CFLW's leaders claim that their message is different while emphasizing that their message is "the best" and "the most" appropriate or adequate compared to other Christian messages. Such claims have to do with their idea that God's will for His children is salvation and prosperity in all areas of their lives and that other Christian messages only address salvation. It is clear, therefore, that the CFLW leadership is careful to present their church's message as something not totally new but familiar, in other words, as a better alternative to other Christian denominations. The fact that most members of the CFLW are former members of other Christian denominations seems to indicate that an important church strategy is to expand by recruiting members (passive or active) of other Christian congregations. Many of the CFLW's activities are designed to involve different Christian members and congregations while promoting an atmosphere of interdenominational camaraderie. Music concerts and contests seem to be the most popular of these activities because, as I mentioned earlier, the Christian music industry continues to grow fast. These activities have caused members of various denominations to visit the CFLW on a regular basis without joining the CFLW permanently.

The other strategies or substrategies employed by Pastor Correa may be divided into four main groups: 1) those that legitimize Pastor Correa as a preacher; 2) those that are indicative of Pastor Correa's preaching style; 3) those that prepare Loízans to receive the church's message; and 4) those that present tangible evidence of the efficacy of the message. They are significant because altogether they help to legitimize the CFLW's message.

Pastor Correa legitimized himself as a preacher by indicating that he, like many other Loízans, had prior false beliefs and by emphasizing the black color of his skin. In fact, the closeness of black preachers to their congregations, or their identification with church members, has been pointed out as one of the most distinguishing characteristics of black spiritual leadership (Lincoln 1974: 67).

The most important substrategies employed by Pastor Correa regarding his preaching style are the use of body language, volume, sarcasm, a direct and conversational style, analogy, and the establishment of biblical legitimacy.

For example, body language and volume came into play when Pastor Correa stood up straight and almost screamingly insisted that Loízans urgently needed another message. Body language and sarcasm were evident when Pastor Correa used facial gestures to ridicule the pessimistic or passive attitude of many Christians. Humor was used in his remark that a Loízan who listens to the Mormons deserves to be hung. A direct and conversational style appeared throughout his preaching, especially at the end when he shifted his message to a more reflexive tone and requested an immediate response from the congregation regarding the sermon. On Sunday, October 26, this style was evident when Pastor Correa demanded the listeners' participation by asking us individually why we followed Jesus and why those in the congregation who were not baptized had not taken that step. The use of analogy was evident in all of Pastor Correa's sermons. On October 26, he used the analogy of the Jewish temple in Old Testament times to explain the effect of the CFLW's message in making people think differently in order for them to obtain more than salvation, to obtain as well a fully prosperous life. On another occasion, he used the analogy of a computer to make the point that many Christians are in need of reprogramming.

Establishing biblical legitimacy is a very important substrategy in light of the fact that within the context of interchurch competition doctrinal authenticity (as it relates to the Bible) is a central issue. This substrategy is closely connected to the substrategies employed to prepare Loízans to receive the CFLW's message. What I mean is that presentation of the CFLW's message as "the most" biblically reasonable and logical doctrine is seen as a major selling point for the church. Moreover, this assertion is tied to Loízan issues of self-esteem. From my interviews it is clear that Loízans believe they are regarded as stupid, passive, or conformist by those outside their community. The CFLW approach in Loíza makes use of this concern. In fact, "stupid" is often used by Pastor Correa to characterize those who oppose the CFLW's message, a message that when accepted becomes a sign of common sense and intelligence.

The CFLW approach in Loíza emphasizes a strong sense of the self and of control over one's life. Pastor Correa indicated many times that Loízans had false beliefs in the past because of ignorance, in this case lack of knowledge or information, and not because of lack of intelligence or bad intentions. He often shaped his message to build up a healthy self-esteem in his listeners. Contrary to the idea behind the phrase "If you caint get the boat, take a log," still circulating in many black churches in the United States (Pitts 1989), Pastor Correa's idea is that taking a log is not an option because how one "gets there" is as important as "getting there." Christians should always take the boat. Here again is the idea that a healthy self-esteem is an important step toward prosperity. The church's open disdain for the "victim mentality" goes hand in hand with this approach. When people feel inadequate they are more likely to conform and less likely to fight to have their needs met. Pastor Correa presents the CFLW's message within this context.

Here I would like to point out that at first I thought that bringing up the issue of black identity was a single response to the Loízans' need as black people. However, a few conversations with members of the CFLW convinced me that this attention is part of a larger initiative of the CFLW to include openly the issue of Puerto Rican culture and Afro-Caribbean modern traditions in its events and activities. Among other examples is the initiative of the radio program "Salsa con sentido" (Salsa with meaning) in which the audience is called to an awareness of Afro-Caribbean elements such as salsa and given historical information about this heritage. Here it is important to understand that salsa is a modern aspect of Afro-Caribbean tradition that has gained great international acceptance (including Asia, all parts of Europe, and Africa). In the situation of the CFLW, supporting salsa is *one* of the strategies employed to modernize and internationalize the church and to be ahead of other churches and even secular institutions. In my recent visit to Puerto Rico (in May of 2003), I heard a Christian radio station playing a wide range of Afro-Caribbean rhythms. At this point, I want to clarify that an increased taste for these rhythms does not mean an embracing of the Afro-Caribbean identity or the issue of color. There is no connection between this awareness and a specifically anti-racist religious or secular agenda. However, it is true that addressing the issue of color is more necessary in the situation of Loíza. Another point related to the issue of self-esteem and color that cannot be ignored is the great interest of Loíza's CFLW leadership in getting its members to participate in activities at the mother church and to integrate into the large CFLW community. This attitude is very significant when considering the stereotype of Loízans as "isolated" and the fact that the mother church is mostly attended by light-skinned and socioeconomically stable members.

Finally, we come to the substrategy that presents tangible evidence of the efficacy of the CFLW's message. The popularity, power, and prosperity of the CFLW are often cited as proof of its authenticity. In different sermons and personal conversations, Pastor Correa often referred to the examples of the CFLW's great financial, physical, and technological capacity; the rapid spread of the message outside Puerto Rico; the consideration of the CFLW's message by important figures; the conversion of entire families; and a great number of healings in the congregation. Testimonies are especially significant as they represent tangible evidence of the power of the CFLW's message. On one of the Sundays I visited the church, the service began with testimony by Pastor Correa's third sister. She is the local pastor who assumed leadership of the church after Pastor Correa's initial term. (He served as pastor for purposes of establishing the mission and he continues to be in charge of the Sunday sermons. His sister handles the rest of the leadership duties and is therefore also called Pastor Correa [in Spanish, Pastora Correa].) Her testimony concerned the large numbers of young people who attended the recent campaign that discouraged sex before marriage and encouraged educational goals for the youth. Additional evidence of the power of the CFLW's message is provided by testimonies that indicate God's supernatural intervention through miracles of conversion/transformation of a relative or friend, of protection, and especially of healing and financial provision. For this reason, the church provides a special section after the sermon at each meeting for testimonies; at the same time, testimonies are also welcomed anytime during the service.

One of the most memorable testimonies was given by Pastor Correa's mother: On one occasion she was sick and wanted to die, but her children requested her healing with strong faith and God healed her. In fact, the CFLW believe that death that results from illness is never God's will for His children. On the morning of October 26, Pastor Correa testified about his daughter's acceptance into the very competitive medical school of the UPR and asked his brother, who had recently accepted the Lord, to testify about his recent promotion and salary increase. In this context, testimonies also conform to the empowerment ventures of African-Americans. By pointing to tangible evidence of the power of the message of the CFLW, testimonies are also as Melvin Williams has argued (1974: 163–64) "a vivid rite of community solidarity," which I argue is very significant because the CFLW members are constantly and strongly criticized by the rest of the Christian community. Testimonies are the result of faith, which is emphasized in the CFLW. The use of testimonies help individuals to exercise their faith and, therefore, to bring to reality tangible evidence of the power of the CFLW's message. Change of verb tense, as in "Bendecida" instead of "God bless you," and the use of imagination are also part of this strategic approach. As Michael Brown (1984) has shown, among Aguaruna people song lyrics allow the imaginary to affect or shape reality, a successful hunting. The use of imagination was clearly employed during the service of October 26, when Pastor Correa asked members of the congregation to close their eyes and to see or imagine a son graduating from college. The emphasis on imagination is also in evidence during the many times members refer to the picture of their new church building that they have in front of the altar.

Clearly, the CFLW regards the church community as the principal arena in which members serve others' needs, including the needs of those outside the CFLW community. These efforts are clearly evident in the CFLW's various resources and physical facilities. The CFLW is a model of society: a combination of community integration and individuals achieving their greatest potential.

Reassessing Possibilities

Almost ten years after the foundation of the CFLW in Las Cuevas, the majority of the congregation is still from outside the area of Loíza and is mainly from the Correa family. A possible reason for this slow growth could be the fact that some of the strategies used by the CFLW, such as emphasizing identity and self-esteem, are not completely unfamiliar to competing churches and other social groups and settings. A case in point was the constant fight of Pastor Rafael Osorio of the Baptist churces of Loíza (interview, October 8, 2002) against low self-esteem and conformism in Medianía Alta, which caused a deep frustration within him. Such was the case despite various accomplishments of the church, including its strong involvement in social ministry and an increase in the attendance to four hundred by the time he left the church. According to Pastor Osorio, he did address the issue of race as directly as he did other social issues. In fact, he related low socioeconomic status more to people's attitudes than to their dark skin.

Other reasons for the slow growth of the CFLW in Loíza surfaced during my conversations with people from Las Cuevas. The following comment is representative of the opinions of many individuals in the community: "Here it not easy simply to claim economic prosperity because of our social and economic situation. The government is corrupt. It is hard to progress and to break with the cycle of dependency when jobs and resources are scant. It is very easy to say that you do not progress because you do not have enough faith. It does not make sense to me. Also, what does progress really mean? We have to be careful because the more we have the more we want." This comment means that modernity and its systems have affected people differently and have caused people to develop different perspectives on or consciousness of social progress. Many elders and even young individuals were cautious about the implications of modernity and prosperity. Some interviewees felt uncomfortable with churches using high technology; they saw high technology as intimidating and as a sign of less spirituality. They associated modernity and prosperity with lack of morality, unity, and sense of community. They pointed out that in the past there was more unity because everybody was poor and depended on each other and therefore respected each other's property. In other words, the prosperity that the CFLW advocates is not necessarily what many Loízans aspire to or feel comfortable with. In addition, the CFLW also has to confront long-term, strongly held religious convictions, for example the CC's and the CFDC's emphasis on humility, sacrifice, and separation from the things of the world, that have already found legitimacy among the people of Las Cuevas. The following statement by Julia, a member of the Baptist church downtown, is an example of these strong convictions: "God is God no matter if we are doing fine or not. He wants the best for us, but sometimes what we think is the best for us is not what He thinks. God said that we will suffer. God also expects our faith to be weak like a mustard seed; this is why He also expects that we depend on Him to have more faith. I lost my son. I was not a super woman, but I depended on Him and He helped me in my weakness. We have to focus on Him and on spreading the Good News of salvation, instead of focusing on how to live a prosperous life."

Only the future will tell what kind of steps the CFLW will need to take to reach other sectors of believers and nonbelievers and what changes in Loízans' mindset and social conditions will need to happen for them to accept the CFLW's message.[4]

"Now there is a church on every corner"

Religious, Socioeconomic, and Family Identities
in a Small Residential Space

The first time I visited the temple of the Heavenly Doors Evangelical Church in Las Cuevas, there were only seven people at the service (the capacity was eighty). Pastor Medero and his wife were the only whites present. During most of the service the pastor kept walking the aisle and checking people during the devotions. One of the girls was seated at a time when all the others were standing and he asked her to stand. I forgot to stand up when he asked me to read from the Bible and he reminded me to do so in a way that seemed to me as though he were talking to a child. At one point, Pastor Medero checked his mail from the main podium while a young lady was testifying and singing *coritos*. The pastor's wife sat the whole time in the very last seat, which was close to the front door, and she played the tambourines completely out of rhythm. The guitar was not in the right key.

The second time I visited the HDEC, I participated in the Sunday school. This time the service was better attended because of the arrival of Pastor Medero's two children and their children. After the Sunday school finished, Pastor Medero invited me to his home upstairs to eat lunch, which he ordered his wife to prepare for me. While eating, I was able to talk with Pastor Medero and his family. I explained that I was there to study religion in the area, a topic that Pastor Medero avoided in our conversations, although at some point he agreed to answer questions regarding the history of the church. However, one day when I was walking in front of the church, Pastor Medero told me he knew about me and my real intentions. According to him, I was a member of the group or had been sent by the group of people who had just left the church because of problems with him. He also told me that I wanted to investigate his church to accuse him before the council. When I started to deny these accusations, his son, who was doing construction work on the church at the time, asked me to stop questioning his father. Both also stated that religion was not something to be studied but to be practiced and that they could not waste their time helping me when they could use it to spread the gospel. I left and decided to make no more attempts to contact them.

Former HDEC members and neighbors who live close to the church told me that the church has always had conflicts because of the pastor's character. A resident told me that the pastor and his family normally were in a defensive posture and suggested that this probably had to do with the fact that they are part of a white minority in the area. Also, the church is surrounded by a small residential neighborhood and is located wall to wall with residences. These residents were quick to say that the HDEC has survived because of the support and protection of the pastor's children. As a resident put it, "If not for the pastor's children, the church would not exist." However, the pastor's family members have been inconsistent with regard to the church as they tend to show up more often when there is a crisis. I heard rumors that the pastor's family members themselves have caused crisis in the church, but I was not able to confirm them. Fortunately, over the course of a few weeks, Pastor Medero began to smile at me when I passed in front of the church. I think this change occurred after he realized that my intentions were not bad, that I was being welcomed in other churches, and that I had no intentions of trying to approach him again.

This experience at the HDEC made me aware of a strong relationship between religious and family identities and the fact that this relationship may be contradictory, ambiguous, and paradoxical (as shown by Rodríguez Toulis 1997: 212–64; Mariz and Mafra 1999), while having effects both ways (Ammerman and Roof 1995).[1] This relationship can be influenced by various factors, such as education, income, race, and color (Rowe 1998; Steigenga and Smilde 1999). It can involve various family relationships: parents/children, brother/sister, niece/uncle.[2] It is also integrated into wider systems of meaning such as nation or state (Collier and Yanagisako 1989), community and ethnicity (Kipp 1993; Brow 1996), and sociophysical space. Relationships created by functions such as adoption and godparenting, among others, make kinship a fabrication (Kipp 1993: 125–56).

Evidence of the above dynamics and situations was not hard to find in Las Cuevas, particularly concerning the sociophysical space that included interreligious interactions. By focusing on the intertwining of religion, socioeconomic stability, family, and space, I address the concerns about looking at religious pluralism or syncretism from the perspective of static or unpenetrating boundaries or components. Along this line of thought, Feeley-Harnik makes the following comment, which she developed when confronted by the relationship between religion and food cross-culturally: "In my view, our comparative analysis of 'religious' pluralism should not stop at ideological boundaries of 'church' in what are too preemptively called 'secular' states, obscuring the interaction of competing approaches to life-and-death concerns that might be common to all" (1995: 571). Feeley-Harnik's statement moves along the same lines as Stewart and Shaw's (1994: 7) preference for studying syncretism as processes and discourses involving power and agency instead of a category referring to a mechanical mixing.

The analysis of religious pluralism in terms of unpenetrating boundaries and of syncretism as a mechanical mixing is in great part the result of denying or ignoring the level of everyday life, as Nasr (1990: 124) has indicated. Solivan (1998: 41) relates the great potential of Hispanic Pentecostalism for interreligious dialogue to its emphasis on the Holy Spirit's work and, more significantly, to the marginal social and economic status of this sector, which promotes an attitude of privileging daily experience over reasoning. In this way he reacts to a view of Pentecostalism as clear-cut. Also, the evidence I present in this chapter shows the fluidity of religious boundaries and, simultaneously, the way these boundaries are constantly re-created.

Emphasizing the level of everyday life while focusing on space in general and sacred space in particular also brings the opportunity to corroborate the validity of Davies's (1994: 55) suggestion to consider people's perspective on sacred space primarily instead of departing from the religious discourse while assuming this a priori. This type of analysis allows seeing the process by which sacred space is a social project of a certain kind. Along the same lines, Chidester and Linenthal (1995: 5–6) favor a situational or political definition of the sacred as opposed to a substantial or poetic definition. According to the authors, a situational analysis locates the sacred at the nexus of human practices and social projects, a notional supplement to the ongoing cultural work of sacralizing space, time, person, and social relations.

General Characteristics of Las Cuevas

Las Cuevas is in one of the six barrios of the town of Loíza and where the town's mayor lived for many years. This barrio is called Pueblo because it contains the administrative center. The other barrios are Medianía Alta, Medianía Baja, Torrecilla Alta, Torrecilla Baja, and Canóvanas. Las Cuevas is officially considered a sector, the name used to refer to a subdivision of a barrio or to a neighborhood. Las Cuevas includes an area larger than the area where 99 percent of the houses are concentrated; however, in this study Las Cuevas refers to the area with the high concentration of houses. Because of Las Cuevas's size and self-contained character, it is also considered a barrio. More specifically, Las Cuevas, like the rest of Loíza, is flat and is situated at the western edge of Pueblo and between the more central area of downtown and the Río Grande de Loíza. The river and a stream in the southwestern part of Las Cuevas give the sector a swampy and rural character, although there is not much vegetation except in the most interior area, where there are serious problems of stagnant waters in need of channeling. The average temperature is 85°F, making Las Cuevas cooler than many areas of Loíza.

As I mentioned earlier, the name Las Cuevas refers to the caves in the area. The caves were formerly known as Cueva de los Indios (Indian Caves) and were used as a quarry for many years. According to archaeological and historical research and oral tradition, the caves were used by the Indians as a cemetery and as a ceremonial place. The eastern area of the mouth of Loíza's river, called Cayrabón by the Indians of the time, was home to the Indian settlement or chiefdom mentioned earlier. It was called Jaymanío by the Indians and was ruled by a chieftess called Yuiza when the Spaniards arrived. According to historical accounts and common knowledge, Yuiza married a Spanish man and was baptized. The most common belief is that "Loíza" derives from the chieftess's name, Yuiza. Over the decades the area of Las Cuevas was owned by *hacendados* or landowners whom people called *colonos*. The *colonos* used the land mainly for agricultural production with labor provided by *agregados*, who in exchange for their labor were allowed to grow crops on the property for their own subsistence. Later, the caves were named after a *mestiza* woman, María la Cruz, who was the owner of the piece of land where the caves are located.

According to my census, the oldest residence in Las Cuevas has existed since 1918, in the area close to the bridge. It was followed by two houses built in 1919, all of them using cardboard, palm tree leaves, and some wood. In the first half of the twentieth century, a great part of Las Cuevas was dedicated to the production of sugar because of the establishment of a sugar mill in the area. As cane production disappeared, part of Las Cuevas became the government's property and the rest of the land, which includes the majority of Las Cuevas, passed through the hands of different families without legal documents.³ The area close to the caves became a recreation area, although at present it is practically abandoned and in bad shape. In Las Cuevas, more than half of the houses were built in the second half of the twentieth century. The peak in building activity came between 1968 and 1978 with 34 percent of the houses built during that period. The construction of eleven houses in 1948 could have had to do with a PPD government agrarian reform to provide property to the poor masses at the time (the slogan of the party was "Bread, earth, liberty"). The great number of houses built in the second period and early third period, most of which were built of cement, were part of the "cement fever" that swept the island during the rapid growth of the Puerto Rican–owned Ponce Cement company. (As I mentioned earlier, the company is owned by the family of former PNP governor Luis A. Ferré and the family is one of the richest families in the country.) In fact, my research indicates that 79 percent of the houses in Las Cuevas are of cement, most of them rebuilt, and only 8 percent are of wood. The average number of years between the building year and the rebuilding year in Las Cuevas was twenty-three, which speaks about the difficult socioeconomic situation of many households in Las Cuevas.

Las Cuevas contains about eight hundred residents, most of whom were raised there. The population is relatively equally distributed by gender and is largely young. The sector contains about 230 inhabited households, highly concentrated. I found an average of three members per household, which indicates a reduction of members per household from several decades earlier. This reduction is mainly attributed by Las Cuevas's residents to contraceptive alternatives, socioeconomic competition, education, and a high number of female-headed households. However, people have dealt with the problems of large households in the past through adoption (mostly informal or without papers), by joining the military, and by migrating to other towns and to the United States.

The reduction in the number of members per household is not completely indicative of the lack of importance of the extended family. In 40 percent of the households with offspring, at least one of the offspring is an adult (older than twenty-one); in addition, 16.3 percent of households have grandchildren. Also, in many cases the houses of the parents, the children, and the grandchildren are in close proximity. The monthly income in 71 percent of the households is less than $900 (ranging from $300 or less to $8,000 or more), which comes mainly from a combination of government assistance, technical occupations, especially construction, and different economic activities, which is consistent with the strategies employed by people in other countries to cope with poverty, for example St. Vincent (Rubenstein 1987: 132–41). But the socioeconomic situation of Las Cuevas is best understood by looking at the experience of one of its residents.

Pablo's Experience

Pablo had been admitted into the UPR to study medicine. When he told me that I said, "Really?" He answered, "Oh yes, don't be surprised. Many people have misconceptions about Loízans. You may see people dressing like me [simply and dirtily, because he was fixing his car], without shoes, who are very smart. Don't let physical appearance guide you." To continue his studies in Mexico or Spain after his graduation from the UPR, Pablo needed a lot of money. In order to acquire the needed funds, he enlisted in the National Guard for three years, where he became a first lieutenant and a television and radio technician. However, Pablo left the military because he felt discriminated against and exploited by the U.S. military establishment. Once he left the military, he became a member of the pro-independence party or PIP and a good electrician working in large companies such as Western Auto and White Westinghouse. While working as an electrician, he suffered a terrible accident in which he was seriously injured. This forced him to leave his job and in 1977 he started to receive compensation. Pablo went to full-time fishing because the $500 that he was receiving was not enough to cover his and his family's living expenses (Pablo has six children) and the many medical expenses of his second wife, who is mentally ill. Pablo got his fishing license for fishing in shallow water (no more than twelve feet of water). At the time, he was fishing principally in Carolina and Loíza. After his father died about four years ago, he moved to Loíza to live in a house he built on a piece of property he inherited from his father (without legal papers).

The situation for Pablo, as for many other fishermen on the island, has been very hard. Pablo compared it to the situation of artisans who only get money during festivals because of the competition with other products from outside and the common misconception that Loízan crafts are satanic or weird. Pollution, especially since the 1980s, has negatively affected fishing in shallow water because it chases fish into deep water. The cutting of trees close to the rivers (where Pablo also fished before the 1992 law that prohibited fishing in the rivers) has made the mud come into shallow water, which also forces the fish to go to deep water. Because of these problems, Pablo tried fishing in deep water for a while, but could not continue because of the great expenses it involved: the acquisition and maintenance of equipment and the salary of his helpers. Pablo discovered that the government does not provide assistance or the necessary infrastructure, such as good port facilities. In addition, fishermen in Puerto Rico are relatively lacking in unity regarding the fight for their rights because of the different socioeconomic backgrounds and needs of the fishers (something that Griffith, Valdés Pizzini, and Johnson [1992: 69] have identified as heterogeneity of trajectories in their study of fishing in Puerto Rico). Pablo gave me a specific example of this situation: In the past, he could catch four hundred pounds in one night. Today, the maximum he catches is forty to fifty pounds a night, which he sells for $1.50 per pound to clients mainly from outside Loíza and Carolina. Sometimes Pablo sells his catch for $1.00 a pound because the kind of fish that predominates is *mojarra*, which deteriorates in quality after twelve days in the refrigerator.

Pablo and his family have survived financially because of the many strategies he employs to keep going, such as doing plumbing and mechanical work to earn extra money. Other strategies include utilizing the phone only when necessary (mainly for job purposes) and watching television only for good purposes (such as educational or cultural local and international programs, which he often videotapes in order to study at his leisure). Pablo thinks that television has opened the world to him, although sometimes he finds it frustrating to see all the alternatives to improve the social system that do not exist in Loíza. All of his efforts require a lot of discipline on his part and are the cause of many conflicts with his children.

Pablo has been a socially active person. Throughout his life he has organized sports teams, protests, and community events and programs. Because of his fighting spirit and strong leadership, he was unanimously elected president of the Organization of Shallow Water Fishermen, a position he held for four years. However, this kind of leadership has cost him and other residents from Las Cuevas local job opportunities. This is particularly the case of individuals who are not afraid of criticizing the local government and making demands of it and who have been part of the political left in the United States and on the island.

Although religion has been significant in Pablo's life, he is critical of it, particularly of the fact that ecological responsibility is rarely requested in the churches. He strongly believes that God has always helped him so that he can help others. When we started to talk about religion, Pablo's attitude was the same attitude he had had when he told me he had been a medical student. He said that many people still think that Loízans are highly superstitious and that the town is full of witches. Pablo does not go consistently to mass, but he usually watches it on television. More importantly, he communicates with God constantly and tries to help others. He feels particularly sorry for so many young people in Loíza and in Puerto Rico who are involved in drugs. He thinks that drugs are the result of moral decay and consumerism (wherein great value is put on material possessions), which he associates with the high rate of bankruptcy. (In fact, in 1998 the bankruptcy rate on the island was at 44 percent.) According to Pablo, all religions are right in their own way. He thinks it is sometimes confusing to see so much antagonism. He has visited different churches, but he thinks the Catholic Church is the most authentic, although he approves of the fact that the Catholic Church lately has adopted good things from Protestant churches, such as identifying more with the people.

Las Cuevas's Physical-Social Space

Street #951, leading to the barrio of Canóvanas, divides Las Cuevas into two major areas, which for the purpose of this discussion I will call the northern and the southern parts. As I mentioned earlier, Las Cuevas contains about 230 households.[4] About 30 houses are unfinished but inhabited. There are also about 20 unfinished houses that nobody lives in. In the closest zone to downtown, bordering streets #187 and #188, there is a gas station, a beauty supply store, a grade school, a food store, and the health center, which is considered to be number one in the area. In addition to the beauty supply store and the food store, Las Cuevas has thirteen other small businesses, which include a workshop and a television repair place. The rest are stores that sell food or house products or both, except for Luisa's small store, which sells mainly traditional Puerto Rican dishes. Three of the stores that sell food or house products or both also sell alcohol. All of the businesses except Luisa's store and the stores bordering street #951 in the northern part of Las Cuevas are attached to or are next to the owners' houses. I should also mention the caves, which are located more to the southern part of Las Cuevas, the recreational area in front of the caves (with some structures), the office of Civil Defense, and the six churches located in Las Cuevas.

I support Cohen's (1985: 20) argument that community should be regarded as an aggregating device rather than as an integrating mechanism because it does not clone behavior or ideas, but rather forms of behaving whose content may vary considerably. If this is so, then we must ask how these similar forms of behaving with potential for a similar content come about. The first thing I noticed in Las Cuevas was the high concentration of homes and the lack of residential organization, although Las Cuevas is more organized than many other sectors I visited in Loíza. Second, the houses are mainly grouped according to the last names of the owners. There I found 102 last names (counting both the father's and the mother's last names). The highest percentages are as follows: Tapia with 13 percent; Benítez with 7 percent; Febres, Cortijo, and González with 4 percent each; and Guzmán, Santos, and Sánchez with 3 percent each.[5]

The areas delineated by last names are subdivided by socioeconomic stability, which I deduced by the house's physical appearance, family income, everyday expenses, and education. However, I was very careful of generalizations because despite the fact that these four variables are good indicators of socioeconomic stability, I found that there were other factors that were just as determinant, space availability and the contribution and care of children not living in the house being just two examples. Furthermore, some residents told me they did not want their houses to look attractive to robbers. A common opinion in Las Cuevas was that some residents prefer their houses to look in bad shape in order to get money from the government (this opinion has to do with the concern of some residents that their answers to the question of income would give the impression that their economic situation was stable). In relation to their homes' appearance, a few people mentioned a sense of critique toward a growing consumeristic mentality in the country. I also found socioeconomic conditions to be more flexible than I had expected, sometimes changing dramatically in the course of a month and therefore keeping people in a constant everyday struggle to maintain some kind of economic balance. This dynamic constitutes the main reason for my use of the term socioeconomic stability instead of class, which I consider to be a less flexible term.

The Tapia extended family is divided, although not rigidly, into three main subgroups. The physical appearance of the areas in which family members live can be considered a partial indication of their socioeconomic stability, but only partial because some of the areas were poor and clean while others were poor and full of trash. The two sections of the Tapia family with a more stable socioeconomic situation live close to a main street in the northern part of Las Cuevas. One of them is close to street #187 and the bridge, and the other close to street #951. The third subgroup of the Tapia family lives in poverty in the interior area of the southern part of Las Cuevas, close to the stream. These members are called hermits by residents of Las Cuevas, who also refer to them as crazy or weird people. Three of the adult children are mentally ill. Clearly, this socioeconomic subdivision relates to the patterns Portes, Itzigsohn, and Dore-Cabral (1994) have found developing recently in some areas of the Caribbean: the deceleration of urban primacy and of spatial polarization between socioeconomic sectors.

The situation of the Tapia extended family points to a general pattern in Las Cuevas, and this is that the houses close to a main street are usually in better shape than the houses in the interior areas. Many of the families who live in the very interior areas have numerous problems with infrastructure. For example, in the northern area I met a family whose house was usually full of stagnant water. The mother came from St. Thomas and married a man from the Ayala family. As soon as I mentioned the situation to the mayor, he promised to do something about it, but argued that this happens often to people who take big risks and then expect the municipality to resolve their problems. To the mayor's comment the mother responded that they had no choice but to build in the area.

There are also physical or spatial strategies or situations that people use in order to interact, although these divisions are also important for security reasons and the avoidance of conflict. The first strategy refers to the accommodation of the houses and their proximity to one another. One can start with the short distance between most of the houses in Las Cuevas, a pattern that is very common in poor communities in other parts of Puerto Rico (Bryce-Laporte 1970: 88) and in other countries such as Mexico (De Lomnitz 1975: 126). In Las Cuevas, the houses are sometimes very close to each other while forming a circle with the front doors facing the center of the circle. I noticed this in about ten areas. In these cases, about twenty houses are built literally on top of other houses. About five houses share a common wall or one or two sections of the structure, for example, the kitchen or the living room. This relates to the practice of sharing a tank or a faucet in an open area.

A large network of small roads and pathways between residences lead outside the residential area of Las Cuevas to the hospital, the school, the downtown, and to other residential areas where friends and relatives live. Most of them created by repeated use, these pathways provide a way for people to travel by foot outside Las Cuevas, especially downtown. Here it is significant to argue, as Berreman (1997: 340) does about the Himalayas, that Las Cuevas cannot be understood without reference to its extensions into surrounding villages with which individuals of Las Cuevas have socioeconomic ties. These pathways are a means to overcome the limitations of poor public transportation. They also serve as a safe alternative for the elderly, who run the danger of getting hit by a car on the main streets of town. Pathway foot travel also keeps neighbors in touch with one another. There are many opportunities for verbal (including whistling) and nonverbal interaction while using the pathways. Because of this, when I was in a hurry I tried to avoid certain pathways, although at times I found myself spontaneously trying to hear inside the houses and to gather information. Oftentimes homeowners will stop a traveler to request a favor depending on the traveler's destination (for example, to buy something in a store or to pass a message along to someone else). I have to confess that sometimes after smelling the delicious food being prepared, I wished I had been stopped. However, some pathways are not that popular and therefore represent a danger because they lead to areas that are not visited much by people and that have been used for drug dealing.

Regarding the third strategy or spatial situation used strategically by members of the community to interact, Las Cuevas has developed designated areas for close sharing or interaction. These are mainly used by relatives and especially by friends of the same age and gender (relatives tend to interact more inside a house, on the back or front porch, or on the balcony of a house). One of the most popular areas in Las Cuevas is *el senado* (the Senate), as everybody calls an area in the northern part of Las Cuevas bordering street #951. Permanent chairs, some of them in bad shape because of the rain, form a circle. The area of *el senado* used to have a small place that sold rum *caña* (a strong, crudely processed alcohol drink). However, it was destroyed twenty to twenty-five years ago. In *el senado,* men, who are usually at least forty years old, get together on weekday and weekend afternoons to talk about general issues and their personal situations. They may play a table game such as dominos or use the time to smoke and drink or both. One of the men who regularly meets there indicated that the area serves as a security network because men can hear from other men, sometimes from outside Las Cuevas, about what is going on in the community and in town regarding crime and problems. Sometimes they discuss the sermons they hear while attending church (particularly the Pentecostal Church of God and the Heavenly Doors Evangelical

Church). Not everybody has good opinions about *el senado*. Some residents, especially women, criticized the fact that *el senado* keeps men away from their responsibilities at home. Other women liked the fact that *el senado* keeps the men inside the neighborhood and within view. The significance of this place was evident during my last session of fieldwork, when one of the men who used to frequent this place died and the funeral procession made a stop at *el senado* for a moment of silence.

Women also have their public spaces in which to chat about general issues and personal matters. These usually vary in location, but still include a range of commonly understood areas, usually close to a house. For example, after a funeral rosary about 9:00 p.m., a group of women (including myself) gathered in front of Rosa's house and talked for about forty minutes. Rosa's nephew, who had just came from the PCG across the street, joined us, as did Rosa's brother and his wife from their balcony (two houses from Rosa's house). They had just come from their meeting at another Pentecostal church outside Las Cuevas. As commonly practiced in other Caribbean countries (Sobo 1993: 82–84), there are a few permanent places for women to cook, eat together, and exchange food, such as the social area close to the HDEC. The idea that these women might think that I was looking for food sometimes prevented me from walking to these areas. As I said, women's public areas for sharing are usually close to a residence, although most of women's sharing, especially among elder women, happens on the balcony or inside the house. This situation also includes doing a favor such as making a phone call, sometimes in a neighbor's house (the only public phone in the area was out of service).

The fact that women's public areas for sharing are usually close to a residence and that most of women's sharing happens inside the house has a lot to do with the idea that women are not to walk the streets. The female teenagers and young women whom one sees walking and gathering in public places are usually accompanied by male teenagers and young men, who gather on a regular basis in public places, such as street #951. Some of these girls and young women, however, are thought to be crazy, involved in drugs, or indecent. This is a great source of controversy between mothers and daughters. There are separate spaces exclusively for male teenagers and young men to gather and practice sports, such as the area of the basketball court and the area of an abandoned ranch close to the caves. Other public areas are used for drug dealing, although in some areas of Loíza this activity is decreasing thanks to the efforts of members of the community, including policemen who reside there.

Small businesses, most of which are attached to the owners' houses, also serve as areas for interaction. Many people think that there have been fewer of these gatherings because of the decreasing use of these small stores (people prefer to buy in big stores) and also because only three of the eight stores sell alcohol. (One of the stores that still sells alcohol is very near to closing because of the building's disrepair, the lack of business, pressure from the owner's born-again Christian children, and the owner's health problems, which are related to his alcoholism.) Regarding alcohol use in Las Cuevas, only 9 percent of the families who participated in the census reported to have at least one member with serious alcohol problems. Even though this percentage represents less than what I saw, people agree that over the years there has been a decrease in the use of alcohol because of the advancement of the gospel, the many health problems associated with alcohol that have plagued users, and the alternative of drugs. Small stores in Las Cuevas have survived because even though people who can shop outside the town do so, they still have need for immediate, local purchases. Also, many people cannot go outside Las Cuevas because of transportation limitations, and some people buy food on an informal credit basis, which requires a network of close friendships and kinship.

Finally, there are the areas centering around church buildings, which also coincide with groups of households whose members are related. This is particularly the case in the areas surrounding the Church of Christ and the Church of the Faithful Disciples of Christ, where church members and non-members interact in front of the church before and after the services. Because these areas involve a church structure, they promote religiously motivated physical divisions, which affect routine social interactions.

The strength of these strategies and the ones discussed below (such as visiting and television watching) comes from special needs and circumstances. The most important of these is the need to safeguard a community that many believe is disappearing mainly because of economic competition. As Carmen, one of the coordinators of the chapel of San Antonio put it, "In the past, everybody had the same things. But today the ones who are ahead have to continue seeking and are afraid that if they stop to help others they will lose what they have gained, and the ones who are behind feel they are too far behind to catch up." To the pressures of economic competition, people added busy routines. Two common expressions that characterize the situation in Las

Cuevas, Loíza, and the world that these people see on television is "Today everybody walks his own path" and "Each person is doing his own thing."

The need for security explains people's preference for gathering closer to residences and for traveling for entertainment to the metropolitan area (mainly the mall or the shopping centers that have cinemas and fast food restaurants) or to *la isla* (outside the metropolitan area), instead of visiting other public parts of Loíza. During my stay in Las Cuevas I heard gunshots several times. As I stated before, on Fridays it was very common to see policemen patrolling and also making arrests on streets #188, #187, and #951. Most of the arrests are for crimes related to delinquency, alcohol, and drugs, although another growing common cause of crime is domestic conflict. The first week I was in Las Cuevas I saw two young men fighting; one of them was drunk. Also, a teenager and a twenty-seven-year-old man who were involved in the drug business were killed and a policeman from another neighborhood of Loíza killed his wife, her aunt, and himself. As I mentioned earlier, a common complaint in Loíza regards the lack of sufficient recreational facilities for the youth (these include sport facilities, theater, cinema, restaurants, parks, and so forth) and the poor conditions of the existing ones. In Las Cuevas, for example, the basketball court and facilities in front of the caves are run down and full of trash. When I asked the mayor about these places, he indicated that he did not want to fix them because people will judge him for the projects he initiates but not for repairing projects initiated by others.

Watching television is a common activity because it represents a combination of strategies involving the issues of community, security, entertainment, lack of recreational facilities, and also privacy, socioeconomic and physical investment, and communication with the outside world. In fact, 98 percent of the households had a television (two of the seniors that did not have television were blind). Televisions were even in homes where the income was very low and the conditions of the houses were extremely poor. As Kottak (1992: 86) argues, television affects people's attitudes and patterns of conduct and is not an isolating device. This is the reason why I would like to finish this section with some observations I made about watching television.

When the topic of watching television came up, residents pointed out the poor quality of television programming and its negative impact on people. They decried the mindless consumerism promoted by commercials. Some people complained about the sensational nature of the news programs that tend to highlight tragedies and how this, as well as the sexual content and violence of many television shows, desensitizes the audience. Some individuals were very affected by the material on television. Doña Inés is a woman whom some call crazy or "mala de los nervios" (schizophrenic), although she sounded very articulate to me when I talked with her. Her children were planning to take the television away from her because when she sees bad news on television her blood pressure goes up and she becomes neurotic (walking back and forth or in circles, talking incoherently to herself, and making unusual expressions and gestures). Her children first noticed this behavior after one of her grandchildren was killed in the United States.

However, despite all the complaints about television content, during my field study television was watched quite regularly by most people in the area and often with no restrictions. This included conservative religious people as well. In fact, as I said before, only 6.6 percent of the participants in the census indicated that they watch Christian television programs. As in Brazil (Kottak 1992: 72), news programming ranked as the most watched of all program categories. Many justified this by claiming that there were benefits to being informed about current events. People also reported that they find ways to combat the negative influence of news programming through sarcasm, jokes, and by watching television with relatives and friends. This explains why the entertainment value of television was thought by many to be secondary. At the same time, however, television held first place as the source of entertainment or recreational activity with 28 percent, followed by visiting or going out with 20 percent, and church social activities with 7.4 percent. The other participants mentioned other sources of entertainment. Soap operas, usually watched with others (including men), were in second place behind viewing news programs, while watching movies occupied third place. The importance of movies rests on the fact that almost half of the households that participated in the survey had a video cassette recorder, especially houses with teenagers. This is because, as some parents pointed out, "It is better to have them at home watching a movie than having them hanging around in the streets looking for trouble." However, in most of the households the video cassette recorder was not used much because there was little money to rent movies or because it was not working and there was no money to repair it.

There was not a significant number of complaints about television watching separating members of the family. On the contrary and similar to what Dávila (2001: 189) has found among Latinos in the United States, some parents use the television to connect with their kids: watching television together brings about conversations that would not start any other way. However, some parents mentioned the fact that television was distracting their children from doing their homework. Some churchgoers did bring up the fact that watching television (including the watching of religious programs) was competing with church attendance. At the same time, many people complained that some churches' use of microphones or that having churches in close proximity was limiting their right to watch television and invading their privacy in general. This is something I have experienced my whole life in my community, where Pentecostal preachers often amplified their sermons so that people in the surrounding homes would hear. They even asked us to turn off our televisions. This situation is so widespread in Puerto Rico that it has forced the government's office of Junta de Calidad Ambiental (Committee for Environmental Quality) to intervene. In fact, the 1980s were a time of controversy, as several cases were presented in the courts involving different churches. Some of these cases and the situation in general were covered by the media. During this time, various denominations joined in the effort to participate directly in the decision making of the committee or to be represented officially on the committee. Since then, churches around the island, especially in urban areas where the problem is more obvious and there is more accountability, have had to make some adjustments.

In Las Cuevas, churches have reduced the number of meetings, shortened the length of the service, reduced or eliminated meetings in open areas close to residences, reduced the volume of the microphones, and are using air conditioners. This explains Pastor Febres's decision to build the Church of Christ relatively far away from the residential area, although as we will see later, for some residents the church's distance was not far enough. The Church of the Faithful Disciples of Christ's low church attendance, minimal use of microphones, and meetings in the mountains have limited its impact on the neighborhood's environment. The location of the Church of the Fountain of the Living Water in the outskirts of Las Cuevas, bordering street #187, and its use of air conditioners also help to control its physical impact. Still, the problem of using microphones at high volume in churches is a major complaint in other communities, especially during evangelistic campaigns when churches feel more entitled or justified to use loudspeakers. Some pastors think that because the secular sector is allowed to have its activities, wherein everyone is expected to accommodate themselves to problems of space, traffic, and loud noise, that churches should also be allowed to have their special events, wherein others should accommodate themselves to the churches' use of more space and loudspeakers.

"There is no more family unity, there is not much of the Holy Spirit": The PCG Experience

Rosa, whom I introduced in chapter 5, belongs to the branch of the Tapia extended family whose socioeconomic situation is more stable. Most of the members of this branch are active Catholics; some of them facilitated the purchase of the chapel in the neighborhood. Most of them agree that religion has helped them to stay united and that it has provided many opportunities for them to help each other spiritually and financially. (In contrast, the poorest branch of the Tapia extended family, whose members live in the very interior and southern parts of Las Cuevas, consists of passive Pentecostals with many family conflicts). The unity through religion that Rosa's branch of the family experiences is so even though a sizeable number of family members became Pentecostal in the Pentecostal Church of God of Las Cuevas and then moved to other Pentecostal churches where they are currently active. The Pentecostal Church of God, the largest congregation in Las Cuevas (with about sixty-five members), was founded about thirty years ago and established with local leadership through the initiative of a member of the PCG in the town of Río Grande. He was mainly described as a charismatic, determined, and strict pastor. The church has been composed of members of various families, principally the Tapia family. There have been four pastors thus far. The third pastor died after less than a month in office and his position was taken by Pastor López, the current leader. Pastor López is a forty-five-year-old white man originally from Lares, a town in the very interior mountainous part of Puerto Rico and with a pro-independence history. He told me that initially he was concerned about coming to Loíza because of the negative things he had heard and also because he and his family are white. However, he agreed to come because he wanted to obey God's call and because he likes challenges.

Pastor López was described to me by different members as an easygoing and flexible pastor. For example, compared to previous pastors he gives more freedom to the leaders in decision making and favors activities such as band concerts and sports, although he disapproves of the festival of Santiago Após-tol downtown and other cultural activities like it. Likewise, Pastor López is also flexible about women's modesty (although his wife, in contrast to his daughter, dresses very conservatively). Old members and those who came from other Pentecostal congregations are happy with these kinds of changes. At the same time, they feel very nostalgic for the old times when there was more unity, discipline, and respect for God's matters among members of the church and the general public. They attribute these fond memories to the higher number of kin-related members in the past and the fact that there were not many churches around. As one member remarked to me, "It was like a big family doing something together." As I indicated earlier, many members of the branch of the Tapia family to which Rosa belongs were members of the PCG. When I was at the church, there was only one member of this family present, Rosa's nephew, who is the son of Rosa's sister who lives close to Rosa and who, like Rosa, is a faithful Catholic. (Rosa's sister also has a son who is a Pentecostal pastor in another barrio in Loíza.) The members of the PCG also acknowledge other factors, such as economic competition and secularism, that now detract from the sense of church closeness.

During one of the Sunday schools, Pastor López indicated that lack of unity, discipline, and respect inside the church was the reason for the decline of the manifestation of the Holy Spirit during the service. During and after the meeting, I learned that lately the congregation had been experiencing behavior problems during the service, especially from teenagers. To support his contention that "we cannot play with or fool God," Pastor López gave the example of a woman he knew who prophesied, spoke in tongues, and danced in the Holy Spirit, but who was always looking for trouble in the church and desired to have much control. One day while she was dancing, God allowed her to hit herself various times to punish her. In addition to this incident, there were three other reasons church members remain skeptical of manifestations of the Holy Spirit: a higher level of education; years of critique identifying these experiences as signs of craziness, ignorance, and an overemphasis on external matters; and exposure to less charismatic styles, which introduces members to the possibility of experiencing God's presence in other ways. This last item is not something that Pastor López fears. In fact, as soon as he came to Las Cuevas, he joined Confraternidad de Pastores e Iglesias Evangélicas de Loíza (Fraternity of Pastors and Churches from Loíza), the association of pastors from different denominations in Loíza. He also began to participate in the group's radio program, which was managed by the Baptist church of downtown Carolina. His interest in working with other pastors was rooted in his concern about the devil using lack of unity within and among churches to accomplish his evil purposes. Pastor López's church also visits other churches.

(During one of the services I attended, Pastor López read an invitation to a special celebration at a Pentecostal church of another denomination.) Pastor López was planning to unite the pastors of the churches in Las Cuevas so that their churches would become "like one big family in God," although his vision of a big family was limited to certain churches, excluding the Church of Christ and the Catholic Church.

Several Sundays after my first visit to the PCG, the issue of discipline and respect was brought up again during the adult class in Sunday Bible school. The subject of the class was knowing the devil and his plans. The class concluded with the opinion that nowadays the devil works less through possession or supernatural events than through a subtle breaking down of unity and destruction of families. The class also agreed that the negative consequences we experience on a daily basis are the result of Christians' weak character as well as the devil's intervention. Then we discussed whether the church should take the role or responsibility of a family. There were differing opinions, but the general consensus was that the state of the family and the world in general is calling for the church to follow the family model. As expressed by a member: "We all have the same last name: Christian." The class ended in a mood of repentance and with an act of recommitment to discipline teenagers and to be like parents to them.

The class was followed by some singing with the rest of the classes present. During the second *corito,* which was sung at least eleven times, a young woman began to dance in the spirit. Mayra, my friend and one of the adult teachers, followed her to keep her from hitting herself and any objects from falling. The woman moved from her seat to the front area facing the altar, dancing rhythmically almost in a circle. The woman hit the podium and it fell to the floor. Mayra, with the help of the man playing the congas, picked it up immediately. Soon the woman stopped dancing. I noticed that the strength of the woman's dancing movements had increased with the volume of people's verbal worship and the music, and that after she stopped, everything slowed down gradually. For members, this was a demonstration of God's forgiveness and support and of His call to obey Him.

After the service finished, I talked with Héctor, a big, strong, energetic, and educated man who at the time was the youth leader. Héctor was concerned about dealing with the church's teenagers because most of them had difficult relationships with their nonconverted parents and were relying on Héctor and the pastor as substitute parents. From our conversation I could tell that Héctor was looking for help. The next time I saw him, I brought him a book about ways to approach teenagers using group dynamics and games and I shared some helpful tips from my own experience working with teenagers at church, most of which he was already using.

Clearly the case at hand points to a close relationship between the emergence of certain ritual experiences (such as spirit possession) or changes in their practice and intergenerational and social relationships, moral values, and economic processes. The case at hand also points to the influence of education and inter-religious interaction. Most members agree that the lack of manifestation of the Holy Spirit and the devil's bad influence can be remedied by adopting a family model of relationships within and outside the church. Here Brow's (1996) study mentioned in chapter 2 is relevant because it focuses on the effects of development on rural Sri Lanka, where disparities, tensions, and rivalries between two communities erupted when one community became more prosperous than the other. The study presents this evidence to coincide with the use of demonic supernatural manifestation (through sorcery and possession) as the explanation for the situation and the source of accusations between the two communities. In Las Cuevas's PCG, reduced community, church, and family unity is considered the main reason for a reduction in the manifestation of the Holy Spirit, although economic disparities are believed to have had a negative effect on these relationships.

"When I see families in the house of the Lord I can only worship Him": The CFLW Experience

The great significance of family values in the CFLW is evident in its message, activities, programs, and organizations. It is also evident in its literature. For example, in its promotional magazine there is a picture of each pastor couple. Both are referred to as *pastores*, despite the unofficial role of the wife. Family networks and relationships were crucial in facilitating the spreading of the CFLW's message in Las Cuevas and in the foundation of the CFLW's Christian mission there in 1989. Pastor Correa and his siblings were raised in Las Cuevas, but by the time of my field study, only one sibling and their mother were living there. Pastor Correa, like Pastor Font, received a special visit from God. From this moment on Pastor Correa understood that he had been called to serve the Lord. He and his family began to attend Fe Es la Victoria (Faith Is Victory), a church known for its strong emphasis on faith as the way to a victorious life. He was joined by some of his siblings and their respective families. From there, all of them moved to the CFLW in Carolina. After some time in the CFLW, they felt the need to bring the CFLW's message to Loíza. Pastor Correa bought the piece of land where the church is located and donated it to the mission. He became the pastor until his sister, Martina, a school principal, was able to lead the church as the pastor, under his supervision and with the help of Luisa, another sister, as the co-pastor. The first time I met Luisa, at her store, which sold traditional Puerto Rican dishes next to the CFLW building, I understood how important family was to her. Constantly and with much excitement, Luisa talked about her five children, her husband, her seven siblings, and her mother. This also happened the second time we met, while we were driving to the property of the missionary couple I mentioned earlier. This couple was from the United States and had lived in Las Cuevas for about twenty years doing missionary work; Luisa had worked with them on a volunteer basis for about ten years.

I learned about Luisa's personal life only little by little (we interacted on several occasions) because she was more concerned that I learn about and accept the CFLW. I encountered this pressure more in the CFLW than in any other church I visited in Las Cuevas. Luisa's father became a member of the HDEC. Her mother only visited it a few times. At some point Luisa's father became so depressed that he went back to drinking and eventually died. But before he died, Luisa's father was convinced God would take care of his children. Luisa's mother worked hard to raise her kids with good morals and determination. In fact, all of them finished school and found good jobs (some of them went on to graduate from the university and became professionals). Luisa herself worked as a secretary for many years until she decided to stay at home to take care of her children. In Las Cuevas, Luisa's family is known as a family that has prospered and honored the family name.

In spite of what happened to her husband and the fact that she herself decided to go back to her Catholic faith, Luisa's mother never discouraged her children from going to the Pentecostal church. Luisa and her siblings taught in the Sunday school and did evangelical work, but their involvement was not consistent. Luisa fell in love with a nonpracticing Catholic man, whom she married in the Baptist church because they could not marry in the Catholic church. During the first years of matrimony they partied, danced, and lived a "good" life. Over the years, they had five children and realized they felt empty. While her husband resorted to alcohol, Luisa joined the Vida Nueva

(New Life) church in Medianía Baja. During this time, Luisa met the North American missionary couple who founded a children's ministry in Las Cuevas. Luisa remained actively involved in the ministry for several years, because she realized how significant the ministry was for the children from different communities and how much they needed her love. One of the things Luisa remembered the most is when girls fought to be close to her and to comb her hair. Like Héctor, the youth leader of the PCG, Luisa saw herself fulfilling the role of mother for many of these kids.

By the time Luisa became involved in this ministry, two or three of her siblings were going to the CFLW. A few years after Luisa's siblings joined the CFLW, she suffered a stroke, which left her paralyzed for five years. During her illness, her siblings from the CFLW visited her and talked to her about the CFLW's message of God's will for physical prosperity. One evening she was anointed by her brother, but nothing happened until the next morning when she felt a powerful force lifting her to a seated position in her bed and she heard God's voice saying, "Luisa, I forgive you, wake up." Luisa screamed after realizing she was able to walk. Immediately, she realized she was saved but was not fulfilling God's plan for her. Then she decided to join the CFLW, to be actively involved in the church, and to share this message with everybody she could. (While all of this was happening, the popularity of the children's ministry was waning.)

Luisa sees her life going from one miracle to another: Luisa's husband quit drinking, her brother (Pastor Correa) bought her a big house with a pool after she lost almost everything during Hurricane Hugo, and she was able to establish a small business selling traditional Puerto Rican dishes next to the church building. Luisa also mentioned that she recovered her car after it had been stolen. However, for Luisa, the greatest miracle and sign of prosperity and of the power and efficacy of the CFLW is that all of her family serve the Lord and are prosperous. Luisa even contrasted the experience of her family with that of a Baptist pastor who recently lost his son. About this she commented that even though he was a man of God, he did not have enough faith to *reclamar* (confidently require from God) God's salvation and protection for his entire family. According to Luisa, the message of freedom, prosperity, and victory that the CFLW preaches is for the whole family and especially for Loízan families. Nevertheless, as Luisa indicated at one point, her desire for other families to join the church in Loíza stems from her desire to avoid the impression that one family is controlling the church. Her concern in this regard was evident in that she did not mention her position as the co-pastor of the church.

Luisa explained to me what was happening with Loízan families and Loíza in general, citing Hosea 4:6, which says, "My people will be destroyed because they have no knowledge." Luisa's life was destroyed even while she was going to church because she was ignorant of God's real purpose for her to prosper. It is significant that Luisa never mentioned her heavy weight as a contributing factor to her stroke, although the CFLW's message strongly emphasizes the need for the individual to assume control of and responsibility for her life by exercising her faith and by doing tangible things, such as taking good care of one's health.

Many elements related to the family played a big role in Luisa's conversion and her decision to serve the Lord actively: seeing how God's promise to her father was being fulfilled (because he had faith despite the fact that the church he was going to was not God's real plan for him); the visits and concern of her siblings, who were becoming so prosperous; her desire that all of her relatives be together because all of them live far away from each other; and the need to honor her father's memory, her mother's sacrifices, and the family's identity. Every time she sees her relatives in the house of the Lord, she "can only worship Him." When she learned that not all members of my household were attending church regularly, she told me that God had a purpose in leading me to the CFLW; our encounter did not happen by chance. According to Luisa, I needed to proceed in faith that all members of my family will commit to the Lord.

"I don't go to church, but I know that what my Father preaches is the truth": The CC Experience

To understand the foundation of the CC in Las Cuevas it is necessary to look at the personal experience of Luis Febres, one of the two CC ministers. I met Pastor Febres while doing the census. Immediately after I told him I was interested in knowing the history and general characteristics of the churches in the community he decided to collaborate.

Pastor Febres is a tall, *trigueño* man in his early seventies and the father of ten adult children. His wife has always helped him in the ministry, three daughters and a son are very involved in the church, and those children who are not actively involved respect and defend the CC doctrines of their father's church. According to Pastor Febres, when he was a child religion was not very important to his family. His parents had some beliefs but they were not active, so they were not an encouragement for him in this regard. He attended religious festivities because his grandfather was one of the coordinators. However, this attendance did not completely satisfy him. As he was becoming a teenager amid a hard economic situation, he was feeling emptier. At a young age, during the Korean War, Pastor Febres joined the military, where he saw injustice and experienced racial and ethnic discrimination. This opened his eyes and made him critical of the Americanized system.

Once back home from the military, Pastor Febres joined the pro-independence party and became actively involved, so active that the governing PPD made a *carpeta*, which was a record of his political participation (this measure was implemented by the government to control "subversive" political actions). While politically active and working with the government, he realized that the answer for his life and for the world was not in politics, but in God. It was then, about thirty to thirty-five years ago, that Pastor Febres became a member of the Church of the Defenders of Faith in Loíza. But even there he felt unsatisfied with the church's practices, some of which he felt were in conflict with the Bible. He did not like the way things were organized. While he was still a member of the Church of the Defenders of Faith, he received a tract about the message of the CC from one of the leaders working in Loíza. He was immediately attracted to the message because of its clarity, simplicity, and the fact that it was tied to what the Bible said. According to him, there was no hidden agenda. Pastor Febres decided to join the CC with his wife. He was baptized by the missionary Dewayne Chaplin from Tennessee and the founder of the first CC in Puerto Rico. The group he joined was meeting in the garage of a house in the barrio of Medianía Baja and was under the financial support of the CC in the United States. Years later, as the group continued to grow and was becoming financially independent, he decided to donate a piece of the land he had inherited in Las Cuevas and to build a church at a walking distance from his house, close to the river. The church was finally finished about four to five years before my field study.

The average church attendance when I visited the CC was twenty-five, almost equally distributed by gender. To get to the church, attendees walk, use their private vehicles, or use the church's bus (which is parked at Pastor Febres's house). Most members have attended church for a long time and participate in all the activities, including Tuesday evening devotions and preaching, Thursday evening prayer and Bible study, Sunday morning children's Bible school, and Sunday evening devotions, preaching, and communion. On the third Saturday of each month they have a special service in a house, upon request. They also plan services in open areas in different neighborhoods. These are very short and quiet to avoid problems. Before, during, and after these services, members distribute tracts about the CC doctrine (the tract has the church's address). The CC members share with other CCs in Puerto Rico through youth and children's camps, women's or men's retreats, collections for missionaries, and their radio program on a non-Christian radio station (WIAC). However, they do not share with other denominations. They help the local community "quietly" by collecting money for the needy, visiting people who are in physical and spiritual need, bringing a service to somebody's home, offering a funeral service to nonconverted people, and so forth.

Despite members' desire for attendance to increase, they understand this is a slow process because what they preach "is not an easy gospel." For this reason I sensed an attitude of pride from the different members I interacted with, pride that they follow a message that is strictly what the Bible says. About this, Pastor Febres told me, "The ways of the Lord are to be followed in order, with meaning, according to what the Bible strictly says, knowing and feeling deeply in the heart what one preaches. This is why the CC is really for brave people." The CC claims to come more directly than other Christian churches from the same lineage of the church that Christ founded. This view relates to their claim that they preach a message distinct from that preached in most of the other Christian churches by strictly following the Bible's text rather than altering it to accommodate parishioners' desires or the interests of the modern world. CC members described themselves as strictly in opposition to current Christian traditions.

The CC avoids the centralization of authority because the only authority is God. It does not have a central headquarters (although in Puerto Rico the individual churches help each other and coordinate activities together: for sharing, spreading their message, and social work around the world; and contributing to common nationwide radio and television programs, newsletters, and their own literature). The two ministers of the CC in Las Cuevas are not paid. They completely avoid the term "reverend" because of the passage from the Bible that says, "Holy and Reverend is His (meaning God's) name." The CC in Las Cuevas has deacons, a secretary, and a treasurer, who is the Pastor

Febre's daughter. Other members help in different ways, for example, by distributing communion, teaching, driving the church bus, and doing construction work. All of the positions have the same importance and are completely voluntary, although the church needs to approve them.

Members believe in simplicity and imitate the Christian church as it existed during the times of Jesus and his disciples. This is why they do not have any liturgical paraphernalia except a simple platform with a pulpit, yellow curtains behind it, some flowers on each side of the pulpit, the table of communion, and the letters of the church's name on the front right wall. Here, for example, there is no cross, no special chairs for the ministers, or a sound system. One important element of the temple, though, is the registration papers, which are kept on the church's bulletin board in the back (it was one of the first things Pastor Febres showed me). Regarding this list, Pastor Febres said to me, "Here everything is vertical, nothing is hidden. Things are presented the way they are."

The simplicity of the CC is also related to the fact that it does not collect the tithe or have any offering during the service and does not allow sales in the church. This position with regard to money is based on 1 Cor. 1:2. There is a wooden box in a corner in the very back part of the church in which people may place donations made completely voluntarily and this is only expected on Sundays. The CC yearly budget is around $1,000 with a monthly income of only $80.00, which is kept in the bank. Pastor Febres, like other members, very firmly criticized the Christian church in general for its emphasis on material possessions and the Loízan churches in particular for wanting to imitate these negative things without being able to do it (in other words, without having the money to spend). From the way he was talking, I got the impression he was thinking of the CFLW in Las Cuevas, wherein Luisa's store is almost attached to the church building. The CC's low budget has to do with its doctrine and with the fact that the average monthly individual income is below $500. Most members are retired, housekeepers, or students. There is a small group of educated and professional individuals, which includes a teacher, a health technician, a dentist's assistant, and a secretary. Two members of this small group are Pastor Febres's daughters and all of the members of this small group are women.

Pastor Febres told me that contrary to most CC members in Las Cuevas, who were pro-statehood, he was still pro-independence. Also, when there is a need to protest, he is the first one to participate, although he admitted he cannot do it as much as he wants. This kind of flexibility is also seen in an open attitude about clothing choices (Sandra, his daughter, wore pants to the service) and in the area of entertainment, since members are allowed to go to the theater and to the beach. (However, most of the congregation does not visit these places.) Despite its flexibility on some points, the CC does have some requirements. For example, members do not celebrate any of the holidays such as Christmas, Easter, and Thanksgiving. Based on what the Bible says, the CC doctrine does not allow women to be in charge of prayers or singing or to teach, preach, or distribute communion during the service. But women teach in the children's Bible school on Sunday mornings and participate in social ministry.

Limiting women's leadership during the service has to do with what the Bible says in 1 Cor. 14:40 about doing things in a fitting and orderly way. This is why members do not use instruments (the latter is also based on Eph. 5:19). They sing hymns from the hymn book *Himnos de Vida Cristiana* (used for many years in the Baptist church). Their solemn style has caused other Christians to accuse them of not experiencing the presence of the Holy Spirit. The CC believes that the Holy Spirit comes to dwell inside the individual when he repents of his sins, accepts Christ as his savior, and is baptized. Divine healing, speaking in tongues, and prophesy were manifestations that happened in the past, but are not necessary for today. According to the CC, the best sign of the Holy Spirit's presence is His guidance in all everyday matters.

Some of Pastor Febres's relatives were not happy that he built the church in the area without consulting the extended family. One of Pastor Febres's nephews complained that he paid to survey and register the piece of land where the church was going to be built instead of making an effort to survey the whole piece of property, knowing his and other family members' difficult financial situations. According to him, this is why members of the extended family and his neighbors prefer to attend other churches. Elena, Pastor Febres's niece and his neighbor across the street, complained for the same reason. The second time we talked, she also complained that Pastor Febres does not allow her kids and other kids from the neighborhood to play basketball around the church facilities, something they used to do before the church was built. She indicated that she did not understand why he was bothered by kids playing in the surroundings of the church (more specifically the parking lot), which according to Elena are not sacred. This attitude, according to Elena, discourages teenagers who need support from religious leaders. It also promotes a negative impression of religion. Neighbors in Las Cuevas see having a church so close by as limiting their activities and use of space. Elena told me that being so close to a church limits her options to have a decent party for the kids, to watch soap operas, to listen to the radio a little bit louder, and to gather outside to talk with her kids. Sometimes she feels she is disrespecting God and jeopardizing her relationship with her relatives in the CC. To resolve the situation, sometimes she accommodates her schedule to the church's schedule. However, many times she just has to forget about it and do what she has to do. An interviewee, who was not related to members of any of the closest churches, insisted that having churches so close to residential areas and having people doing their routine activities so close to church activities, makes religion lose "something," which he was not able to describe despite my insistence to him to be clear and specific.

When I met Elena, she was beginning to attend the CC mainly to support her husband's conversion and, therefore, the family as a whole. On the day I visited her, she was getting ready to help her mother-in-law clean the house and to prepare some refreshments for that evening's service, which was going to be held at her house. Elena was feeling happy because her relationship with her relatives at the CC was favorable, although she felt that their only motivation was that she commit to the CC. They knew she preferred to go to different churches. In fact, I heard from some individuals that the idea that "all churches seek the same God" is one of the ways they resolve the confusion brought about by having so many different churches so close by. Elena, like other individuals I talked to, was trying to overcome feeling obligated to attend a church. She told me that converting and committing permanently is something that you have "to feel in your heart." For this reason she was skeptical of the real motivations of many churchgoers.

The fourth time I visited Elena, she did not respond when I called to her from the front door. I was disappointed because she had firmly committed to meet with me. As I kept calling, I became aware of her presence inside the house and wondered what was going on. Eventually, I decided to leave. But Elena called to me while I was walking away. Her eyes were red from crying. She brought out two chairs and we put them under a tree next to her house. I thought she wanted to talk privately. She immediately apologized for her attitude and explained that she had had a fight with one of her sisters. This time, when we talked about having churches so close to the house, Elena said it was a good thing, especially because she did not have to walk long distances and could avoid crime. On this occasion, Elena indicated that the CC was not that close. We even laughed that the church was closer to the river than to residences and that this was the reason why there were so many mosquitoes in the church, which necessitated screen doors and the use of Off spray before each church meeting. This time Elena also told me that having many churches made her feel that her kids were protected in a good atmosphere. She even defended the CC doctrine by saying it was very close to what the Bible says. She pointed out the positive things, for example, the leader's lack of authority, the simplicity, and the soft and a cappella style, which she contrasted with the "scandalous" Pentecostal style, which she has never liked. At some point Elena said with much difficulty because she was crying:

> It is always good to hear the word of God because it helps people to respect each other and have good morals. It makes a difference in the family and my uncle's family is a good example. We all have the same last name, but religion has really made a difference. My father was an alcoholic and my mother was not close to us. We do not get along very well. My sister is envious of me, of everything I do. (She looked back in the direction of her sister's house.) I tell her the good things that happen to me because I am glad when good things happen to my sisters. The other day I told her about a new refrigerator my kids' father got for me and she was not happy. She is probably envious right now because you are interviewing me. We never had much. We lived very poorly and now that we have had some things, there is much competition. She was not happy I moved from Carolina to here. They [Pastor Febres's family] care for each other, even those who live afuera [in the United States]. However, we live so close to each other and are always fighting. They help the father, even those who do not attend church regularly. He is a responsible father. They help each other. They do not have to feel ashamed of being part of their family. They live [economically] comfortably. I think what they preach is good despite the fact that it is hard to follow everything that the doctrine requires.

Elena also pointed out the fact that Pastor Febres and his children took good care of their property, keeping it clean while contrasting it with her siblings' property, which was full of trash. Elena's change of attitude and views directs us to overcome the general thinking that an individual's actions follow a single and coherent logic, instead of being socio- interactionally situated, as Mannheim and Tedlock (1995: 5) insist.

Similarly to Luisa, Elena made the connection between the efficacy of the message and the quality of family relationships, including those overseas. I was able to confirm Elena's favorable opinion about Pastor Febres's family through my interaction with him and his wife and my friendship with Sandra, one of Pastor Febres's daughters. She considers her father to be a good husband and a good father, as does Pastor Febres's oldest son, Daniel. (Like his father and a brother who is living in the United States, Daniel was in the military.) When Pastor Febres and I met for the first time to have a formal conversation about the CC, Daniel decided to come along. He strongly defended his father and the CC doctrine throughout the conversation and showed a kind but defensive attitude, more so than his own father. Daniel helped his father explain the CC doctrine by reading the verses that give support to each doctrine. At that point I thought Daniel was a main leader in the CC. But later Daniel told me that although he was not going to church, he was strongly convinced that his father was preaching the truth.

"Praise God for My Sister Living Close to the Church": The CFDC Experience

The founding of the Church of the Faithful Disciples of Christ in Las Cuevas is also closely related to the religious experience of its main leader, Pastor Tapia, who is a member of one of the three main branches of the Tapia family. I met him through Delia, his oldest sister. When I told her that I was interested in knowing the history and characteristics of the churches in Las Cuevas she told me that I should not leave out her brother's church, which was located in front of her house. In fact, she arranged our meeting. Pastor Tapia, who was seventy-four years old when I met him, is a humble man with a cheerful personality, which is manifested in his constant repetition of "praise God," "Alleluia," and "Amen." On the occasions when we interacted in his church, he also constantly shook his arms, clapped his hands, and lifted his feet while laughing. Pastor Tapia was raised in the northern area of Las Cuevas; his parents built the first house I registered in the area in 1918. When Pastor Tapia married he moved with his wife to another barrio in Loíza, where they had four children. Pastor Tapia, like Pastor Febres (and two other pastors I met from Las Cuevas), joined the military during the Korean War, which is one of the reasons why they have good relationships with each other (although they do not see each other much because each is busy with his own church). In war he had many disappointments and developed a clear understanding that it was ultimately not in man's hands to fix the world.

When Pastor Tapia came back in 1953 from the military, he converted to Christ. He was baptized on the beach and became a member of the Missionary Church of Christ or MCC, a Pentecostal church located in the barrio of Medianía Alta. The MCC council (formerly Church of Christ of the Antilles) was founded in 1934 in the town of Río Grande (it was registered in the Department of State of Puerto Rico a year later) thanks to the efforts of former members of historical Protestant churches who wanted to follow the Bible strictly and were motivated by what the Holy Spirit was doing in different campaigns through prophecy, healing, dancing, and speaking in tongues. Today the MCC is known in Puerto Rico for its ultraconservative doctrine, which has led to a low rate of participation among the youth. The MCC has also kept relatively isolated from the rest of the Pentecostal community (for example, it did not participate in the evangelistic campaign with Billy Graham in 1995). However, the strength of the MCC has been its strong appeal to mostly poor and uneducated Puerto Ricans.

While actively involved in the MCC, Pastor Tapia visited and helped other churches of his denomination and also small missions of the Church of God, Incorporated or CGI. He helped in both denominations by teaching, preaching, praying, and doing carpentry work. After the war, Pastor Tapia developed his carpentry skills and has worked in this field for many years. The CGI, known in Puerto Rico as the church of the veil because of the belief that the women should wear white veils, originated in the 1930s in the town of Fajardo under the initiative of former members of some historical Protestant churches and Pentecostal churches. They were also motivated by their desire to allow the Holy Spirit to manifest itself freely and to follow the Scriptures strictly. In 1939 the CGI was registered in the Department of State of Puerto Rico. The council began under the presidency of Aurelio Tiburcio. The CGI, like the MCC, is known in Puerto Rico for its ultraconservative doctrine, low participation of youth and women, and a very hierarchical structure. Also like the MCC, the CGI continues to appeal to the poor and uneducated sectors of Puerto Rico.

Pastor Tapia began to go to a mountain located in another town to seek the presence of the Lord in a quiet and peaceful place. Having gone to pray and meditate in the mountains on various occasions with members of different churches when this became a fad during the late 1980s, I could understand why Pastor Tapia might try to set himself apart from the confusing atmosphere, spiritually speaking, especially in light of the dramatic, environmental, economic, social and political changes the island was experiencing and the high level of interdenominational competition. He deeply wanted God to guide him to serve Him "in spirit and truth." While praying, fasting, and reading the Bible on the mountain, he felt guided to join the CGI. God revealed to him that the doctrines of the CGI (for example, the women's use of white veils, the use of burlap, and the Sabbath) were completely meaningful because they were based on the Bible. Thus, after six years in the MCC, he finally joined the CGI. Pastor Tapia was strongly opposed in his decision, especially by his former pastor. I must clarify that Pastor Tapia really joined the First Church of God, Incorporated or FCGI, a branch of the CGI that was founded by Aurelio Tiburcio, the first president of the CGI, in 1947 after the directive committee of the CGI asked him to leave his position. Today, the FCGI includes fifty-five congregations under the direction of the Reverend Tiburcio's son.

As a FCGI leader, Pastor Tapia continued spreading the message in evangelistic campaigns in open areas and through home visits. He kept praying, fasting, and reading the Bible on the mountain. One day God called him to be a full-time minister. Weeks later he was anointed, despite some disagreements by leaders of the denomination because of what Pastor Tapia calls his honesty. Pastor Tapia did not care for religious competition. Over the years he got tired of "too much noise" (he was referring to singing, dancing, prophecy, speaking in tongues, and praising God loudly). He said that people worshipped God in a disorganized way, without meaning and love. People heard themselves and did not let God speak. They did not like to pray. There was no humility or sacrifice. Over the course of the years, Pastor Tapia's disappointment kept accumulating and one day he finally decided to raise a mission in Las Cuevas. But because the FCGI and the CGI leadership disapproved of his decision, he registered the church as independent. With the help of his brother, who is Catholic and lives next door to the church, and the help of the current co-pastor, Pastor Tapia built a small temple on a piece of property he inherited in Las Cuevas. He also gained the support of other members of the family.

The CFDC has the simplest structure of all the churches in Las Cuevas.

The church inside has a small altar with no decoration, an old podium, about eight chairs, a simple sound system, one microphone, an electric guitar, and some folk instruments. The church is also the smallest because it only accommodates around fifteen to twenty people, although the average attendance during the time I shared with them was only six (attendance has never been more than twelve). Pastor Tapia and the co-pastor complained that the members were not very involved. They have a prayer meeting on the mountain on Saturdays at 10:00 a.m. and every evening at 7:00 p.m., except Sunday. All of the meetings are very informal and include singing, praying, offerings, praising God loudly, testimonies, preaching, and Bible discussion. For studying the Bible they use a very small doctrinal manual, less than the size of a hand, sent by a church of their denomination in California that they visited once. Involvement in other activities such as evangelistic home and hospital visits, distribution of tracts, and visiting other churches are almost exclusively done by the pastors. The congregation is mostly composed of men and also members with less than a high school education and an average monthly family income of $300. The latter explains why the church's budget is so low and mainly depends on Pastor Tapia's income from his veteran status.

Pastor Tapia explained the low attendance at his church by using Matt. 13:57, which says, "A prophet is honored everywhere except in his own town or in his own home." Also, Pastor Tapia insisted that the church has been experiencing "great persecution" or "has been in war" because of competition and the interest of several pastors in his property. In addition, some residents dislike the idea of having the church in their neighborhood. Religious leaders, knowing the church is registered, have sent government officials to check the church's registration and permissions. This was the reason why Pastor Tapia insisted that I write down the church's registration number. The great number of clandestine churches in Loíza has led the government to take action. In fact, at the beginning Pastor Tapia thought I was a government official until he asked Pastor Febres about me and the latter explained who I was. Members also thought I was going there under a church leader's order to get information about the situation of the church.

However, after Pastor Tapia and the co-pastor knew my intentions and were convinced that I was "a real Christian" (they referred to me like this), they invited me to become a leader. They indicated that they were blessed by my presence, which they took as encouragement from God. Pastor Tapia told me, "People do not like small and humble churches. It is all competition. It is good that you stopped by. This church is small, but the Bible says that when there are two or more grouped in His name there is God. This is why we go to the mountain too, to get away from so much noise, disappointment and lack of true love." I understood what Pastor Tapia was talking about because in my rural Baptist church we were discouraged by the lack of interest shown by famous preachers and singers in visiting us. Pastor Tapia strongly criticized contemporary Protestant emphasis on physical and material well-being. He considered this emphasis to be ironic in light of the fact that Catholics have long been criticized by Protestants for worshipping idols or things. Many Protestant churches are now worshipping famous preachers, big temples, and money. According to him, in Loíza this emphasis is even more ironic because Jesus, like many Loízans, was poor and humble and did not want to become wealthy.

Pastor Tapia gave me an example of an encounter with persecution. Once Delia's pastor sent a missionary from the Dominican Republic to preach for several nights in front of Delia's house. Delia's pastor knew that Pastor Tapia's church was very close to Delia's house. As Pastor Tapia told me, "They did not consider that this was a sacred place." Guided by the Holy Spirit but with the help of his church members, Pastor Tapia decided to stay quiet and to close the church during the evenings of the evangelistic campaign. Pastor Tapia told me that he was not a "warrior" and that he simply put things in God's hands. He kept praying on his knees for justice, and several days after the end of the campaign the missionary came to his church to ask for forgiveness and admit that he had been used. Pastor Tapia was very disappointed with Delia, but she also apologized to him and admitted that she had been used by her pastor. Pastor Tapia was so thankful for her apology because Delia has always supported him and his ministry despite the fact that she is very committed to the Assembly of Christian Churches in Medianía Alta, where she has been a member for many years (this church is one of the twelve most important congregations of this denomination in Puerto Rico).

The many times I interacted with Delia, she was always defending the integrity of Pastor Tapia's ministry and him personally. She always referred to him as a hard-working and humble man, like her father, with a lot of love for God. Delia told me that her brother is better than many pastors because he does not depend on the ministry financially. In fact, he does not take any money to pay himself; instead, he uses the money he gets monthly from his veteran's check to cover the church's expenses. Every once in a while, Delia gives food to Pastor Tapia. To show me her brother's sense of sacrifice, one day she took me by the hand to see his old car, which was in very bad shape. Delia allows him and other church members to park their cars in front of her house because the church does not have a parking lot. (Pastor Tapia said he was working to resolve this legal requirement.) I also learned from Delia and from Pastor Tapia himself that he has helped different churches and their pastors with their personal problems; some of them are from Las Cuevas.

Delia, like other relatives who live nearby, cleans the surroundings of the church. She and her other brother, a passive Catholic who lives next door to the church, keep an eye on it to make sure it is not robbed. Pastor Tapia's brother is able to do this because he spends a lot of time on his house's balcony, which is protected with bars. Robbing churches is a common occurrence. In fact, two common expressions are, "Today people even rob the nails of the cross" and "People do not have any respect for sacred things." Delia herself commented while trying to explain why this happens so often, "The truth is that now there is a church on every corner." Delia and other neighbors (some of them relatives) do these things because they feel they have the responsibility to protect "God's things," because they have to set an example, especially to the youth, to show respect for God's matters, and because they care for Pastor Tapia. Every once in a while Delia attends and participates in her brother's church by singing and witnessing. She especially likes to visit her brother's church with her sister, also Pentecostal, when she comes to visit from the United States.

Delia told me that the three have become more "spiritually" united since they converted, despite living far from each other. Delia was also considering attending her brother's church in the future, when she gets older and sicker. For now she prefers her church because she was converted there and is used to it. Also, Delia considers the challenges of going to a church headed by a brother. According to her, this in-between situation, which she characterized as neither one thing nor the other, has allowed love to be manifested and conflicts to be avoided. She also mentioned the fact that she wanted to avoid rumors like "those Tapias fight a lot among themselves" and said that fighting brings shame to the family and to the gospel. When I told Pastor Tapia all the good things Delia had said about him, he jumped from his seat and praised God loudly while clapping his hands. He told the co-pastor, "You see? What did I tell you? That is the Lord!" And he immediately indicated that these are the things that stop him from quitting and closing the church. I immediately wondered what might have happened if Delia had not been around.

Religious Re-embedding

In light of all these events, I began to consider the question: How can I explain the fact that 80 percent of the participants in a questionnaire I distributed in different churches in Las Cuevas indicated family was more important than church community? The first easy answer is that in many cases blood and church relationships overlap. The second easy answer is that individuals in Las Cuevas still think in terms of the extended family and that almost everybody is related. Therefore, blood relationships are wide and not limited to church relationships; in other words, they are inclusive, and this greatly contributes to religious tolerance (as Kipp [1996: 253] argues has happened among the Karo people in Indonesia). However, each church situation leads to a more complex or elaborate answer by pointing to different ways of safeguarding the family's socioeconomic stability and family relationships, including those members who do not live close to one another. The conditions of a high degree of kin-related ties and a high concentration of churches in such a limited residential space as Las Cuevas bring about situations of conflict and at the same time opportunities for nourishing and maintaining family interreligious relationships, while giving a sacred character to these relationships. This may have various implications. Elena, for example, was bothered by the idea that the most important motive her relatives in the CC had for approaching her was her conversion, but at the same time she valued their concern for her salvation. Conditions such as these cause the people of Las Cuevas to see the sacred as place-related: in the community, inside a cement building, and in the individual's heart. Residents have also become more aware of how the sacred place is something given (by God) and, at the same time, something they have to work for, to (re)create, and to protect.

Without reducing religious experience to family issues, I argue that these dynamics of family relationships give great legitimacy to religious identity, religious practice, and attitudes toward religion in general and to the social and sacred place. Like family, social space or community is very important in this context because it informs religious experience at the same time it is influenced by it. Members of these families, including those living outside Las Cuevas, care for Las Cuevas so much and are greatly committed to helping the difficult situation of Las Cuevas and Loíza with the message of the gospel. Most of them consider that this mission is better accomplished if they keep the unity of their families.

Clearly, the situation in Las Cuevas promotes a tension between distancing and attachment that makes me prefer to use the concept of re-embedding to situate the events in Las Cuevas. Therefore, I think re-embedding is a more descriptive term than the concept of disembedding, which in chapter 3 referred to the distancing of religion from social structures such as kinship or family, neighborhood, and a certain space or place. I believe that in Las Cuevas religion has found "new" ways of embedding that are clearly manifested in everyday life through community and family relationships, routine space management, and at the level of ritual and individual experience.

"As God is my witness,
I don't have anything to hide"

Woman, Hair, and Spiritual Identity

Throughout this work I have emphasized the management of identities within a broad religious framework while emphasizing a struggle for identity and resources, everyday life spatial-social interactions, and an atmosphere of religious competition. Here I examine the strategies of rebuilding identity in the faith-based lifestyles of Lydia and Alfonsina, both of whom are from Las Cuevas, while closely looking at the body's involvement, particularly the hair. Regarding the body's involvement, one must be aware as is Csordas (1994a: 5) of the reductionistic manner in which the body is sometimes understood, such as when reducing religion to unconscious motivations associated with the body. Csordas (1994b: 4) also identifies the problem of equalizing body to the self or person while forgetting the dimension of materiality through the physical-emotive experience, to which he (89) gives much attention to specific physical-emotive processes such as chills, trembling hands, and burning queasiness, as I try to do here.

In her study of elderly Jewish women in Jerusalem (a majority of them Kurdish), Sered (1992: 72) mainly argues that within the context of male-oriented religion, women clearly find strategies for constructing a meaningful religious life, emphasizing rituals (or ritual aspects or elements) that require women's involvement and delimiting modesty as an issue between God and women and not between women and men. Along the same lines, in her cross-cultural study about religions dominated by women, Sered (1994: 4–5) also argues that women give spiritual meaning to their everyday lives and develop strong leadership by emphasizing rituals and symbols that sacralize their domestic lives or that domesticate religion. Cucchiari (1990: 693–95) notices a significant strategy among Pentecostal women in Sicily to affect the patriarchal system: to emphasize and strongly develop an area of ministry that is informally or ambiguously ascribed to a specific gender. Also, Rodríguez Toulis (1997: 258) has found possibilities for African-Caribbean Pentecostal women in England to transform their identity in the coexistence of biblical models: one with the man as the head and the other with the two genders as saints. According to her, although each biblical model supports the other, the interlocking of gender identities constructed in these two models provides areas of inconsistency in which women can contest and change ideas about their role.

These studies demonstrate that these women's strategies amplify the range of possibilities for women within and outside religion, rather than reducing women's religious experience to a female-male antagonism as many studies of women and religion have done. Thus, in this chapter, it is important, as Díaz Quiñones (1998: 129) has suggested, to consider Puerto Rican and Loízan religious experience not in opposition to but in relationship with the religious experience of men, with the social context, and with the sacred. I believe that this can be better accomplished by considering, as Watkins (1996) suggests, personal factors and conditions (such as age, life cycle, marital situation, and formal status) that promote similarities and varieties of women's religious motivation, meaning, participation, and social contribution.

Women, Religion, and Body Issues in the Context of Study

For most Loízan women, the situation of women in Puerto Rico has improved, despite the new challenges they are facing (which I will address when discussing the experiences of Lydia and Alfonsina). They assert, in agreement with Sánchez de León (1994) that socioeconomic changes brought about by industrial development, as well as changes in the Catholic Church and the presence of Protestantism, have encouraged wider participation by women and their visibility in the public sphere. But what is it about religion that has promoted women's wider participation and leadership in the last decades? According to Loízan women, wider religious participation cannot be attributed to their knowledge of the existence of female deities or of the Mita cult, which is centered on a woman prophet (mentioned earlier). Many of these women agreed that the Marian model of submission has been very powerful and even necessary to control women's extreme (nonreligious) behavior, such as prostitution. This is something old residents of Las Cuevas experienced first hand. According to many of these residents, one of Loíza's brothels was located in Las Cuevas, on street #951. The Marian devotion has also helped women to understand and feel honored about their role in society: especially their role in raising children, providing for their physical needs and teaching them the good moral and spiritual way. However, it is precisely the strong devotion to an image exalting the virtue of submission that, according to Boudewijnse (1998), caused the conversion of many women in Curaçao to Pentecostalism or to the charismatic movement. Some Loízan women Catholics indicated they have been inspired to participate widely and to develop themselves as social and religious leaders by Mary's example of leadership, her independence from her husband, and her dependence on God. However, as we saw in the experience of Rosa (discussed in chapter 5), which is in agreement with Safa's (1986: 1) statement based on Latin American and Caribbean women's experience, Marianism has not been the only weapon Catholic Loízan women have used to counter male dominance or the only source of inspiration for their religious participation and leadership. Thus, there must be other factors within the religious experience.

In Loíza, as in many other Puerto Rican Catholic communities, despite the great advances regarding women's role and position, one can argue that there is still no complete gender equality regarding leadership because women leaders are still subordinated to the higher leadership of men. I suspect this relates to the fact that I never saw the deacon of the San Antonio chapel in Las Cuevas or the coordinators' husbands, most of them church leaders themselves, attending any meetings at the chapel led by their wives and other women. Also, in the rosary I attended in honor of the deceased wife of the deacon of the San Antonio chapel, of fifteen attendants (the rosary's female leader included), only two were men and these were the deacon and his son. They only entered the house at the end to help serve refreshments. All of this may indicate a kind of paternalistic concession to women's leadership (this informal ritual placed it in a lower position anyway) and also a serious and deep consideration of women's leadership that is difficult to admit or to handle.

Protestantism, more precisely Pentecostalism (or neo-Pentecostalism), has also provided possibilities for women's participation and leadership in Las Cuevas. In fact, women like the sister of Carlos (whom I introduced in chapter 3) were key in spreading the Pentecostal message and in helping to establish the PCG of Las Cuevas. Women in this Pentecostal church also became prophets and solo singers, although I heard this happened under the leadership of men. In the CFLW in Las Cuevas, the role of women, including their role as pastors, has been very significant, but as in the Catholic Church, men take all of the highest positions in the CFLW at the council level.

But if Catholicism, in one way or another, has opened space for women's leadership, and Protestant churches, especially Pentecostal churches in Loíza, have not surpassed the Catholic Church in matters of women's leadership, then what else has attracted women to Pentecostalism? In agreement with Brusco's (1995) findings in Colombia, women in Las Cuevas acknowledge the great benefits to them and their families of strict codes of behavior imposed by Pentecostalism, even in situations where men did not convert but displayed some respect. Contrary to what Burdick (1998: 16) found in Rio de Janeiro, where seven of ten evangelicals are women, in Las Cuevas there was a only slight difference between men's and women's Protestant affiliation. Therefore, we can expect the benefits for women and their families to be greater. In many instances, money for alcohol and for gambling is saved for the family. Another benefit women of Las Cuevas brought to my attention is the openness (not always that obvious) of the Pentecostal church to birth control and divorce. For a few women I talked to from Las Cuevas, it is better to have a good husband and family stability than to be a great leader in church, since there are many ways to serve God.

As I discussed in chapter 7, women in the CC cannot participate in any leadership role in the ritual; however, they are actively involved in charities, teaching of children, visiting, administration, and other essential jobs such as cleaning up the church facilities and cooking. Through my friendship with Elena, the CC minister's niece, and with Sandra, his daughter, I learned about the great examples of fatherhood and husbandhood that the minister and many men of the CC represent. I was somewhat surprised to learn about Pastor Febres's strong support of Sandra, her sisters, and other young women from the congregation in their progress against a conformist attitude, their pursuit of higher education, and their development of social leadership. This opinion was also shared by men in the congregation. In fact, all of the educated members in the CC were women, which makes applicable the argument of Simon Harrison (1985) that ritual does not "reflect" social reality or the relationship between sexes and generations, but temporarily alters them. In the case of Sandra, her father was agreeable and encouraged her to move to the United States with her husband, who was joining the Navy in search of a better life, just as he has supported his sons who joined the U.S. Army.

He offers this support despite his reservations about the armed forces and his pro-independence and leftist ideals. Pastor Febres also wanted Sandra to continue graduate school.

Likewise, my experience with the CFDC demonstrates the flexibility of this alleged "ultra" conservative church regarding women's participation and leadership under certain circumstances. The CFDC pastors attempted to recruit my services after they were convinced I was a "real servant of the Lord" because of my biblical knowledge and my conservative style, which they pointed out as an example of modesty. I asked myself if they would have thought the same if I had worn shorts, a sleeveless shirt, and jewelry, if I had colored my nails or used makeup. One day, while we were praying together on our knees, Pastor Tapia asked me if I wanted to become the leader of the church to continue God's work. The pastor and the co-pastor were thinking of retiring in the near future and did not want to close the church. They would not be able to call me *pastora* (female pastor) because the Bible says that God calls *pastores* (male pastors) and not *pastoras*. However, I could be the main leader "as if I were a pastor" because Pastor Tapia passionately believed that the most important thing is to continue spreading God's word by any possible means. I answered, somewhat startled by his directness, that I was not prepared to make such a commitment. At the same time, his attitude did not take me completely by surprise because of the church's desperation for new members.

My personal experiences and association with Mayra, a main leader of the PCG, support other reasons why women stay in churches with conservative views regarding female leadership and modesty. Women in these churches have compensated for strict codes of modesty and body appearance in a number of ways: by having elaborate hair styles and hair pins; by having long nails; and by wearing elaborate clothes pins, fashionable high heels, lots of face powder, and strong perfume.

Over the years, the attitude of and toward Pentecostal women regarding codes of modesty and body appearance has changed—or been forced to change—significantly. In her teens, Mayra became a Pentecostal in a church outside Las Cuevas, where the doctrine was so strict that women were not even allowed to use curlers in their hair. She joined the PCG in Las Cuevas about fifteen years ago, when the doctrine was stricter than it is today, but less strict than that of the church she had been attending. In the PCG, Mayra has experienced changes that are manifested in her appearance: long nails colored with clear polish (some of them are fake), semi-short skirts, very fashionable high heels, a relaxed coiffure and hair cut, and shaved legs. Mayra defended these changes by arguing that the Bible should not be interpreted "too literally" and that nature itself expresses God's will for beauty and balance. Women's beautifying practices also confirm God's design of a man and a woman. (In addition, many young women believe that if they do not beautify themselves they are judged to be lesbian.) Mayra feels that God condones the act of women beautifying themselves "decently" for their husbands, considering the many worldly temptations men are exposed to. Also, her husband's artistic sensitivity justifies beautifying her body. More significantly, Mayra insisted that religion is more than following rules or doctrines and that it is relating to God personally.

Changes regarding women's perception of themselves, self- esteem, participation, leadership, modesty, and body appearance in the PCG, as in other Pentecostal churches in Loíza, have been greatly influenced by broad secular forces. In Loíza itself there are many obvious examples of women taking a leading social role, such as Rosa's running for the mayor's office under the PPD and Laura becoming the director of Loíza's cultural center. Also a woman from PIP ran for the position of Loíza's mayor in the last elections. During the six years I spent studying and working at the UPR and also during the many years in which I interacted with clerical or office workers (including my mother) from various public service facilities, I heard many expressions and witnessed behavior that pointed to the use of the body as some sort of affirmation (which Aparicio [1998: 151] has also noticed in dancing salsa). On Fridays and special celebrations at work, women dress more extravagantly, adorning themselves with expensive jewelry and colorful clothing in a non-verbal friendly competition to decide who has out-dressed her female associates or counterparts, even to see who can look nicest for men. Yet social pressure emanates from the media too as it pushes standards of beauty for women and men. This is common in Loíza.

Changes in the PCG, as in other traditional Pentecostal churches, have also been influenced by religious competition with Protestantism, neo-Pentecostalism, and/or individual big ministries such as the CFLW. In Puerto Rico the number of female pastors continues to increase. The CFLW supports female pastors and also promotes woman's upward mobility and personal progress in all areas, including body appearance in a strategic balance, as described in a CFLW newsletter article about "how women can be fashionable, look good, and keep their professionalism, while giving a good testimony."[1] Pastor Wanda Rolón, whom I mentioned in chapter 3, is an example of the relationship between neo-Pentecostalism and a less conservative view about women's body appearance. When she was first invited to our church, she wore long black hair, a long skirt, and no makeup or jewelry. Today, she is still a charismatic, but now sports a short blond hair style, shorter skirts, makeup, and jewelry. She therefore represents the movement from Pentecostalism to neo-Pentecostalism.

However, I must emphasize that for Sandra and other female church members from the CC, female leadership in the ritual is insignificant when compared to the experience of relating with God personally and obeying His word. For Mayra from the PCG, whatever she does with her skills and physical appearance is ultimately to please God, an issue between her and God. These statements remind me of the strategy, mentioned earlier, adopted by elderly Jewish women in Jerusalem: these women considered modesty to be an issue between God and women and not between women and men.

Hair Matters

Right after I asked Lydia to answer the questions for the census, she touched her hair and told me, in a semi-defensive and firm tone, that she might look like a *loquita* (little crazy person) or a *brujita* (little witch), but she was not. Lydia repeated this verbal and nonverbal behavior the third time we met. At the same time, she indicated that she did not much care what people think of her. She also alluded to the stereotype that Loíza is full of witches. Her hair seemed unusual to me, but not that messy. She called it *pelo parao* (meaning literally "hair up high"). It was unusual because it was very long, unrelaxed, and set up very high, an uncommon hairstyle for a fifty-three-year-old woman.

Similar to Caldwell's (1999: 89) observations that in ancient Dravidian culture hair was regarded as the source of great force, aggression and supernatural energies, in Puerto Rican tradition, witches, whose primary characteristic was their out-of-the-ordinary or unnatural behavior, had messy hair. In fact, some residents of Las Cuevas argued that messy hair was one of the characteristics of María la Cruz, the former owner of the area of the caves in Las Cuevas, and one of the reasons people believed she was a witch, crazy, weird or spiritually mysterious. Still today, the words *loca* (crazy) and *bruja* (witch) are interchangeably and are normally used to describe a person with messy hair, as in the case mentioned earlier of the internationally known musician William Cepeda, whom Loízans in Connecticut and New York know as "Toñito la bruja" because of his long dreadlocks. The use of the feminine *bruja* despite Toñito's male identity is interesting, as if there is a strict relationship between being a witch and being a woman. This is also quite common. During my first weeks in Las Cuevas, I was warned, jokingly, about a woman who was crazy. When I asked how they knew she was crazy, people said, "Because she talks to herself and walks corner to corner with messy hair." Also, two expressions reveal a connection between the hair and the person's unusual behavior or bad humor or both: "Se levantó con la moña pará" (She woke up with her hair rolled up high) and "Tiene el moño virao" (She has her hair rolled upside down).

Cross-cultural data confirms that each culture associates particular hairstyles with particular sexual behaviors and gender hierarchies (Delaney 1995) and that these are connected to sexual processes in the unconscious (Obeyesekere 1981; Caldwell 1999:89). Hair also has different sociopolitical functions such as affirming group and personal identity (Rowe 1998: 76–78) and protest. These last functions of hair were demonstrated during the controversy surrounding the Puerto Rican Barbie when it came out in 1997. Puerto Ricans in the United States and a relative few on the island protested the fact that Barbie's hair was straight (see Negrón-Muntaner 2002). During the course of my research, I regularly observed women of Las Cuevas helping each other with their hair, curling, styling, relaxing, and coloring it, often on the front and back porches of their homes. Such communal interaction, observed by Burdick (1998: 37) in Brazil, was more evident among young women with small incomes, who could not afford beauty salon services, including the beauty salon in Las Cuevas, which was owned by one of the coordinators of the chapel of San Antonio. Some women in Las Cuevas relaxed their hair, but would never consider coloring it because it would mean too many chemicals in their hair and because they were proud of their hair's color. Elderly women, such as Lydia and Alfonsina, prefer to wear a handkerchief, dreadlocks, or simply make a big roll with their hair on the back of their heads, although some of them, including Lydia, do not care much for hair appearance in protest against consumerism and established standards of beauty that discriminate against poor and black women in Loíza specifically and in Puerto Rico at large. Here, Lydia, without knowing it, is protesting something larger because as Dávila (2001: 223) has noted, African-Americans outspend whites in hair and nail accessories in order to improve their image and to compensate for their lacks; in Brazil, as in Las Cuevas, Burdick (1998: 36) found that this spending happens even to the point of sacrificing other necessary expenses, including food.[2]

The Unconscious and Conscious in Lydia's and Alfonsina's Religious Identities

I met Alfonsina after I met Lydia. Several individuals, including Rosa and Lydia, had described Alfonsina as a long-time Spiritist and midwife who knew a lot about Loízan history. (Lydia's father had been a Spiritist for many years until he accepted the Lord before dying, which is one of the reasons why Lydia and Alfonsina knew each other.) Some residents referred to Alfonsina as a Spiritist witch. I have to confess that the first time I walked to her house, I felt a little bit nervous. That first day, she was talking with her animals when I found her. Alfonsina's voice and her body comportment were strong despite the fact that she was thin and small. Her hands were calloused and she gazed at me intently. After she answered the questions on the census, Alfonsina voluntarily told me that she was willing to talk to me about anything I wanted to know because "as God was her witness, she did not have anything to hide." About one week later, I saw her again giving food to her birds and talking to them. She looked at me and smiled, nonverbally saying, "Don't think I am crazy." Then we sat down on the balcony of her unfinished cement house. It was surrounded by the strong smell of her animals and plants, most of them with medicinal properties, which she took great care of. (I saw different people coming to look for Alfonsina's medicinal plants and for her recipes.) Once she was seated on a moldy rocking chair, Alfonsina slapped her thighs firmly, making me almost jump from my seat. After rocking herself for several seconds, she stopped, got close to me, and with her eyes wide open told me that I could start asking her questions. Gesturing to her body and especially her hair, she said, "Go head. Here I am. This is all I am." She was dressed in a cotton robe and dirty sandals and her hair was short, unrelaxed, and messy. Neither Alfonsina's hair nor her whole appearance seemed as unusual to me as Lydia's hair because elderly women are not expected to take much care of their hair (although many elderly women, including my grandmothers, were very careful concerning the appearance of their hair).

When I met Alfonsina she was eighty-seven years old. Like Lydia, she and her parents grew up in Las Cuevas. I consider both of them *jabá,* a category used in Puerto Rico to refer to people with white or yellowish skin, black people's facial characteristics, and *pelo malo* (meaning coarse or kinky hair, or literally in Spanish, "bad hair"). Lydia was emphatic that she was a proud *jabá*, which is one of the main reasons why she did not relax her hair. She had been inspired by a black Puerto Rican woman on television who expressed herself in the same way and who followed that reasoning for not relaxing her hair. (Through television, Lydia also learned about other women around the world with the same attitude.) Lydia contrasted her attitude with the attitude of many Loízan women, especially young women, who seem to feel ashamed or unhappy with the way they are "naturally." I suggest this relates to the previously mentioned fact that the majority of the participants in the census who declined to classify themselves as black and said things like "Put trigueña, negro sounds ugly" were women.

Lydia and Alfonsina have been widows for several years and have lived without a male companion. They are heads of their households. In Las Cuevas, 11 percent of the households were headed by men only and 40 percent were headed by women only. Forty-nine percent of the households were headed jointly by husbands and wives or unmarried couples, although in many of these households the women had the control (or more control) in decision making. This phenomenon explains why, based on data from the Caribbean, Safa (1986: 10) makes the distinction between the symbolism of the head of the household and the actual decision making. The phenomenon of female-headed households is highly common in developing countries, such as those in the Caribbean (Horowitz 1967: 43). Some of the factors contributing to this phenomenon that are clearly evident in Las Cuevas include new laws that protect the mother and the children (such as the child support law established in 1986), political and social entitlement programs such as government welfare, and family networks and physical proximity (which facilitate the care of the children, freeing women to work and to access resources in general, and which provide a sense of security). There is also an increase in women's expectations regarding male companionship and the development of women's less conservative view of themselves (Muñoz Vázquez 1986). In Las Cuevas, both elder and younger women were very much aware of discrimination and subordination because of the extreme cases involving violent domestic crimes in the neighborhoods. Some of them admitted having experienced domestic violence and acknowledged it to be growing in Puerto Rico. In fact, adultery and domestic violence were very common topics of conversation while I was in the field because of the scandal regularly commented on in the media regarding a case of adultery involving Loíza's mayor.

Moreover, Schmink (1986: 149) reminds us to pay close attention to the ideological and subjective determinants to understand women's experience. The high number of female-headed households and women's standards of behavior in Las Cuevas are positively correlated with a high value of motherhood and a strong opposition to abortion, although sterilization was seen by a sizeable number of men and women as helping the family's well-being. The high value placed on motherhood explains expectations regarding women's proper behavior. During daily interactions with both men and women, including Lydia and Alfonsina, women's issues surfaced incessantly in the theme of *libertinaje*, which in this case people defined as that which women do at the expense of the well-being of their families. Both men and women mentioned lack of modesty (which many agreed has grown rapidly since the 1970s, with the popular Puerto Rican artist Iris Chacón singing and dancing "almost naked" on television), and, in the extreme case, delinquent behavior, which is growing rapidly in Puerto Rico. Clearly, this shows that the experience of women in Las Cuevas is more complex than what Collier (1986) has argued has been the case in a village in southwestern Spain, where female chastity gave way to a concern for "personal" capacities and preferences in a context of inequalities in income.

Lydia and Alfonsina are also mothers and grandmothers. For them motherhood is the most fulfilling experience in their lives, and they share this with younger women. Both of them maintain strong relationships with their children (in both cases, at least one adult child lives in the same house). Lydia has three children and Alfonsina twenty (several of them died when they were very young). Lydia told me that feeling her son growing inside her was the happiest experience in her life. She found it amazing to feel a human being, a piece of her, inside her. Alfonsina told me how much she respected the human body because of motherhood and her work as a midwife. Her greatest suffering in life was seeing some of her children die. Both Lydia and Alfonsina had strong relationships with their parents, Lydia more with her father and Alfonsina more with her mother. Both related their relationships with their parents to their education or general learning experience.

Lydia's father always encouraged her to study and learn, as did the fathers of a few other women in Las Cuevas. He read to her about Spiritism and politics of the left. She began to see these two as connected and reacting to the main system. He also encouraged her to help him manage his small store, which was attached to their house. After several years of a difficult marriage, Lydia decided independently to go to school while working as a cook and kitchen supervisor in the public school system (the last years as the supervisor) and grieving over her father's death. Though her husband opposed her studying, she finished her B.A. in social work with a minor in special education and graduated with a 3.8 grade point average. She worked as a social worker and as a teacher in the public school system until she suffered a fall that disabled her, preventing her from walking well. In Las Cuevas I discovered that only one-third of the employees were women between the ages of thirty and sixty; most were educated in the areas of health, office work, and education. Lydia thinks her most important attribute is not her degree or the 3.8 grade point average, but the fact that she is a fighter and has overcome many obstacles in life. Lydia emphasized that her education specifically contradicts the idea that Loízans are stupid, ignorant, conformist, or that they like to live "del mantengo" (dependent on welfare). She acknowledged that this characterization is applied to Puerto Ricans in general.

Alfonsina's father was a policeman. He was killed by a machine in a hacienda when Alfonsina was five years old. Alfonsina suffered at his death, but his death did not bring about many changes at home because her mother had been always the *macho* of the house. This was not unusual in those days. In fact, Alfonsina remembered when her mother insulted and hit her father because he did not fulfill his obligations. Alfonsina's mother was a determined woman, a hard worker, and a good provider. She gathered coconuts from the beach, made coconut oil, and transported it to her clients from eight *centrales*. For this she acquired some land and cattle and was able to loan and even give money to needy people. Alfonsina's mother was also very active in helping individuals through spiritual means and in planning religious events that involved the community, such as *rogativas* (chanting and prayers) during crises such as the hurricane season. Alfonsina's mother's practice of Spiritism and midwifery were related to her leadership in organizing secular events as well, which involved the attendance of people from within and outside the community, including famous musicians, actors, politicians, and professionals. Alfonsina's father resented all of this, but especially the gifts of mediumhood (the ability to communicate with spirits), midwifery, and community leadership, which Alfonsina inherited from her mother.

Alfonsina began practicing midwifery by helping her mother and doctors when she was about ten years old, and for many years she practiced midwifery independently. Later she decided to take nursing courses to be able to work at one of the medical clinics in Loíza. She had a lot of experience in midwifery, but had to compete with women who were getting a formal education. Consistent with Burdick's (1998: 48) recent findings in Brazil, nursing and medical assistance are two of the most appealing careers among women in Loíza, although the numbers in office work and teaching are also growing. Like Lydia, Alfonsina always confronted the opposition of her husband, who used to say that midwives were whores. According to Alfonsina, her husband objected because of his taboos about sex and nudity. On different occasions Alfonsina and I talked about how in midwifery you deal with the intimate parts of another woman, become very knowledgeable about sex and procreation, and develop an open attitude about sex. Alfonsina's husband's insecure personality made him feel envious of her independence (at a time when this was interpreted as a sign of a man's weakness) and social prestige. Her husband's envy, according to Alfonsina, was one of the main reasons for their antagonism, which over the years turned into a strong spiritual battle. Alfonsina believed her husband had made a covenant with the devil and used his faculties to do harm. She said he did it partly to bother her (she used a stronger word); however, the more harm he did, the more she bothered him by doing good to others. On several occasions, he threatened her with a gun and once tried to kill her by burning the house. These stories were corroborated by several of Alfonsina's close neighbors, including Carlos, whom I introduced in chapter 3.

Lydia described her relationship with her husband as antagonistic, but less harmful than Alfonsina's. She contrasted her father's character with her husband's. Proudly, Lydia told me that thanks to her father there was always food on their table and they were the first family with a television in the whole neighborhood. But Lydia always thought it was absurd that her mother referred to her father as *usted* (the formal form of you) despite the fact that they knew each other intimately. This is why she made up her mind to be different than her mother by doing the opposite. Lydia's husband was a man of weak character who was not a good provider; later he became an alcoholic. This is why she was in charge of bringing food to the table, of making decisions at home, and disciplining the children. According to Lydia, her husband had low self-esteem and was not a fighter. However, despite that fact that their relationship was fraught with conflict over his character, they loved each other. She suffered much after his death and stayed in a depressed state for five years, until she reconciled with God. After her reconciliation with God in the Mission Board Pentecostal Church (in another sector of the barrio of Pueblo), Lydia even thought that in some manner she had contributed to her husband's low self-esteem.

Like Alfonsina, Lydia also referred to her husband's taboos about sex and the body as a great source of antagonism, while relating these taboos to his low self-esteem and weak character. According to Lydia, she had crazy or unusual ideas about sex and nudity. (She meant that she was open-minded.) Her husband never liked her to walk almost naked inside the house. Her mother, who became a deacon in the Pentecostal church (while Lydia's father was a Spiritist), never liked that Lydia, who became Pentecostal as a child, did not wear slips. (Women from her church have also criticized her for the same reason.) Lydia told me she always felt free sexually and even more so after reconciling with God. She also connected her sexual freedom to her hair practices and in that context told me the following: "I felt dirty, but I learned to be open with Him [God] and here I am, a free person. I don't look at the mirror. I feel relieved, free. I can breath freely [while breathing deeply]. If I wake up in the morning with a desire to have dreadlocks I have dreadlocks. When I want my hair up high I have it like that, especially for church. When you are in Christ you feel you do not have to please others. You are honest with yourself. You only please God."

In more than one conversation, Lydia made the connection between her free hairstyle and other aspects of her lifestyle. In the same way she felt free to wear her hair the way she wanted, she dressed up and arranged the house the way she wanted. For example, when I met Lydia, she was wearing old clothes that she had collected for herself and for other people. (She criticized the fact that some needy people have rejected clothes in good condition that she has given them.) She was also recycling many things for reuse, such as greeting cards, washing machines, and old car tires for planting flowers in her garden. In her living room, she showed me the old curtains her sister, who also lives in Las Cuevas, had intended to throw away. Lydia's sister, nieces, brother, and her two sons who live with her protested because she insisted on keeping them; the curtains' color did not match either the other curtains she had in the room or her furniture's fabric. They also criticized the color she used to paint her house and her idea of moving her furniture to the balcony and having a hammock in the living room. Also Lydia was not using the phone system and was planning to build a water tank. She has been critical of the consumerist mentality in which many Loízans are trapped (with bills), the Puerto Rican government system, and the terrible services provided by the government. Finally, Lydia felt she was fulfilling part of her mission on earth by being an example of self-affirmation and of a critical outlook, which she claimed many Loízans have, contrary to what others commonly perceive.

According to Lydia though, being a role model is not enough if concrete actions are not taken. When Lydia was a supervisor in the public school kitchen system, she was known in the Department of Education as controversial. She earned this description because she encouraged her employees to fight for their rights. This fight as well as the fight against crime have often motivated Loízan women to organize and protest publicly. On various occasions Lydia personally requested of the mayor, in a confrontational attitude, various services for the community and the solution of different problems. She often complained to the mayor about the water filtration plant close to her neighborhood, which receives sewage from other towns and brings a strong bad odor to the area. She also showed great concern for elders, whom she took to their doctor's appointments.

Lydia believes the most important part of her mission is to be an example of a free and personal relationship with God in order to bring others to Christ, instead of an example of following certain rules. She prays constantly and reads the Bible to nurture herself, helps the church in different ministries and charities, especially with children and the elderly, and tells nonbelievers about God and also helps them if they have some need. Lydia interconnects the two parts of her mission by, for example, bringing her critical outlook to the church despite disagreements. She originally accepted membership in her church because members are free to express their thoughts and to disagree. Most importantly, the pastor does not force people to do things or to follow doctrines, but leaves it to the Holy Spirit to guide members. Yet, she explained, the pastor is clear about preaching the truth from the Bible. Lydia also mentioned that her church does not limit women; its philosophy of marriage, for example, is "fifty/fifty." Lydia made the point that she was telling me these things to demonstrate that Pentecostals in general and Loízans in particular are not blind or ignorant.

Alfonsina was critical of some Loízans' status as victims and their lack of proactive mentality while at the same time she claimed to be proud of being a Loízan with a fighting spirit. She also tries to be an inspiration to others and

to be proactive through her daily behavior and concrete action, such as helping people to resolve their problems by giving general counseling, by healing people with rituals and medicinal herbs, and by communicating with the
spirits. However, she does not organize Spiritist meetings anymore because
many clients fail to appear, in great part because of the misconceptions about
Spiritism. Furthermore, she feels too old for those meetings and would rather
help people spiritually one by one, as she did with me when she prescribed
a prayer to destroy bad thoughts against me by envious people whom she
asserted were around me. Once I said I wanted to have a baby (she asked me
first), she also prescribed medicinal herbs for getting pregnant and for preparing my body for pregnancy.

Alfonsina was clear in communicating the importance of her mission to
help others. According to Alfonsina, she has helped rich and poor, black and
white, Loízan and non-Loízan, Puerto Rican and non-Puerto Rican people
because, she said, problems are problems everywhere you go and the spiritual
world does not have a nationality. She was also clear that her mission and her
age make owning a beautiful house, dressing up beautifully, and even having
her hair combed insignificant. With a similar opinion to that of Romberg
(2003) about the partnership of modern Spiritism in Puerto Rico with materialism, Alfonsina criticized the fact that more people are using Spiritism to
obtain physical and material things rather than for the most important things
in life, such as being able to love and be at peace with one another. This is
why part of Alfonsina's job has also been to reorient people about their real
needs. In more than one conversation, Alfonsina acknowledged that this is a
big problem in Loíza, where decades of marginality and lack of recognition
and resources have made many people desperate for material things and less
concerned about what should really matter in life.

Two more things are important to note about Alfonsina's affirmation of
social identity and of a certain religious stand within Spiritism. First, Alfonsina indicated that some people still think that all Loízans are Spiritists in a
negative way. She said that many have criticized Spiritism as a sign of ignorance and blindness, but that in the type of Spiritism she has practiced, even
though it is not scientific or sophisticated, it is clearly established that spirits
are not responsible for all events and circumstances such as poverty. Another
misconception is that Spiritism's goal is to do harm. According to Alfonsina,
some individuals, such as her husband and other men of Las Cuevas with
whom she competed for best mediumhood for many years, have used their

faculties to do wrong, including deceiving people for money. This is why, she claimed, that some of them, including her husband, came to the end of their lives miserably (spiritually, financially, and physically). In this regard she commented, "What you do on this earth you pay [for] on this earth." I wondered if she was referring to Toño Lacen (mentioned in chapter 1 as the number one Spiritist in town), whom I met when he was very ill and in a wheelchair. However, I decided not inquire. Later I learned from Marcelino (the deacon I mentioned in chapters 4 and 5 who is Toño Lacen's nephew and *hijo de crianza* [a son that is raised by a nonbiological father]), that a few months before my fieldwork, Don Toño had "accepted the Lord" and the Catholic doctrine. This may explain why Don Toño was hesitant to talk about Spiritism with me, but willing to talk about life and traditions of the past. (Years earlier he served as an informant in Romberg's study about witchcraft [2003: xi].)

Alfonsina emphasized that corruption and heresies exist in all religions. To expand on this point, Alfonsina distinguished Spiritism from Santería and also Vodou, despite national and local efforts to mix them verbally and in practice. According to her, in Santería (mostly practiced in Medianía Alta) spirits are pagan idols, which are often used to do evil. Practitioners also perform animal sacrifices. She did not like the fact that Santería and Vodou are seen as inherent to the Loízan experience and that these religions are attributed, in a negative way, to all Loízans. To counter that, she emphasized the fact that Santería came from Cuba and that it did not came to Loíza right away, but through intermittent contacts with people who were practicing it in the area of San Juan (especially Río Piedras). Alfonsina's attitude clearly confirms the fact that Spiritism (even folk Spiritism) and Santería (and Vodou) are seen, in Puerto Rico as well as in Loíza, as distinct from one another and that Spiritism is usually the favored of the three. It also confirms that the Spiritist identity is more complex than the distinction between scientific and folk Spiritism allows. Alfonsina's experience with Spiritism, which she characterized as "a little bit by the book and a little bit by inspiration" also differs from what one would expect after reading Haydeé's characterization of witchcraft as the "uneducated ways" of Spiritism (Romberg 2003: x).

Moreover, Alfonsina clarified to me the centrality of Jesus in her practice of Spiritism. She acknowledged that this opposes the principles of official or Kardecist Spiritism, where Jesus is simply the best spiritual guide. For Alfonsina, Jesus is the source of life, the creator, the savior, and the only way to

God. The focus and influence of Jesus were evident and obvious in the saints' icons and Catholic paraphernalia I observed inside her home, particularly the image of Child God. This was also evident in the type of prayer she prescribed for me to gain God's protection from envious people and the great significance she gives to the Bible.

Alfonsina quit attending parish worship because of the strong attacks against Spiritism by Father Antonio and some parishioners, including those she knew and whom I learned consulted the horoscope in the newspaper, psychics on television, and sometimes tarot cards hidden in homes. In fact, I learned from various individuals and from Alfonsina herself that she had serious problems with Father Antonio. Once, she confronted him with the argument that exorcism is a sign of the belief in spirits within Catholicism. Alfonsina told Father Antonio that he could not play with God's matters and therefore with the spiritual world. Alfonsina commented that even Pentecostalism contains some Spiritism, but that one should avoid offending Pentecostals, including her oldest son (who was working in one of the individual ministries mentioned in chapter 3), with such a statement. Pentecostals' beliefs and non-Pentecostals' negative stereotyping of Spiritism would offend non-Spiritist believers. However, Alfonsina has faithfully attended postfuneral Catholic rituals. In fact, she was one of the first women to show up at the postfuneral ritual, in which I participated, in honor of the wife of the deacon of San Antonio chapel. Alfonsina attended this ritual because of her good relationship with the deacon's family (they have been her neighbors for many years) and because of her strong belief that the spirits should be treated rightly so that they do not bother living people. She has the respect of religious leaders, even those who have completely rejected Spiritism publicly, and she has attended a selective number of activities sponsored by their churches. A few months before I met Alfonsina, she had been asked by the leader of a popular religious and social ministry in the country to participate in a community parade where she was given an award for her many years of community work. The municipality also honored her by placing her picture in the town's new health center.

Finally, more than once Alfonsina mentioned to me her strong and intimate relationship with Jesus and exclaimed in a loud voice while almost clapping her hands, "If I catch Christ I will consume him with kisses." As much as she repeated this phrase, she also repeated another phrase, "When you do things the way God wants you to, you are at peace with God and your conscience, and you can breathe clean air and you can say that you don't have anything to hide."

Alternative Religious Exigencies

Political participation by women with no "specific" feminist agenda has been characteristic of countries such as Jamaica (F. Harrison 1988) and one can argue that this has also been the case in Puerto Rico. Here, women's political participation has been mainly expressed through commitment in various degrees to platforms and candidates surrounding the issue of the country's status among other social issues. However, in her study of Philippine Muslim women, Angeles (1998) argues that nationalistic participation coalesced a strong sense of female identity with women's strong and wide-ranging capabilities. In Puerto Rico in the last decades, women's political participation has become more informed by specific gender issues. Lydia's and Alfonsina's religious lifestyle points to a kind of political participation that can be considered nationalistic and feminist, collective and personal. Like Rosa's religious lifestyle, that of Lydia and Alfonsina can also be represented by the interplay of conscious and unconscious motivations and by a hierarchy of motivations with an overall mission to help others and an intimate relationship with God at the top. This forces one to reconsider the exclusive idea of "politics" and "feminism."

Giddens's (1991: 214) concept of "life politics" is applicable here: a politics of lifestyle, of self-actualization given changing external circumstances. Religion defines proper actions in an era that has abandoned final authorities (142). This conclusion is true; however, Lydia's and Alfonsina's religious stand challenges Muesse's (1996) statement that fundamentalism defines the world in terms of binary oppositions and does not provide a place for mystery, critique, or analysis of social or structural forces. Additionally, my study has demonstrated how their religious stand involves affirmation of their Loízan identity and of themselves as individuals (with a soul, a mission, a body with a color tone, a hair texture, and with physical and emotional expressions).

Giddens (1991: 218) argues that reflexive appropriation of bodily processes and development is a fundamental element of "life politics." As Lydia's and Alfonsina's sense of responsibility toward body appearance increases their concrete action to help others does likewise. These observations affirm Becker's (1995: 85) argument, based on her study of the Fijian people, that responsibility for cultivating the personal body is removed from the sphere of the individual to that of the collective. Here the example of Rosa is revealing because her efforts to look good and take care of her body are driven by her sense of responsibility to lift up Loízans' image (to demonstrate that Loízans have cachet, she told me) and, very importantly, by her desire to make others and herself feel good from an emotional and spiritual point of view. This effort is being challenged in a different way because, as I noticed in the parish downtown, the women do not dress up so elaborately, contrary to the black women in the churches of the United States studied by O'Neal (1999).

But before continuing to compare Rosa with Lydia and Alfonsina, I would like to provide some explanations for these women's attitudes. One explanation is the existence of other social and cultural spheres where an individual may express this type of elaboration, such as cultural activities, and a consequent resistance to a reductionistic type of folklorization of Loíza. I witnessed some women ridiculing other women by comparing them to *vejigante* masks because of their "extravagant" dressing. Their comments reminded me of the many times when I rode the bus to the university and witnessed black, usually heavy, girls making fun of *trigueña* or white girls who dressed up very nicely. I thought that because these black girls could not fit in with or be part of these white girls' standards that they did not have another choice but to convert themselves into the audience for some sort of spectacle. I also found women who were strong advocates of Loízan folklore while promoting a kind of sophistication in their personal taste for clothing. I was able to identify with this group when interacting with academic women at the University of Michigan, most of whom wore somber colors and clothes of a refined simplicity. In Las Cuevas, I also found a reluctance to dress as though one's socioeconomic situation was better than it actually was for fear of not being able to receive government financial assistance. Even in the few cases where there is money to spend, there is pressure to be like the rest, which is tied to a strong religious emphasis on humbleness. As some women in the parish downtown told me, in Loíza you learn that appearance is not the most important thing; you can be very smart and look homeless, crazy, or criminal. However, it was also clearly evident that the younger generation was more concerned about dress codes and that there is a constant struggle between generations regarding this issue.

Similarly to Rosa, Lydia and Alfonsina establish a connection between body appearance, their mission to help others, and being able to "breath," which I take as a metaphor for having internal peace or being at peace with themselves and with God. Lydia's and Alfonsina's strong character is reflected in their body comportment, which is different from that of Rosa, who dresses more fashionably but who seems more physically and emotionally vulnerable than the other two women. I believe the latter has to do with Rosa's dark skin color (as opposed to that of Lydia and Alfonsina) and with her greater exposure to a socially competitive atmosphere: the majority of her competitors were white students when she studied at the university and when she was a teacher, and the majority of PPD candidates and leaders in her church were men. At the same time, Lydia's and Alfonsina's defensive/affirmative/critical attitude with respect to their bodies has to be placed in a context where the majority is dark skinned. Another way of looking at it is that by being *jabá* they are in an obviously ambiguous situation because they are white but have characteristics of people who are dark skinned, their kinky hair being the most distinct.

I argue that the conscious involvement of the body and hair in Lydia's and Alfonsina's mission to help others comes from three main interrelated sources. First, they have an appreciation for and serious consideration of their bodies, which emanates in a strong physical-emotive power from the experience of maternity, which they regard as the most fulfilling experience in their lives. Second, there exists the social moment/context where attention is given to body appearance and hair in particular during community interactions. The physical characterization of Lydia and Alfonsina as in-between makes their hair appearance more significant. At the same time, messy hair is commonly accepted or expected from old people as normal elderly behavior. Here I want to mention Mayra, who is a lot younger than Lydia and whose husband has artistic expectations, for whom the Pentecostal emphasis on the external status has a less liberating effect. The assumption that older people tend to be more conservative allows more freedom, which Rowe (1998: 76–77, 80–82) indicates has happened in the Rastafari movement, which allows only older women to wear locks. Third, the physical properties of hair, especially its manageability, allow hair to reflect Lydia's and Alfonsina's personal religious stands: Lydia wears her hair *parao*, but long, as required of Pentecostal women, although she selectively fixes it a little bit, for example, when posing for me to take her photo; Alfonsina wears her hair messy, but selectively covers it with a handkerchief for ritual purposes (as she did in the postfuneral ritual in which I participated, where she was also well dressed and wore panty hose).

Moreover, body and religion in women's experience have been important research areas for psychological interpretations. Both Lydia and Alfonsina verbally and repeatedly associated their specific religious lifestyle with issues of female and male antagonism. This antagonism was somewhat ambiguous, especially in the case of Lydia, who even before her husband's death acknowledged that she was contributing to her husband's low self-esteem by constantly criticizing his personality and his role as the "head" of the family. She also acknowledged the social pressures on men when resources are scanty and the man is considered the main provider of the family. Lydia and Alfonsina also related their religious experience to their personal takes on issues of sexuality, which coincide with Olivelle's (1998: 35–36) analysis. Olivelle (37) persuasively explains the unconscious displacement that occurs when individuals are prevented from dealing directly with an issue on a conscious level, for example, the issue of sexual maturity. This kind of displacement is manifest in the verbal connection Lydia and Alfonsina made between their religious stands and experiences with female-male antagonism and issues of sexual maturity, despite their conscious denial of such connection because it seemed reductionist or even irreverent.

Finally, relating Lydia's and Alfonsina's social and political contribution within the religious experience with empowerment, I strongly support Abu-Lughod's (1990) comment that recent studies have emphasized people's resistance against hegemonic powers to the point of romanticizing it instead of seeing the emphasis as a "diagnostic of power." Perhaps my analysis may be seen as emphasizing empowerment. However, I have been sensitive to Ingersoll's (2002: 164) concern about the pushing of ethnographic research to find women's empowerment amid structural limitations instead of exploring the experiences of women in the subculture who actively participate in the process of change. This may happen in different forms—sometimes ambiguous and contradictory—and degrees (Brink and Mencher 1997), and a multidimensional perspective allows us to see it that way. Feminists and researchers on the topic, particularly in Puerto Rico, should become more aware of this broad perspective in order to significantly understand and affect women's collective and individual lives in and outside the religious experience.

9

"When they call my name from the Book of Life, I will respond happily"

Re-identifying Through Witnessing at an Advanced Age

By looking at the witnessing experiences of Delia and Bartolo, two elders from Las Cuevas, this chapter becomes a continuation of the previous chapter, where I examined religious experience at the level of the individual lifestyle. By focusing on witnessing, this chapter is also a continuation of chapters 4, 5, and 6, in which I examined elements or strategies employed in the ritual context to legitimize changes in religious ideas and practices and a certain religious message.

The first part of my main argument is that witnessing is fulfilling, particularly at an old age, because it allows elders to make an active, practical, and creative social and spiritual contribution with earthly and eternal implications. Demonstrating the significant role of religion in advanced age is nothing new.[1] For example, studies (Chatters and Taylor 1994: 209; Coke and Twaite 1995: 99) have found that among black or African-American elders in the United States, religion provides a sense of pride and personal satisfaction, of self-worth and personal control.[2] However, I have found few answers to the question of *how* religion provides these qualities, or what elderly people are able to contribute through it. One study that has approached this question is Sered's (1992) study of elderly Jewish women (mentioned in chapter 8). Here, the author demonstrates that in a religious context dominated by men, elderly women construct meaningful religion by emphasizing rites (funerary) that depend on them for their practice and efficacy. Therefore, the second part of my main argument is that the social and spiritual contribution that comes with witnessing derives in great part from its referential and constitutive nature. By this I mean that witnessing is not only referential or indicative of religious identity and experience but also reenacts what is being narrated, and that this is possible because of verbal and nonverbal mechanisms and and specific processes taking place.[3]

Inspired by the works of Rosaldo (1982) and Stromberg (1993) about the referential and constitutive nature of narrative, I followed Bauman's suggestion (1983: 17) to make the speech event (or situation or scene) the unit of analysis. Bauman (4) has also assisted this study by pointing out the areas to look for while doing a speech analysis. He enumerates the areas as follows: participants' identities and roles; the expressive means employed in performance; social interactional ground rules, norms, and strategies for performance and criteria for its interpretation and evaluation; and the sequence of actions that make up the scenario of the event.

Bauman's suggestion resembles the model Mannheim and Van Vleet (1998: 326) apply to the Southern Quechua narrative whose elements I will use here. According to Mannheim and Van Vleet, the Southern Quechua narrative is constitutive or dialogical for the following reasons: it is produced between interlocutors; it implicates discourse within discourse (by means of quotations or indirect discourse); it refers to coexisting narratives; and it involves multiple interactional frameworks. About this last point, they argue that a dialogue is created in the very event of speaking, in the mutually constitutive dynamic between the organization of participant roles in the speech event and the social field within which it occurs. Emphasizing the second and third points, Mannheim (1998: 61, 90), who was also inspired by the Southern Quechua narrative, indicates that its conversational and coparticipative structure is part of a larger pattern of interrelations between narratives within a larger discourse field.

For the purpose of analysis, looking for narrative structures, processes, and their social and spiritual implications, I divided Delia's and Bartolo's witnessing narratives into various fragments (keeping the information of each fragment as it was given, except for the deletion of confidential information at the request of the subject). I then organized these fragments by major topics. By doing this I may contradict the very argument that witnessing is constitutive of religious experience because witnessing does not happen in fragments but as part of a whole. However, if I were to decide to incorporate the entire experience of Delia's and Bartolo's witnessing as it happened, I would probably have needed to make it the whole topic of this book. But before getting into Delia's and Bartolo's narratives, I will talk briefly about the significance of witnessing in the Protestant community.

Witnessing in the Protestant Community

Witnessing or *testificar* is considered one of the most important elements of the Protestant ritual and experience (S. Harding 1987; Stromberg 1993), although in Puerto Rico Catholics (particularly charismatic Catholics) have also incorporated it into their experience. In this context, witnessing is an individual's description of his or her encounter with God. This could be rephrased in many ways, for example, "what God has done in one's life," "how one got saved," "how one knew the Lord," "how one converted," or "how one was born again." Normally, witnessing also includes the witness's experience before and after the encounter with God. This is why *testificar* or *dar testimonio* (giving a testimony) among the Protestant community may also refer to describing how God helped one in a specific situation, for example, through healing, protection, provision, or saving a relative or a friend. Witnessing can follow an established format or style in terms of the structure or organization of the information, language forms, and the use of phrases and terms. For example, to describe the witness's situation before the witness's encounter with God, he or she may say, "I was lost," "I lived in darkness," or "I belonged to the world."

Witnessing can be as creative as the witness's religious tradition, education, gender, and age allow. Regarding religious tradition, for example, most of the witnessing narratives I heard in the Church of the Fountain of the Living Water in Las Cuevas emphasized experiences of healing and material provision. However, the witnessing narratives I heard in the Pentecostal Church of God emphasized how God helped the witness in the middle of a difficult situation. In this study, the variable of age is significant because of the common understanding that elders talk too much. Because of this generalization, it is commonly understood that the elders' witnessing is usually long and detailed and full of childhood experiences relating to how things were in the past as opposed to the present. I suggest that the relationship of advanced age and lack of education and economic participation that exists in Las Cuevas has to do with the elders' lack of participation in leadership and, consequently, with the fact that witnessing is the most preferable and available means of church participation for elders and has become greatly integrated with everyday life. Some elders believe that demonstrating their usefulness by witnessing encourages more respect toward them and maybe even helps them avoid being put in a nursing home.

Witnessing is expected to happen normally in a ritual that can be cele-brated in church, in a home, in the park, in the prison, or in the hospital, often in the presence of a group of people. Some rituals *(servicios* or *cultos)* are specifically for witnessing, for example, during Thanksgiving or New Year's Eve. However, witnessing may also happen outside the ritual and between two individuals. This is why witnessing is addressed to both believers and nonbelievers. On the one hand, when it is addressed to believers it is with the purpose of *edificar*, which means to reinforce or to encourage the faith, life, and well-being of the congregation. On the other hand, witnessing is expected to make nonbelievers have an encounter with God through a public act of *profesión de fe* (profession of faith) or acceptance of Christ as savior. Witnessing is also expected to bring to a reconciliation with God those who at one point had an encounter with God but who kept themselves outside the church community. Profession of faith and reconciliation with God usually happen after raising one's hand or walking to the front (altar) or both.

Witnessing and preaching can overlap to the extent that witnessing may become the main source of an individual ministry or that witnessing may become the identity of a ministry. This often happens when the witnessing contains a supernatural experience such as a miracle of healing or an extraor-dinary experience of transformation, as when a person is changed from a criminal to a follower of Christ.

Delia

My assistants and I met Delia while doing the census. Later, Eunice, the el-derly lady with whom I stayed in Las Cuevas, told me that Delia was a mem-ber of the Tapia extended family. Immediately after explaining that her house was first built in 1918 by her parents (an answer to a question on the census), Delia began to give me information about her life, pointing to her conver-sion and relationship with God while saying repeatedly, "Christ is my life." When I told her we had to leave, she asked us to come back to hear her whole testimony because I could easily write a book about it, and week later we were at her house. This time we drank some refreshments in her kitchen while she narrated her encounter with God, told us about her childhood, and described how different things had been in the past. I told her that because she had given us a lot of information, I wanted to come back and record it. Delia said she would not mind telling it to me again because I had not heard even half of it, because she was very used to witnessing (in church, on public buses, and in her home when kids and teenagers from the neighborhood visit her, as they often do for company, food, or money) and also because of the strong responsibility she felt for the youth. Finally, she mentioned that she was living alone. And about four days later, I came back with my recorder but without my assistant, which disappointed her (she had cooked for us). Delia stood in front of the kitchen cabinets and narrated her encounter with God and other experiences.

Delia, who was eighty-six years old when I met her, had come from Canóvanas with her whole family (including her grandparents) when she was a child to work for a *hacendado* in the northeastern part of Las Cuevas, close to the bridge. They planted sugar cane and pineapples and also raised animals. The oldest of six children (including Pastor Tapia, whom I introduced in chapter 7), Delia quit school after the sixth grade to help in the house and to take care of her grandparents. At the age of nineteen she married a man with whom she was very much in love. However, she was unable to get pregnant and her marriage lasted only until her husband left her for another woman who was able to give him children. Consequently, Delia got so depressed that once she tried to shoot herself to death, but thanks to her family's support she kept going.

Delia then moved in with her parents, whom she took care of until they died. Years later, one of her brothers, who had cancer, moved in and Delia cared for him until he died. To raise his three children, Delia sold pigs and traditional Puerto Rican dishes because the government's assistance was not enough. It was at this stage of her life, more than twenty years ago, that Delia had a profound encounter with God.

All along, Delia knew that God was someone "big" and "distant" who deserved to be respected. Her parents, especially her mother, encouraged her and her five siblings to attend the Catholic Church and to have good morals. Her father was more concerned that she be knowledgeable about life matters and so he took her to political meetings. Delia's sister, with whom I spoke several times, had already converted in the Assembly of Christian Churches in Medianía Alta before she decided to move to the United States. She and her brother, Pastor Tapia of the church close to her house, were constantly encouraging Delia to convert. The following is Delia's narrative of her encounter with God:

The doctors gave me an appointment to see if there was a need to cut off my leg. That morning I did not have anybody to take me to the hospital in Río Piedras. I tell you that I have been through . . . [a lot she meant to finish]. Nena [girl], I asked, "God who will take me to the hospital? It is so dark . . . ," but God always provides. My cousin's friend took me. When I was walking to the hospital, I asked a nurse, whom God had put in my way, to help me find the clinic, so she took me where I had to go. She bendito . . . was very nice to me. Nena, you see how God is with me. I always say that God is planning something for me because my life has been suffering and suffering. Nena, you do not imagine how much these eyes have cried. They [the doctors] did everything in my leg quickly in the bed. I cried and cried. I told God, "I cannot resist anymore, help me, please!" My heart was burning. But I say that God was planning something for me. The doctors and the nurses were wondering what was going on since the surgery was successful, but I kept crying and crying. I did not know what was happening. Then, Vitito [her cousin's friend] came and picked me up. I came back and in severe pain cooked some food for my brother. That same afternoon my sister came and asked me if I wanted to have a service at home. I do not know why, but I jumped and I answered, "Yes!" A week later, the whole church came. They sang some hymns that said exactly what was going on in my life. Nena, I tell you that the message was clearly a picture of my life. The pastor invited me to stand up and asked the congregation to pray for me. I felt burning inside and cried and cried like nobody could stop me. [She said this while touching her chest as if she were feeling something.] The next week I went to church with my sister and converted. I said to myself, "I have to raise my hand," but that was not necessary because I felt like somebody pushed me to raise my hand. After that I took the microphone. [She began to laugh.] Can you imagine, nena, me with a microphone . . . in my hand? [She kept laughing for a while.] I began to testify about everything that had happened to me. I said that I was healed in the name of the Lord. You hear me, nena, I was healed! God healed me! Since then I have not had any problem with my leg. My life has been suffering and suffering. This is why I say that God was planning something for me. I . . . a crown when I am in the Heavens . . . [She laughed.] I always think God is planning something for me. I laugh when the pastor says that a book can be written about me.

In this first fragment, Delia quoted her conversations with God, using gestures to bring them into the present. This direct quoting occurred when she recounted the occasion she had nobody to take her to the hospital, after the doctors treated her leg, and during the altar call. She used repetition to establish the intensity and length of her suffering before the encounter with God. By repeating the phrase "God is planning something for me," Delia reassures herself of God's control of her life. Repetition and change of verb give meaning to her suffering and minimize it. Pauses and incomplete sentences with phrases such as "I . . ." and "a crown . . ." lead her to expect something good, and beyond her imagination, also giving meaning to her suffering.

The expressions "My heart was burning" and "I felt like somebody pushed me to raise my hand" mark the supernatural intervention in her physical-emotive experience when encountering God. Touching her body while narrating her story influences her ability to reexperience the physical-emotive sensation. Delia used pauses and laughing when she mentioned that she took the microphone to testify in front of the congregation right after her conversion. By this, Delia emphasized the significance of the transformation in her life.

Delia's life is still full of much suffering, for example, the suffering caused by the treason of family members. However, God and the way she cultivates her relationship with God (through praying three times a day and reading the Bible, regular church attendance and active involvement, and fasting whenever she can) have given her the strength she has needed.

Delia indicated that the greatest signs of her transformation are her strength and lack of fear, the emphasis of her message. She considers herself blessed by the love and respect of her ex-husband until his death and of his children and by the way God has provided for her financially. For example, after Hurricane Hugo (in which she lost her old wooden house and everything in it), she received $14,000 from FEMA (Federal Emergency Management Agency) and collections from members of her church to build a cement house. Delia was happy with the $250 she was receiving monthly from Social Security and with the fact that every now and then she receives gifts and money from her relatives in the United States, with whom she has contact by phone. About this Delia said, "I have learned to receive little by little. God gives us according to what we really need. Jesus was poor anyway. Christians should be poor like Jesus." She continued, "Jesus came for Loízans, for the poor. Jesus is for the people of Loíza." In other instances she mentioned the word poor along with the color black, as in Jesus is for these "poor negritos" and making gestures to include herself. As mentioned before, "negrito" is the diminutive of black and can be used as Delia did, in a self-effacing way. Finally, she compared her life with Jesus' life and said, "My life has been like Jesus', suffering, betrayal, suffering, suffering, humbleness, suffering . . . but victory."

About her experience with God after her encounter, Delia narrated the following:

> I think, nena, that all this [the difficult situation of Puerto Rico and Loíza] means the coming of Christ. Everything is in the Bible. The devil is exercising his power and . . . The devil takes the mind of the youth. Ay bendito [meaning Oh God]. Satan is Satan. The Bible says he wants to destroy. He always has wanted to have more authority than God. But he does not. God is more powerful . . . well sometimes . . . he [the devil] seems more powerful . . . God seems tardío [late]. You think so? It is like I say . . . [She was making eye contact, frowning, and attempting to touch one of my shoulders.] Because God is . . . late. I say [while looking up high and touching her chest], "God, do not take so long. Put your hand . . . Stop all this, God. It is enough." I say, "God, why do you enjoy the evil things that are happening and why do you let the good people suffer? Why do you let your own people go through a lot?" I tell all this to Him praying. One does not understand . . . He knows . . . his own mysteries. And then I say [while laughing and touching my arms], "God forgive me that I spoke to you in this way. You know everything. Your word says that the evil prospers only in appearance." But I think God seems late. "God, why this and that?" Here in Loíza you hear that a father killed his son, a son killed his father, a teenager killed an old lady . . . Look, nena, when God will decide . . . I do not know who will be able to tolerate so much punishment. I think "van a pagar justos por pecadores" [the righteous will be charged like sinners]. [She laughed.] But God is righteous and He has His people separated.

In this fragment where Delia mainly explains the difficult reality that surrounds her, two narratives coexist: the biblical reference, which by itself gives legitimacy to Delia's words, and the use of Jesus' life or journey on earth as an analogy or metaphor of her life. Quinnan (1994: 151) found the metaphoric use of journey in the narrative of elderly parish priests to describe their Christian experience. The same mechanism has also been found in Judaism (Goodman 1999: 67) and in the Indian tradition (Tilak 1989: 52–53) to make sense of the process of aging and of life in general. According to Stromberg's (1993: 55–75) analysis, the shifts between the referential and the constitutive forms of communicative action are the strategies used by individuals in narrative to reframe consciousness for self-transformation. Here, Delia's suffering makes sense as it symbolizes Jesus' suffering and vice versa.

The metaphorical or analogical use of Jesus' journey of suffering on earth is tied to the issue of religious identity, which coincides with Quinnan's (1994: 151–53) finding of the relationship between the use of journey as metaphor for Christian life and identity by elderly parish priests. Delia is also tying the two with ethnic and class identity when she argues that Christians should be poor like Jesus and that because Jesus came to this world for the poor He is for the people of Loíza.

Pauses and incomplete sentences while narrating her experience with conflict-doubt suggest that Delia is presently struggling with it. These two, together with repetition and facial expressions, communicate the intensity of the conflict-doubt. In her interest to resolve her conflict-doubt, Delia talked to herself in confession to convince herself (or even force herself) to leave doubt and to trust God. Whitehead (1987: 21, 128) has found a similar strategy in the technique of "solo auditing" (a specific and more advanced technique of "auditing," meaning "listening") employed in the Scientology sect that originated in the United States in the 1950s. This is defined as a solitary method in which the practitioner assumes alternately the role of the auditor (listener) and the role of the "pre-clear" (the individual who is listened to). The use of quotation is indicative of this process, which for Delia was not complete without the mechanisms of touching me and asking me to respond affirmatively to what she was saying in order to find solidarity.

After Delia talked about her view of life, she moved to a section that for me is like a summary. Getting to this point was precipitated by Delia's concern that I was probably hungry and she wanted me to eat her food.

> Look, nena, you are starting now . . . but I feel satisfied. I say, "Lord I am in your hands. Do whatever you want with me." You cannot wish to die, but I say [while looking up high and touching her chest with her hands in the prayer position], "God I am in your hands. I am ready when you are." I am not scared that someday . . . But I would like when the hour comes not to be alone in the room in the night. I would like it

to be that I have a pain in the morning and they take me to the hospital and there . . . I am content with what I have lived already. I keep doing what he wants me to do. I do not waste my time talking about politics. I just vote. A Christian should be careful about what he says. Hear me nena now, one cannot be scared because the person who is with Christ should not be afraid of death. [She said this as though it were a command.] You are a Christian. You cannot be scared. When I was young I was afraid, but nena, I have followed the gospel for about twenty years and I feel very satisfied.

In this fragment where the main themes are contribution and after-life redemption, Delia makes obvious her struggle with death. Through repetition as in the expression "I am in your hands," quotation of her dialogue with God, and expressions of surrender such as "Do whatever you want with me" and "I am ready when you are," she reinforces her communication with God while trying to resolve her struggle with death. With the expression "I am content," Delia trains herself to feel happy about death and to enable herself to "really" contribute as she is authentically witnessing. This relates to what she told me, "You cannot preach what you do not live. How can you preach joy if you are not happy?" The fact that Christian adults are not examples of what they preach, according to Delia, is the main excuse the youth use for not seeking God.

The change from talking in general to addressing me directly makes Delia's life worth living as she is making a contribution to my life. By referring to me as *nena,* Delia confirms her role in coaching me in the Christian life while establishing her authority as someone of higher standing.[4] This authority is also affirmed by the expressions, "A book can be written about me" and "You cannot imagine how much these eyes have cried." The idea of multiple participation elaborated by Mannheim and Van Vleet can be applied to my person as a fellow Christian with whom Delia tried to find solidarity and as a *nena* starting in life and in need of a superior guidance.

After almost preaching to me about death, Delia told me, "*Nena,* before I give you food I want to finish with my song. That song is my life. I always sing this song when I witness. Many people have cried and have come to the feet of Christ." Delia made sure the recorder was working. Then she stood up straight, said "In the name of the Father, the Son, and the Holy Spirit," and sang:

Señor, tu eres mi amparo, eres mi abrigo.
Señor, tu eres consuelo en mi aflicción.
Señor, mientras yo duermo tu vigilas.
Quédate conmigo aquí, no te vayas mi Señor.

No te vayas mi Señor, quédate conmigo aquí,
aquí en mi soledad.
Sin ti no puedo vivir,
si me falta tu calor y tu santa bendición

Señor, tu le diste vida a mi vida.
Señor, tu me diste salvación.
Con tu sangre derramada en el calvario
Tu curastes las heridas que habían en mi corazón.

Lord, you are my protection, you are my shelter.
Lord, you are my comfort in my affliction.
Lord, when I sleep you watch over me.
Stay right here with me, do not go away.

Do not go away, stay right here with me
in my loneliness.
I cannot live without you,
without your warmth and your holy blessing

Lord, you gave me life.
Lord, you saved me.
With your blood spilling at Calvary
You healed the wounds that were in my heart.

I was personally touched by the song of an unknown author, and by the passion with which Delia sang (I accompanied her on the last verse).

After Delia finished singing, there was a pause and I did not know what to say. She wiped away her tears with her own clothes, touched her chest, and said, "That song is my life. Oh my God, that song . . . I encourage myself." Then I told her that I had been touched by her song and that I had been encouraged in my faith and she said, "You see. That is why I keep doing it."

The song talks about Delia's experience and summarizes it. Delia expects that her song, as well as her whole testimony, will have an effect on others, something guaranteed by past experiences. The effect of the song is also on Delia herself, helping her to continue experiencing the Christian faith and as an act of obedience and requirement for eternal redemption.

I continued meeting Delia almost regularly during my field study. She was constantly giving me food at her place and to take home. In almost every conversation we had, she repeated much of the information I presented here, but we also talked about many other things woman to woman. In the next section I examine Bartolo's witnessing from a comparative perspective.

Bartolo

I met Bartolo a lot earlier than I met Delia. I saw him several times listening to the radio while sitting in an old chair in front of his rustic cement house surrounded by a fence. The house was close to the main street. I always felt compelled to talk to Bartolo because he looked weak and lonely and because he reminded me of my grandfather, who had died a few years earlier. Rosa told me that he was living alone, that he did not receive many visitors, that he had been divorced a long time, and that his son, who had lived with him for many years, had been killed several years ago. She also told me that for a while Bartolo had lived with one of his daughters (a missionary and a pastor's wife), but then he had insisted on coming back to his house in the compulsive manner of many elderly people.

Passing by I saw that his eyes were inviting me to talk to him, although I waited until I had to interview him for the census. I introduced myself as someone who was studying the people of Loíza and their religion. Immediately, he turned off the radio (he was listening to a Christian radio program), opened the fence, and told me that he was Pentecostal up to his eye balls, that he was one of the founders of the Pentecostal cause in Las Cuevas (he helped found the Heavenly Doors Evangelical Church in Las Cuevas), and that for many years he had been a preacher who never charged. Then he began to tell me about his conversion when he was a child and how things were in the past. He said, "I like to witness every time I can." So for him there was no distinction between telling me his story and witnessing.

The second time I visited Bartolo, he invited me inside his house. I asked his permission to record him and, like Delia, he told me almost exactly what he had told me before as though it were for the first time. Bartolo was born in 1916 in Maturí in Medianía Alta. His father abandoned him and his four siblings. Bartolo's mother moved to San Juan and left Bartolo with her sister when he was only seven years old. He was constantly trying to work to gain money for food because there was not much food in his aunt's house. When he was about nineteen, he left his job as a cane cutter and moved to San Juan, where he became a good mason, married, and had children. About his encounter with God and some experiences afterward, Bartolo narrated the following:

> It was seven o'clock in the evening and my stomach had not seen any food. I had tried and tried many times without catching any fish. Oiga [hear], I was hungry, hungry. Things were not in the past the way they are now. Food was hard to find. I was there lying down . . . Then I heard a hymn [he showed some emotion] and what they were singing, oiga, was a picture of what I was living. Usted [formal you] understand me? It was like . . . that it began to speak to my heart. That song . . . Have you seen lights in the sky and the wind blowing so peacefully? That I saw. The hymn said:
>
> ¿Cómo podré estar triste?
> ¿Cómo entre sombras ir?
> ¿Cómo sentirme solo o en el dolor vivir?
> Sí, Cristo es mi consuelo, mi amigo siempre fiel.
> Si aún las aves tienen seguro asilo en él.
>
> How can I be sad?
> How can I be in the shadow?
> How can I feel lonely or live in pain?
> Yes, Christ is my consolation, my faithful friend.
> Even the birds are secure in him. (author's translation)[5]

[He was crying as he sang and I joined with him in this popular hymn.] I decided to seek that God that I heard in that song and here I am. That song was my life. Oiga, I went to bed that night with an empty stomach but with my heart full of God's presence. Oiga, I am still alive thanks to God. Mire [look], God has given me everything that I have. He has given me good health. He has given me life. I have been a person . . . I could not go to school, but look! [He showed me some certificates hanging on his wall that proclaimed his various evangelistic training.] All the people about my age who went to school are dead. I have been a happy man because of the life I have lived. I have had no problems. I have not had to work to pay a lawyer to take me away from a legal problem. The gospel made me a true man. I have not had to beg because I have always liked to work to be able to sit in my own house built by myself. [Bartolo began to cry.] I have been a happy man. Usted . . . The only thing . . . [He cried loudly.] I have had a happy life . . . but they killed my only male child. My best child, Israel. He took me to doctor's appointments, to church. This happened about three or four years ago in Medianía. He lived with me. [He showed me the bed where his son used to sleep.] He was divorced and had a son. One day he told me, "Pai [Dad], if somebody calls me, tell them I am in Vega Baja." He had a lady there. I told him that I did not have anybody to take me to church. They called him to work. He was a policeman in the office of human resources and some kids coming from school shot him to death in the back. Mire, I have been through . . . [a lot he meant to finish]. They killed my son. [He could not stop crying, took his big glasses off, and dried his tears with his shirt. He waited to be calm and continued talking after I said some words to comfort him.] Mire, he was a good son. He did not smoke, he did not drink. He read the Bible in his room. [He showed me the room again.] He did not deserve to die like that. I have had to continue with my life. I was lucky that I had the Lord. That same night I was preaching and I heard the gunshots. That was for me something terrible. I did not resent God, but I told him, "God, if you knew that I was preaching why did it happen to me? Why did you allow this to happen to me, why?" That was a big prueba [test], usted oiga, a big, big prueba. You think so? [I responded to him affirmatively.] And recently, they almost stabbed to death one of my daughters, who lived in government housing. If it is not because God is with me . . . But I have two daughters who are professionals in Boston. I helped them to study at the university. Oiga, I have a daughter who is a missionary in the church that I go to. She is the pastor's wife . . . she is almost the pastor. This is the greatest happiness in my life. I have had a happy life. I had so much fun when I was a child. We danced bomba in Maturí where I grew up close to my grandparents, close to the cockfight court. We played in the water. When it rained we played under the rain. Nature is something beautiful. God's creation is beautiful. We played, splashing the water with such innocence. One day somebody showed my father to me, "Look that is your father." I ran after him, "Papá, Papá" and he turned around and walked away. He died . . . I started to let my anger out. God helped me. When He transforms you, He truly does. I hated him, but God helped me. God really helped me. I said once, "He is a coward." "You are a coward, a coward." He left me. "You were never there for me. You did not care about us. [He began to cry.] You were not there when I needed you most." I always cried during the Three Kings Celebration. Oiga, what I have been through . . .

In this first fragment Bartolo uses the repetition "hungry, hungry" to establish the intensity of his suffering before his encounter with God. The experience is amplified by the use of supernatural marks such as lights in the sky and the peaceful blowing of the wind. Another way to legitimize his conversion is by contrasting his empty stomach with his heart full of God's presence: the first experience disappears with the second, making a hierarchy of experiences. While Delia uses a song as a metaphor of all her experience, Bartolo uses it to express his situation at the time of his conversion.

Of some interest is Bartolo's use of contrast to give meaning to the difficult situation in his life, as when he compared himself with people of his age, who unlike himself, went to school but now are dead. This contrast adds to his emphasis on the good things in his life, such as his good reputation, his strong work ethic, and his longevity. In fact, Simmons (1970 [1945]: 221) has noticed among elders in traditional societies (which he refers to as "primitive") the strategy of making longevity a privilege, a reward, in order to cope with reality. This privilege is also significant considering the high incidence of crime in Loíza.

By repeating the sentences "I have been a happy man" and "I have had a happy life" while talking about a difficult situation, Bartolo convinces himself not to let himself down. When he told me about his son's death and I told him that my mother lost her young brother (also named Israel) to gun violence, Bartolo acted a little bit surprised and somewhat comforted.

The statement that while he was preaching he did not resent God for allowing his son to be killed, his crying, and the use of quotation are indicative of some sort of therapeutic technique he was using to minimize the pain he was still suffering. Evidence of this is the use of repetition, as in the phrase "big, big *prueba*." It seems that Bartolo is also telling me, himself, and God that he should not feel bad about his continuing struggle with his son's death. Telling me that, or asking me if I thought what happened to his son was a big *prueba* was his mechanism for finding solidarity.[6] A similar therapeutic mechanism is employed when he narrates his relationship with his father and moves from talking in the third person to talking directly to his father.

Bartolo told me he strengthens his faith by reading the Bible, fasting, and praying. Regarding praying he said, "You cannot imagine how much these knees have bent to pray" (an expression similar to the structure of Delia's expression "You cannot imagine how much these eyes have cried"). He showed me his callused knees with much pride, but with a humble attitude. (I took a picture of his knees.) He was also thankful for the spiritual and emotional support of people from his daughter's church and for the $344 of Social Security benefits he was receiving monthly, which was a little bit higher than Delia's. In Las Cuevas, the majority of households with a monthly income of $500 or less had elders depending on Social Security and government assistance.

According to Bartolo, the main explanation for what is happening in the world is man's disobedience, which began with Adam and Eve. Then he explained his worldview the following way:

The desert the people of Israel walked through was physical, but ours is spiritual. We have to continue walking. This [desert] is even more dangerous. For example, usted were coming so young and respectful . . . but you did not have an idea what you would find. Usted probably did not know if I was a lion or a dove or a snake. But this will stop some day. All this is written in the Bible. Oiga, sometimes I have to hide myself under the bed [to avoid a bullet coming from the street through the window (I told him I was afraid I would have to do the same thing at Eunice's house)]. In the past, things were not like they are now. Usted probably do not know. Usted look like you know a lot, but usted are so young and do not have much experience. In the past, there was only one policeman with his gun and a tamarindo (common fruit in Puerto Rico) branch to spank the kids. But today . . . usted know what some kids did the other day to a poor old man on the main street [referring to an alcoholic old man I saw most of the time in street #951]? They took off his clothes, hit him, and laughed at him. Recently two kids were killed here. But that happens when you do not have God. I grew up in the gospel. I have had my ups and downs because we are still on this earth, but I have kept myself walking.

In this fragment, Bartolo, like Delia, refers to the Bible to make sense of his difficult reality and to give legitimacy to his point of view, which he contrasted with what people say. Bartolo uses the journey of the people of Israel through the desert to explain his journey on this earth.

To Bartolo, the fact that he does not have much time left on earth is the reason for taking things seriously, for sharing the gospel with people. Bartolo told me that for eight years he had services in front of his house to preach to the youth. About the kind of message Bartolo preaches to the youth, he said the following: "My message is: Look, Christ changes you as He changed me. He changes you because he created heavens and earth. God created you. He has blessed you. God gives you air, warmth, cold, he gives you life abundantly. He is your creator. Everything that you have is given by God freely because he created you and does not want that you lack anything, but you have to serve him." While preaching this message he seemed another person, full of energy and strong, speaking loudly and gesturing energetically.

However, Bartolo acknowledges that today it is harder to preach than in the past because at his age it is harder to get around, his health is poor, and crime and lack of respect have grown. He also indicated that young people think older people are boring and do not know much about life. This is why he prefers to keep tracts very close to his front door in order to distribute them easily. Another factor about which Bartolo is cautious he expressed in the following words:

Here usted find some white girls like you, of good presence, well dressed but half dressed. Their faces have so many colors. They look like . . . [He began to laugh]. But usted see . . . usted . . . maybe if usted would have come like one of them I would have not invited you to come inside. Things natural are more beautiful, like the pastor said the other day. Usted see the colors in nature. Nature is beautiful. The Creator made things beautiful. I am against the destruction of nature. Once a girl came in her roller skates and fell. She asked me for some water. I told her . . . well, I sent her to go around the corner where there was a faucet, but I did not let her come inside the house . . . She was almost . . . naked. But I like to talk with anybody about las profundidades de Dios [God's profound ways]. I like to witness what God has done in my life with people like usted. Usted are a Christian, but you are just starting in the walk. Some people do not like to talk with Adventist or Jehovah's Witnesses, but I talk with them because they are willing to talk about las profundidades de Dios. Mire, I listen to the Adventists' radio program. One has to live what one preaches. We have to love. Christians should not waste time. Maybe I die tomorrow. I do not know. My days are numbered and yours also.

Pauses and incomplete sentences speak about Bartolo's sense of impotence regarding sharing God's word, principally with young females. This partly explains, without forgetting his loneliness, why Bartolo has made his options broad in terms of audience and why he exposes himself to criticism.

By witnessing to me, Bartolo makes his life worth living, especially when time is running out and considering Bartolo's strong belief that "a Christian should die like a soldier, with his boots on." Also, Bartolo's emphasis that my days are numbered comes from the high incidence of death among young people on the island and in Loíza. Like Delia, Bartolo legitimized his authority by emphasizing his long-term Christian experience and experience with suffering. By referring to me as "usted" and by using verbs in the second person, he showed respect for me without losing his authority; his long experience as a preacher represents enough authority.

The second to last time I saw Bartolo was during the second part of my large research trip (March and April of 1998), about two or three weeks after my previous day in Las Cuevas. At the time he looked sadder and less alert. I told him that I just wanted to stop by to say good-bye, but he seemed hesitant to talk to me; there was an expression of distrust on his face. Bartolo told me he was not going to answer more questions because another lady had come asking for some information, which she gave to Roselló (the governor at the time). He did not want any trouble and did not want to get involved in politics because of the many problems this brings, although he recently protested against the construction of hotels in a swampy area of Loíza. I felt disappointed because I thought I had lost his trust.

Nevertheless, I insisted on talking with him and promised not to ask him more questions. I did not want to dismiss what I knew was probably my last chance of seeing him. He told me he was very sick and needed prostrate surgery and that he was ready to go to be with the Lord. For a while we engaged

in a dry or cold conversation until we began to talk about the Bible. I immediately noticed a change of attitude and he offered me some pop. I promised that I would come back with a surprise, and the next Sunday my cousin
played her guitar and we sang the hymn of his conversion. After we sang, Bartolo told me, "I never expected this kind of visit. How *usted* . . . [He laughed
and laughed.] What an idea you came with . . . and *usted* came from far away.
I really admire *ustedes* being so young . . ." We took pictures, he gave us coconuts to take home, we shook hands, and said good-bye. Finally, he asked us to
come back, but said, while smiling, that if we could not there would not be a
problem because anyway we would see each other in Heaven. I immediately
thought about the lyrics of the hymn I use in the title of this chapter: "When
they call my name from the Book of Life, I will respond happily." This hymn
has been popular in funeral services where it is sung by members of different
denominations; the song is considered a unifying religious element.

Through Witnessing: After Witnessing . . . ?

The interest in the significance of narrative in the human experience is old
within anthropology. For example, Levi-Strauss (1963) was interested in explaining the efficacy of the South American Indian shaman's chanting during
difficult labor. His answer lay in the comparison between the shaman's chanting and Western psychoanalysis to help "abnormal behavior," because in both
the technique for helping the situation is to reorganize experience concep-
tually through symbolic mechanisms. Inspired by the practice of witnessing
in the Protestant community and by the religious elderly in the community
under study, I looked at witnessing outside the ritual context to conclude that
the efficacy of witnessing derives from its great referential and constitutive
potentials through certain cognitive and physical-emotive processes, delineated as surrender, confession, conflict or doubt resolution, transformation,
identity/solidarity, contribution, and after-life redemption. These processes
occur in combination with certain linguistic mechanisms (verbal and nonverbal). These mechanisms are quotation, repetition, incomplete sentences,
pauses, changes of pronoun and verb tense, contrasting, questions, metaphor,
analogy, coexisting narratives, multiple participant identities, changes of volume, eye and body contact, and facial gestures. Whether these mechanisms
have been employed intentionally or not and whether these mechanisms are
the result or the cause of reexperiencing is not clear here. But the experiences

of Bartolo and Delia tell me that the relationship between the linguistics mechanisms and what is inside the individual is not transparent, since, for example, the witness may continue with internal doubt, but may not show any sign of doubting in order to encourage the listener.

Moreover, by following Chatters and Taylor's (1994) suggestion to adopt a multidimensional perspective, one is able to assess what kind of contribution witnessing represents in the lives of Delia and Bartolo at a more personal level. This perspective involves considering the different social conditions and variables of elderly people, for example, gender, racial identity, family relationships and marital status, and personal religious trajectory.[7] For Delia and Bartolo, witnessing is significant and both take it seriously. Experiences with lack of integrity in the Christian community make truth an important element of the efficacy of witnessing. Rosaldo (1982: 222) found that unlike in Western speech, in Ilongot speech social bonds and interactive meanings are more important than issues of sincerity and truth. For Delia and Bartolo, truth is essential precisely when considering the well-being of other individuals and their interrelationships: this becomes one of the reasons for their lack of political activism. Because the Bible is implicated, the truth is thought to be legitimate in itself.

Bianchi (1982: 162) has observed that old age provides a kind of flexibility so necessary for assuming control of one's religious philosophy because satisfying others is not a big concern.[8] This point leads to establishing differences between Delia and Bartolo. For example, Bartolo's religious philosophy and his loneliness have greatly contributed to his willingness to talk and witness to Adventists and Jehovah's Witnesses and to expose himself to much criticism. Bartolo's situation was unique in Las Cuevas because his close relatives were living outside Las Cuevas, and here the percentage of elders (sixty years old and up) was about 20 and the percentage of elders living alone was only 12, most of them living close to their children and other relatives.[9]

Bartolo's loneliness may also explain his caution about talking with young people, many of whom he considered untrustworthy. As I stated earlier, in Las Cuevas I always sensed some distance between the elders and the youth, particularly between males who were not related, although this also happened between those who were related. Bartolo's caution about talking with young people, especially when approaching young girls, is also explained by his gender identity. This last point has to do with the higher value of motherhood than fatherhood in the context of study: a relationship between an old lady and a boy is seen in mothering terms; however, a relationship between an old man and a girl is often seen in sexual terms and viewed suspiciously. For the same reason, Delia is less reluctant to interact and share her religious experience with young people, especially male, whom she has even invited to her house or her backyard despite the constant advice from her relatives. However, here I would like to mention Delia's need to experience mother-hood and to probe her abilities in this area to prove them to herself (and even to her ex-husband, who was on her mind most of the time because he had abandoned her because of her incapacity to have children). This is also demonstrated in her decision to adopt her brother's children and in her mothering relationship with her ex-husband's children; she felt so proud telling me that they loved her more than their own mother and that her ex-husband admitted it.

Both Delia and Bartolo manifest a great sense of contribution and mission in the way they explain and resolve reality and in their great interest in legitimizing their role and authority. In addition, they resolve the tension between the value of experience, where they are located, and the value of knowledge, where they locate the researcher, by privileging the value of experience. This strategy coincides with the preference for the value of experience over knowledge found in a study about the point of view of the elderly in Christian churches (Rismiller 1964: 21–22). Differences in style between Delia's and Bartolo's witnessing are also evident. Delia stood up throughout the whole witnessing, but the tone of her voice and her body movements were not as intense as Bartolo's, especially when he got to the point of telling me the message he has for young people. In terms of their messages, Delia's message focuses on God changing the individual and on the benefits of strength and joy. Bartolo's message emphasizes God's power to transform the attitude and action of individuals, particularly their morals, although happiness is a significant topic. These messages relate to their concepts of Loízan authentic identity: Delia associates Loízan identity with poverty and humbleness, Bartolo with natural environment and high morals. Also, both messages value strongly a personal or intimate relationship with God. I cannot propose that the differences in these messages do not reflect differences in the intensity of their relationships with God. I cannot conclude either that Bartolo's emphasis on God's concern with man's behavior is a way of keeping some distance between him and God, as Eilberg-Schwartz (1996) suggests is one of the measures Jewish men have (unconsciously) taken to avoid homoeroticism with a male God.

Clearly, witnessing as identity reenactment/crafting can be situated, practical, effective, and socially and spiritually meaningful for the witness and for the listener. However, I hope that the church, the government, and the community at large will continue encouraging and searching for other means besides witnessing by which elderly people may reinforce their religious experience and contribute to society in general.

Conclusion

"If we do not get involved, then the 'witches' will
absolutely overtake us": Recatching Identity for the Future

"It is not a festival of blacks that we are having here; we are not commemorating the freedom of blacks. We are commemorating the freedom of the Puerto Rican people." These were the words (my translation) of the ex-director of the ICP, Luis Díaz Hernández, when he spoke to a small group of people at the 2002 celebration of the abolishment of slavery in Ponce. According to Díaz Hernández, the poor turnout at this celebration was due to the lack of knowledge Puerto Ricans have of their history, meaning the country's experience with slavery and racial mixing. He also blamed this poor showing on the results of the 2000 census, in which a large majority of Puerto Ricans, including a majority of Loízans, classified themselves as white; classifications that a simple look at the population contradicts. Even when the classifications are black or white most Puerto Ricans either preferred white to black or declined to answer the question.[1] Of course, one does not expect the entire Loízan population to consider itself black, especially after the recent immigration of light-skinned residents to the high-cost residential areas. Also, in the results of the census I distributed in Las Cuevas and discussed in chapter 2, many Loízans rejected using the "black" category or used it hesitantly when it was appropriate. Here it is valid to ask: Are these results an exact reflection of Loízans' whole perspective on their black identity, and did these results come about because Loízans do not know their history or because they have experienced their history "en carne propia" (in their own flesh)? To begin, Loízans are aware of the reality of slavery and also of the little significance given to this part of Puerto Rican history and reality. They have also experienced the aftermath of discrimination and social and economic deprivation. Therefore, it seems that these are the reasons why many Loízans have opted to "ignore" or "avoid" these issues. Having said this, in recent years a larger number of Loízans (and non-Loízans) have come to believe that their problems can be resolved in great part if they give more significance to slavery and openly confront racial discrimination.

Nonetheless, as this study has shown, over the decades Loízans have managed identity within and outside the religious framework in their own way, sometimes in a seemingly contradictory way. To begin, the majority agree on the general significance of identity but not necessarily on the degree. There are also different identities that are significant, for example, ethnic, color, community, and town identities. Some individuals believe, for example, that African and black identities are truer and deeper; in essence, they equate the issue of identity with affirming African heritage and blackness. Some understand that African heritage is more important than black skin color and vice versa. The same identity can be managed differently depending on the situation. To be more precise, many Loízans agree on a connection between identity and the social and economic condition but hold different views about the type of connection. For some, identity is prior to or a step toward improvement. For others, crafting a sense of identity is improvement in-the-making. For still others it is necessary to leave behind the issue of identity in order to improve. To make things complicated, for some Loízans social improvement means mainly economic development, individual mobility, and movement toward a progressive mentality; for others, it requires high social, moral, and spiritual standards, a great sense of community, and, more than anything, going back to their roots. The scene becomes more tangled when these views confront each other closely, making it difficult to identify when they represent the consistent view of any social or religious group.

Such complexity of the management of identity, however, does not make it impossible to formulate a general idea of the role of identity and religion together for broad sociopolitical action to improve Loíza's difficult situation. This is an essential issue considering the popular opinion based on present facts that Loíza's problems continue to exacerbate despite much promotion of identity reaffirmation and religious ideology and practice. Here it is necessary to point out that a multidimensional religious and multi-identity perspective, as used by this book, does not prevent one dimension (of religion) and one identity (in relation to religion) from standing out over the others, as in the following example. During my latest brief visit to Loíza (in May of 2003), I was invited to the parish of Santiago Apóstol in Medianía Alta for the twenty-fifth anniversary celebration of Father Francisco's priesthood. Father Francisco has served in Costa Rica, Mexico, and the United States (in Los Angeles, California) and during the last five of these twenty-five years he has served in Loíza. The celebration took place during a Sunday mass on

May 18 at 9:00 a.m. The celebration also honored the twenty-six years of priesthood of Father Eduardo, who in the last few years has been helping Father Francisco in Mediania Alta. Members from the different chapels under the jurisdiction of the parish of Santiago attended, as did friends of Father Francisco from the religious community. The church was full, although, as a parishioner told me, they were getting used to full services because of the recent growth in the number of participants in the mass.

In this event, the priests stood out as part of a small minority of white participants that also included a few elders accompanied by their children. These elders looked rich and seemed to have been living in the area for quite a while. Other white participants were from the newly constructed residential areas. This was not the old typical scene of a financially poor congregation; most people were dressed very well. I was glad to see Marcelino, an old-time deacon of the parish downtown, whom I interviewed for chapters 4 and 5. He seemed excited to help in the liturgy for the occasion, but when I asked him about the parish downtown he said with obvious frustration that they were fighting. (Remember that the church downtown recently endured the resignation of Father Marco Antonio, who left the church allegedly because of serious conflicts among members and their discontent with his "strong" promotion of Loízan identity.) A large group of participants of the drug rehabilitation program Hogar Crea, whom Father Francisco has helped for several years, also attended the event, bringing a large flower and fruit bouquet. The atmosphere was open and inviting. Before mass, people were laughing aloud as they greeted each other. A few members were preparing the last details of the mass and of the feast to follow. This included the music team, which was composed of elders and young people with a keyboard, a guitar, and percussion.

Father Francisco preached while walking up and down the aisle, using a conversational style and simple Spanish (spoken with a strong and peculiar accent). In his sermon he focused on his experience entering the priesthood and his growth in the faith. He grew up in the state of Virginia as a *jibarito*, by which he meant that he did not know much about the rest of the world. The Trinitarian Catholic leaders with whom he had contact affected him because of their outreach to marginal people and their way of challenging the evil system of Jim Crow laws. One day he went to a hospital and sat in the section for black people. Everybody looked at him in surprise. A nurse told him that if he wanted to be seen by the doctor he would have to move to the area for white people. But even this did not discourage him from "fighting the evil system," and there he stayed until he was finally seen by a doctor.

Father Francisco's concern about discrimination and social justice is related to his emphasis on an intimate relationship with Jesus, which he stressed in his sermon is more important than following the rules of the Catholic institution. He preached about the three ways in which Christ is intimately involved with his people of color: the Eucharist, the Word, and the Holy Spirit. He finished his sermon by asking the congregation to mention the ways they have learned Christ is present among his people today. Members of the congregation mentioned the words "love," "compassion," "mercy," "forgiveness," and each of these concepts was further elaborated on by Father Francisco. He then discussed the connection between these concepts and the idea of a god who is very concerned about the marginalized. Father Francisco's commitment to fighting racial discrimination and promoting social justice and the way these values direct his pastoral efforts have much to do with the high esteem in which he is held by residents of various communities and with the congregation's rapid growth in recent years (surpassing even the downtown parish). Here I would like to ask: Is the Loízans' support of Father Francisco's ministry a sociopolitical action and if so what kind?

The experience of Loízans with the issue of color forces me to ask: How many Puerto Ricans (including religious leaders and church members) would protest racial/ethnic prejudice, including that which exists against Haitians and Dominicans, with the same intensity they have protested the U.S. military presence in Vieques to the point of being jailed? I also wonder how many Puerto Ricans would admit that racial prejudice exists in the country but still ignore it or address it superficially. With the U.S. invasion of the island in 1898 and the creation of the commonwealth of Puerto Rico in 1952 came the need to define and reaffirm Puerto Rican identity, which was based on the harmonious coexistence of the Spanish, Indian, and African elements. Another point to consider is that (using Dávila's words [1997: 83]) the issue of color has been an important element for the construction of the "moral" Puerto Rican in the nationalist ideology. Accordingly, only "immoral" Americans are branded as racists. Here it seems appropriate to offer a reaction to Blanco's (1975 [1942]) earlier idea, which is still in many Puerto Ricans' minds, that admitting an exaggerated type of racial prejudice is intellectual colonialism: Is denying or only providing a cursory look at racial prejudice any better? To many Puerto Ricans the issue of racial prejudice or discrimination has no more significance than—or should not be as much of a priority as—the issue of the country's political status. Other citizens think that the issue was automatically addressed or resolved politically by allying with the United States and by the idea of the three components of Puerto Rican culture and religiously by the idea of God's love for all and brotherhood (as discussed in chapter 6). There are other more internal factors that have contributed to the denial of racial prejudice or to the little attention the issue has received (even after all of the recent advances discussed in chapter 7). One of these factors, which I discussed earlier, is an increased marketing of the folkloric and modern Afro-Caribbean or Afro-Rican elements (through *vejigantes* and salsa). In addition, a few Puerto Rican blacks, such as the famous champion boxer Tito Trinidad, have had the chance to lift the name of Puerto Rico up high. Puerto Ricans are able to "disarm" any real dialogue about the issue of racial prejudice by substituting genuine, daily work toward racial equality with a superficial public celebration of the Puerto Rican black identity or contribution.

Loízan experience as discussed in this book brings to light the need for both a distinction and a connection between everyday decision making and public political demonstrations. This idea is reflected in a resident's observation that brings us back to Puerto Rico's relationship with the United States and the events in Vieques: He claims that many Puerto Ricans have used the issue of Vieques as an opportunity to blame the North Americans for all of the country's problems and to excuse themselves for not doing something revolutionary at the level of everyday life.

There seems to be a relationship between these protests and a recent initiative to affirm *lo criollo* (the authentic Puerto Rican) and this involves both the secular and religious sectors in a battle. This affirmation also seems to be a response to the strong push for privatization by the recent PNP governor Pedro Roselló. (This happened within the context of a growing global market, an accelerated consumption modeled after the United States, and a movement in Latin America toward neoliberalism.) Similar to what Derby (1998) has observed in the Dominican Republic, to many Puerto Ricans privatization is the antithesis of Puerto Rican authenticity. In many cases privatization represents *lo americano* (often understood as synonymous with *lo extranjero* or anything foreign). This is why the promotion of *lo criollo* was a driving force behind the protests against the privatization of the Puerto Rican Telephone Company (a government-controlled company for several decades) in 1998 and in daily discussions about the growing foreign control of public services and the media.

However, what many Puerto Ricans seem to forget is that *lo criollo* does not always represent the interests of the Puerto Ricans masses but rather those of the Puerto Rican (white) elite. For example, a controversy erupted several years ago around the use of *criollo* cement culverts, produced by the company Cemento de Ponce, for a large sewage project. The local production of cement has been considered a source of Puerto Rican pride and a source of great wealth for the Ferré family. Outside experts recommended a composite material produced outside Puerto Rico to be used for the culverts. In the end, "Puerto Rican" cement was used for the project against the recommendations of the outside experts and the culverts soon deteriorated and needed to be replaced. Another point is that these public demonstrations to defend *lo criollo* are contradicted by Puerto Ricans' high daily consumption of U.S. products. (However, it cannot be forgotten that *lo criollo* has become very expensive or a luxury. Still, it is important to ask: To what extent have Puerto Ricans allowed this to happen?)

After considering the attitude toward race of many Puerto Ricans and of Loízans (such as those in the parish of Santiago Apóstol), similar to Burdick (1998), I still do not want to romanticize "the people's religious everyday way." This has been argued (in discussions in a few of my university courses) to be the case in Scott's (1985) book about Malay peasants, *Weapons of the Weak: Everyday Forms of Peasant Resistance.* I do not want to pretend either that resolving Loíza's mounting social and economic problems must involve a distancing from religion (assuming that any social agenda away from religion is better). This book's findings clearly establish that the issue is not that religion (as a platform for managing identity) has not worked for people, but that the way it has worked (in a highly religiously competitive environment) has followed multiple logics and has influenced the development of complex attitudes in regard to sociopolitical action. I refer to them as "complex" because they are not always easily detectable or verbally articulated. In agreement with Burdick (1998: 182), I hope this study can help activists and anyone interested in improving Loíza's current situation to develop an awareness of these complex attitudes or "forms of consciousness" (using Burdick's term) within and outside the religious framework, a deeper and realistic understanding of the sociopolitical situation, and insight into how to proceed with this matter.

As I indicated earlier, in my graduate courses at the University of Michigan we discussed the position of the ethnographer in relation to the subjects of study. We also touched upon the applicability of ethnography. Recently Maduro (1995: 49), a scholar of Latino religion, invited researchers in his field to reposition their objectives in terms of research and practice, to move from lived experience (of oppression) to critical reflection of that experience, to transformation of the world outside and within us. It is hard to avoid thinking seriously about these issues after tasting a little of Loíza's good and challenging experiences. I have felt obligated to be as direct as possible by offering the following suggestions (which were requested by many Loízans, by the way). The topic of color has been an issue in Loízans' everyday life and they need not fear the criticism that too much attention is paid to this topic. At the same time, while moving ahead with sociopolitical action for the town's improvement, they need to ask themselves seriously how much racism is to blame for all of their problems. Furthermore, Loízans need to engage in systematic actions (such as meetings, elections, and protests), while intentionally connecting these efforts to their daily experiences (programs, organizations, and policies), to continue making their voices heard and to further their interests. They should be more persistent. (One lesson to be learned from the case of Vieques is that persistence pays off.) The local government should listen closely while encouraging the participation of different religious, political, economic, color, geographical, age, and gender groups. They should be open to what can be learned from the experience of Loízans and non-Loízans abroad. Pro-Loíza/black national secular organizations should also listen more carefully to the various issues that are affecting the quality of life in the town. They should be mediators for the common good, using their contacts, resources, and public relations power to advocate for Loíza.

Finally, Loízan religious leaders must overcome the fear that interreligious social action will compromise the uniqueness of their religious identity and their legitimacy. This fear of cross-group collaborative effort also hinders cooperation between the various political parties or subgroups within the parties. Church leaders should acknowledge that some things are better accomplished as separate units and through individual actions, while others require a systematic collaboration between different religious groups. After completing this book I am convinced that the Loízans' complex attitudes or forms of consciousness across religious boundaries and experiences (and political affiliations) are where one can find points of commonality and the potential for collaborative work. However, it takes actual interreligious dialogue to discover and confirm these points and potentials.

I hope this book will encourage further research about current and future plans regarding Loíza's development. During my latest visit to Loíza, I heard about more criminal activities and socioeconomic problems in the town and in Las Cuevas. I also heard about new secular and religious initiatives to prevent crime and to help or further develop the town socioeconomically. One of the plans included the building of thirty-one low-cost homes with $4.6 million provided by the Hortense Disaster Recovery program of the U.S. Department of Housing and Urban Development.[2] Also, the Autoridad de Desperdicios (Waste Management Department), the Junta de Calidad Ambiental (Council of Environmental Quality), and the coordinator of the residential program Comunidades Especiales (Special Communities) had recently begun an environmental health educational program in Loíza. [3] I hope these recent events as well as the contents of this book will encourage stronger, pro-Loíza, sociopolitical action in these political, economic, and educational circles.

Certainly, there are Loízans who prefer to believe witches are still around as a way of keeping a critical perspective, while others declare that the witches are gone as an act of faith. However, there are also Loízans standing on a middle ground: They stay involved in their community, many of them with God's help, to make absolutely sure the "witches" will not overtake them.

Notes

Introduction: Catching Identity and/or/in Religion

1. Social and historical data about Loíza was found in Arroyo (1981) and in the material distributed by the municipality office of Loíza and the office of tourism, such as "Los municipios de Puerto Rico, su historia y su cultura: Loíza" by Departamento de Educación, Estado Libre Asociado de Puerto Rico. Statistical information for different years was found in *Indicadores Económicos y Sociales* by Junta de Planificación, Oficina del Gobernador de Puerto Rico; *Perfil Demográfico y Económico,* by Junta de Planificación, Oficina del Gobernador de Puerto Rico; and the 1990 U.S. census.

2. Gobierno Municipal Loíza, Puerto Rico, 1998, "Presupuesto Modelo Año Económico 1997–98, Ferdín Carrasquillo Ayala Alcade."

3. The adjectives "North American" and "American" are used in this book to refer to the United States.

Chapter 1. "But it isn't just about Loíza": Encountering Loíza

1. An article covering this performance appears in the newspaper *Diálogo* (November-December 1988): 14–15. Another conference and performance at the university was covered in *Diálogo* (January-February 1991): 12.

2. The terms Afro-Caribbean and Afro-Rican are often used interchangeably, although Afro-Caribbean is more inclusive. Afro-Rican is used interchangeably with Afro-Puerto Rican and Afro-Boricua. Boricua is the Taíno Indian native word for a person who is from Borinquen, Boriquén, or Puerto Rico.

3. See also Fahim's (1982) edited work about indigenous anthropology and Spickard, Landres, and McGuire (2002) about the recent reshaping of the ethnography of religion.

4. In a recent visit to the town of San Germán, I noticed an outdoor mural of the triad with a Spanish woman. This woman is not only placed in an equal position with man, but she is also highly elevated because the Spanish element has been the most valued of the triad in the national discourse.

5. The article does not mention other national or foreign rhythms that were also incorporated into the church, such as danza and bolero.

Chapter 2. "If God were black, my friend . . .": Loízan African Identity in the Puerto Rican Experience Here and There

1. A reluctance to acknowledge black beauty inspired Tite Curet Alonso, a Puerto Rican musician and composer in the Afro-Caribbean genre, to write the song entitled "Las caras lindas de mi gente negra," which I use in the title of this section.

2. In Loíza, Indian identity has been connected to Spiritism and Santería. In Las

Cuevas, I heard rumors that Spiritists and Santeros met together or separately at the caves because they were places where they could connect with ancestors or dead people, including Indians who settled there centuries ago; these residents used old Indian bones as a symbol of this connection. According to Stevens-Arroyo (1995: 131), another example of the identification of indigenous traditions with African religion is "El Indio" (the Indian or the "cigar store" Indian), a guiding spirit in Afro-Caribbean religion. The figure, part of the iconography of Santería, is frequently found in *botánicas* or stores selling religious articles.

3. The video was produced by Banco Popular, which was founded in 1893. The bank adopted the populist discourse of the PPD.

4. The festival has been covered by the following local sources: *El Diario,* July 29, 1993, 42–43; August 5, 1993, 2–33; May 13, 1995, 13; *Imagen* (April 1995): 146–50; *El Nuevo Día,* July 22, 1994, 51–58.

5. From 1990 to 2000 the population of Loíza increased by only 3,230; in 2000 the population totaled 32,537.

6. For some media coverage about this controversy see *El Nuevo Día,* April 3, 1996, 24 and March 23, 2002, 26. Members in favor of developing the area of Piñones pointed out the fact that the project was expected to provide many jobs for Loízans in order to respond to the concerns of the people of Piñones, most of whom own *kioskos* to sell Puerto Rican dishes in the area.

7. Information on the accusations came from the following sources: *El Mundo,* January 28, 1973, 2–4; January 16, 1985, 54; *El Nuevo Día,* February 3, 1986, 6.

8. The video *Raíces* celebrates the social and artistic connections of transnational Puerto Ricans. These are exemplified by William Cepeda's compositions and performance in both countries.

9. FLECHAS has collaborated with students from Yale University in various community and cultural projects. In 2001, an exchange program began between graduate students in social work from the University of Connecticut and the UPR under the initiative of Professor Julio Morales from Connecticut. In 2002, the program was supervised by Professor Esterla Barreto from the UPR.

10. *La Voz del Gigante*, Gobierno Municipal Autónomo de Carolina 12, vol. 59 (March 2003): 8.

Chapter 3. The Restructuring of Religious Identity in Puerto Rico in the Last Few Centuries

1. This information was based on various phone interviews with the executive secretary of the Evangelical Council of Puerto Rico, the Reverend Moisés A. Rosa. The Reverend Ángel Luis Gutiérrez indicated that the number of Protestants must reach around 1.5 million (*El Nuevo Día,* March 15, 1998, 7). However, Pérez Torres (1997: 69–70) considers 800,000 the correct number.

2. This experience with persecution and the fact that Spiritism is waning made it difficult to find up-dated information in Las Cuevas.

3. There is relatively scant and inconclusive information about the Taínos.

4. For more about this topic, see Zayas Micheli (1990: 19) and Scarano (1993: 197). In Cuba, evangelizing slaves was not important or was only a secondary matter for the slave owners, including the clergy (Arguelles Mederos and Hodge Limonta 1991: 55). However, providing the best conditions for the expansion of Catholicism was a concern of some Catholic leaders, such as Fray Damián López de Haro (Santiago Otero and García y García 1986: 9, 21, 29).

5. Zayas Micheli (1990: 32) indicates that the popular campaign against witchcraft in Europe, where people were remunerated for catching witches, encouraged weak doctrinal instruction and rampant accusations of witchcraft.

6. In fact, the island at one point in the eighteenth century had 44,883 individuals but only 25 priests (Silva Gotay 1985: 57).

7. In Spain, monasteries were closed and in Puerto Rico ordination was even more controlled (Silva Gotay 1985: 59).

8. In Cuba, Spiritism also adopted various forms in accordance with the socioeconomic conditions of the members (Castañeda Mache 1998: 50).

9. For more specifics about these early Protestant meetings, see Gutiérrez (1997: 70). About Spiritist meetings, see Rodríguez Escudero (1978: 42).

10. The second assembly was celebrated a year later in San Juan (*El Mundo,* July 26, 1945, 10).

11. They are the Presbyterian, the Baptist, the Congregationalist, the Methodist, the Disciples of Christ, the Brethren United in Christ, the United States Christian Church, the Christian and Missionary Alliance, the Evangelical Lutheran Church of North America, and the Episcopalian Church. Today, the CEPR incorporates the Baptist, the United Evangelical, the United Brethren, the Methodist, the Disciples of Christ, and the Presbyterian churches. The following churches or denominations also exist in Puerto Rico (some of which at some point belonged to the CEPR): the Wesleyan, the Mennonite, the Lutheran, the Nazarene, the Christian Missionary Alliance, and the Southern Baptist.

12. The main Pentecostal churches on the island, most of which originated in the 1930s are the Pentecostal Church of God, International Movement; the Assemblies of God, District of Puerto Rico; the Church of God, "Mission Board"; the Defenders of the Faith Movements; the Missionary Church of Christ, International Movement; the Assembly of Christian Churches; the Pentecostal Church of Jesus Christ; the Church of God, Incorporated; the World Missionary Movement; the Fountain of Salvation Missionary Church; the Universal Church of Jesus Christ; and the Church of God of the Prophecy.

13. Regarding Puerto Rico, see Rodríguez Escudero (1978: 44). Regarding Cuba, see Castañeda Mache (1998: 50).

14. Regarding Puerto Rico, see Silva Gotay (1997: 111–15). Regarding Cuba, see Pérez (1992: 105).

15. In 1899, only 8 percent of the school age children attended school (Silva Gotay 1997: 198).

16. I participated in this program and my parents got their first full-time jobs in the program.

17. This information was provided by Sonia J. C. de Guadalupe, who was the president of the Association of Private Schools of Puerto Rico from 1987 to 1989.

18. For other accusations see *El Vocero,* November 29, 1991, 3; April 1, 1991, 1–2.

19. About one of the conferences held in San Juan, see *El Mundo,* July 29, 1964, 4.

20. Rodríguez Escudero (1978) states clearly at the beginning of his writing that the purpose of his book is to distinguish Spiritism from folk religions, and he invites other Spiritist groups to do the same. Similarly, Machuca (1982) begins his book by claiming that his purpose is not to proselytize but "to separate the wheat from the chaff."

21. I also experienced the emphasis on supernatural healing and exorcism in my Baptist high school during my participation in the Movimiento Estudiantil Cristiano (Christian Student Movement or MEC). Allegedly, there were satanic groups in school.

22. In the United States, see Wuthnow (1988: 197) and in Latin America, see Stoll (1990: 80).

23. One of the main reasons for this success is the increased conversion of famous secular singers, including the musician and composer Tite Curet Alonso, whom I mentioned in chapter 2.

24. This information was confirmed by Luis R. Juarbe, for thirty years a performer, arranger, and composer who is mainly popular in the Christian community.

Chapter 4. From State to National to Loízan Catholicism

1. Within the theme of management of power, ritual has been considered a vehicle of forms of authority (Kelly and Kaplan 1990) and a vehicle of protest because of racial discrimination or social injustice (Spencer 1990).

Within the theme of alteration of social reality, while Duranti (1992) argues that Samoan ceremonial greetings, through their fluid style, provide ways for diminishing the significance of social hierarchies. In Bianco's (1996) analysis, songs are a way of channeling by reformulating religiously imposing ideas and social conditions within the framework of the singers' own reality, in which communicating with the divinity is the most inclusive and ultimate goal. This leads us to the theme of transcendence. Imagination is seen by Fernández (1986) as greatly contributing to a sense of wholeness and connection with the transcendence.

2. For written information about the history of the parish downtown see "Parroquia Espíritu Santo y San Patricio" (material distributed by the church).

3. The fact that in 1798 the parish structure named Holy Spirit was described as constructed of cane and *yaguas* with an altar of stone and mortar indicates that the parish was built sometime between 1798 and 1821.

4. In 1765, Loíza included 938 inhabitants: 672 free individuals and 266 slaves. In 1797, the town had a total population of 1,146 (*Los municipios de Puerto Rico, su historia y su cultura: Loíza*, Departamento de Educación, ELA, 19).

5. An attempt to improve Loíza's situation occurred in 1902, when a law was approved to regulate the establishment of the municipal limits and the annexation of Loíza to the municipality of Río Grande. At this time, the parish services were under the charge of Father Ramón Martínez Girod, who came to town every two weeks. In 1905, the law was repealed and Loíza separated from Río Grande.

6. For details about this fight for the separation between Loíza and Canóvanas see Rivera Correa (1974) and Calzada Rivera (1988). See also *El Mundo*, October 11, 1961, 21; October 27, 1961, 27, 25; November 2, 1961, 8; June 28, 1962, 8; June 16, 1967, 1; July 25, 1967, 14; August 25, 1967, 44; April 19, 1969, 6B; July 1, 1969, 3A; September 3, 1969, 20A; February 3, 1970, 15A; July 2, 1970, 5A; July 25, 1970, 5A; September 15, 1970, 1A.

7. For evidence of the difficult situation of Loíza and the favorable position of Canóvanas particularly in the areas of health and education, see the report alluded to in Puerto Rico, Estado Libre Asociado, Junta de Planificación 1968. See also *El Mundo,* January 22, 1965, 18; March 13, 1968, 5; March 29, 1969, 4D; July 26, 1969, 4C; May 13, 1971, 6B; January 12, 1972, 10A; April 29, 1970, 18D.

8. About housing problems see *El Mundo,* September [not legible], 1953, 3, 12; July 2, 1960, 35; March 24, 1962, 5; July 23, 1963, 7; August 13, 1969, 7E. About problems with utilities see *El Mundo*, September 4, 1953, 3; October 11, 1961, 21; July 23, 1963, 7; January 28, 1967, 28. About problems with employment see Puerto Rico, Estado Libre Asociado, Junta de Planificación 1968, 43; *El Mundo,* September 4, 1953, 3; October 22, 1953, 3.

9. For information on closings and the enthusiasm of Loízans for sports, see *El Mundo* October 7, 1945, 11; July 20, 1955; September 29, 1964, 24.

10. These relationships were one of the most challenging areas to investigate. Most of the time people avoided the subject or discussed the issue superficially. However, everybody seemed to agree that relations are improving. In fact, during the celebration of Saint Patrick, Catholics from the parish of Santiago Apóstol had a special presentation and helped with the preparations of the celebration.

Chapter 5. "No more Latin": Toward a More Meaningful Loízan Catholic Experience

1. This information is from *Directorio Católico de Puerto Rico A. D. 1994* (The directory of the Catholic church of Puerto Rico, 1994).

2. I considered the religious affiliations of adult participants only.

3. A Santero in Puerto Rico is also a person who makes wooden saint figures.

4. For the integration of Spiritism and Santería in the United States, see D. Brown (1999).

Chapter 6. We are the King's children!": Creating a New Consciousness in Loíza

1. *La Voz del Gigante*, Gobierno Municipal Autónomo de Carolina 12, vol. 59, (March 2003): 6–7.

2. This and other information about the CFLW come from free literature distributed by the CFLW, interviews with members of the CFLW, and the secular media.

3. *Nueva conciencia: Un periódico positivo* 2, vol. 4 (March 1998): 12–13.

4. In addition to all these issues, the CFLW is currently under investigation because of serious accusations of financial corruption. Rodolfo Font has also been accused of adultery. He is now living in Florida and the church is under the direction of his son.

Chapter 7. "Now there is a church on every corner": Religious, Socioeconomic, and Family Identities in a Small Residential Space

1. Most works have studied one direction: the influence of religion on family size, family structure, family roles and practices, family relationships, and ideals of family (of Puerto Ricans in the United States, see Matos Salgado [1974]; in Puerto Rico, see Dohen [1967] and Ramírez de Arellano and Seipp [1983]).

2. The influence of religion on the family is often examined through the woman's experience or adult gender experience and not by considering the family as a whole or the experience between different family members.

3. In the 1980s, Loízan families were evicted from their homes (*El Mundo*, August 7, 1980, 15A; August 8, 1980, 7A). "Illegal" settlement has been an old problem in many parts of the country. Between the 1960s and 1980s thousands of families settled "illegally" in emptied pieces of land as a reaction to the lack of public residential facilities. The names these communities adopted speak of these residents' attitudes: Villa Cañona (mentioned in chapter 5), Villa Sin Miedo (Village Without Fear), and Villa Justicia (Justice Village). There have been many violent confrontations between police officials and these residents, which the media has covered extensively. During the 1980s, I accompanied a group of students from my Baptist school, led by a group of young adults from the Baptist community, to Villa Sin Miedo. There we shared the gospel and showed our support for their rights to property ownership.

4. The number of houses does not necessary correspond with the correct number.

5. I am using fake last names to protect the identities of the participants.

Chapter 8. "As God is my witness, I don't have anything to hide": Women, Hair, and Spiritual Identity

1. *Nueva conciencia: Un periódico positivo* (December 1999): 13.

2. Synnot (1998: 103) indicates that in the United States sales for hair-care products amounted to 25 percent of the total cosmetics and personal care industry. In 1990, $4.6 billion was spent, with sales increasing 8 percent over the year before and faster than the rate of growth of the U.S. economy.

Chapter 9. "When they call my name from the Book of Life, I will respond happily": Re-identifying Through Witnessing at an Advanced Age

1. Several years ago, Keith (1980: 342–43) observed that the research on old age in anthropology has focused on the status and treatment of the aged at more descriptive and comparative levels. Similarly, interdisciplinary work has focused on difficulties elderly people face from a cross-cultural and historical perspective. Along these lines, a body of more recent literature has established that religion helps the elderly to cope

with difficulties: for example, those associated with racial identity (Chatters and Taylor 1994; Coke and Twaite 1995), ethnic identity, and migration (Maldonado 1995).

2. Amoss (1981) also found prestige to be a significant way for culture to compensate the elderly.

3. Brenneis's (1996: 43) and Roof's (1993: 298) emphasis on the process-like nature of narrative leads us back to the "doings" of ritual discussed in chapter 4. Some of the processes that have been identified in narratives include: confession(Behar 1995), surrender (Bauman (1983), transformation of reality (Roof 1993), conflict resolution (Breinnes 1996), and redemption (Whitehead 1987).

4. Susan Harding (1987:174) argues that coaching the unconverted in the linguistic dimension of conversion is very important in the fundamental Baptist rhetoric.

5. This is the first verse of a hymn that was originally written English by Civilla D. Martin and composed by her husband, Charles H. Gabriel. Its title is "His Eye Is on the Sparrow."

6. In Drew and Water's (1987) study about Puerto Ricans in the United States, family relationships and family interdependency proved to be very important for survival. Low's (1994: 153) study about *nervios* (nerves) in Puerto Ricans in the United States also demonstrates that most generally *nervios* was an embodiment of loss and family disruption while underlying social and economic crises.

7. According to Chatters and Taylor (1994: 205), a by-product of this perspective is to prevent us from assuming religious differences based strictly on racial, ethnic, and social group characteristics. Drew and Waters (1987) want to make the point that in looking at the negative perceptions Puerto Rican high school seniors have of their elder compatriots living in the United States one has to be careful to take this as intrinsically cultural. The study shows that despite the fact that family interdependency was much emphasized, economic exigencies were more strongly affecting the younger populations' perception of elderly people. Therefore, economic pressures cannot be taken as cultural forces.

8. Summers (1999: 51) uses the example of an old Quaker man's tolerance for sound and music and of his view of spoken liturgy as enriching (therefore opposing Quaker worship, which is framed in silence) to demonstrate that the experience of aging allows boundaries of faith to be expanded.

9. I did not hear of any elders from Las Cuevas living in the municipality's nursing home or any other center for the elderly.

Conclusion. "If we do not get involved, then the 'witches' will absolutely overtake us": Recatching Identity for the Future

1. *El Nuevo Día,* March 23, 2002, 52.

2. *Todo* (Carolina) 19, no. 1078 (April 16, 2003): 10.

3. *Todo* (Carolina) 19, no. 1066 (January 22, 2003): 3.

Bibliography

Abu-Lughod, Lila. 1990. "The Romance of Resistance: Tracing Transformations of Power Through Bedouin Women." *American Ethnologist* 17: 41–55.

Agosto Cintrón, Nélida. 1996. *Religión y cambio social en Puerto Rico, 1898–1940*. Río Piedras: Ediciones Huracán.

Alegría, Ricardo E. 1954. *La fiesta de Santiago Apóstol*. San Juan: Instituto de Cultura Puertorriqueña.

Alonso, J. E. 1922. *Fundación Nuevo Loíza*. San Juan: La Correspondencia de Puerto Rico.

Álvarez Vega, Bienvenido. 1996. "El Movimiento Pentecostal." In *El campo religioso dominicano en la década de los 90s: Diversidad y expansión* (3 and 4), 101–50. Santo Domingo: Departamento de Estudios de Sociedad y Religión-Desyr.

Ammerman, Nancy T., and Wade C. Roof. 1995. "Old Patterns, New Trends, Fragile Experiments." In *Work, Family, and Religion in Contemporary Society*, edited by N. T. Ammerman and W. C. Roof, 1–22. New York: Routledge.

Amoss, Pamela T. 1981. "Cultural Centrality and Prestige for the Elderly: The Coast Salish Case." In *Dimensions: Aging, Culture, and Health*, 47–64. New York: Praeger.

Anderson, Benedict. 1991 [1983]. *Imagined Communities: Reflections on the Origin and Spread of Nationalism*. London: Verso.

Angeles, Viviennes, SM. 1998. "Philippine Muslim Women: Tradition and Change." In *Islam, Gender, and Social Change*, edited by Y. Y. Haddad and J. L. Esposito, 209–34. New York: Oxford University Press.

Aparicio, Frances R. 1998. *Listening to Salsa: Gender, Latin Popular Music, and Puerto Rican Cultures*. Hanover, N.H.: University Press of New England.

Arguelles Mederos, Anibal, and Ileana Hodge Limonta. 1991. *Los llamados cultos sincréticos y el espiritismo*. Havana: Editorial Academia.

Arroyo, Vanessa. 1981. "Estudio socio-económico de la esclavitud en Loíza: Siglo xix." Master's thesis, Centro de Estudios Avanzados de Puerto Rico y el Caribe, San Juan.

Babb, Lawrence. 1995. "Introduction." In *Media and Transformation of Religion in South Asia*, edited by L. Babb and S. S. Wadley, 1–18. Philadelphia: University of Pennsylvania Press.

Babín, María T. 1973. *La cultura de Puerto Rico*. San Juan: Instituto de Cultura Puertorriqueña.

Bauman, Richard. 1983. *Let Your Words Be Few: Symbolism of Speaking and Silence Among Seventeenth-Century Quakers*. New York: Cambridge University Press.

Becker, Anne E. 1995. *Body, Self, and Society: The View from Fiji*. Philadelphia: University of Pennsylvania Press.

Behar, Ruth. 1995. "Rage and Redemption: Reading the Life Story of a Mexican Marketing Woman." In *The Dialogic Emergence of Culture*, edited by B. Mannheim and D. Tedlock, 148–78. Urbana and Chicago: University of Illinois Press.

Belanger, Marc. 1992. "Counterinsurgency, Ethnicity, and the Politics of Evangelical Protestantism in Guatemala." In *Competing Gods: Religious Pluralism in Latin America*, 41–73. Providence, R.I.: The Thomas J. Watson Jr. Institute for International Studies.

Berreman, Gerald D. 1997. *Hindus of the Himalayas: Ethnography and Change*. Delhi: Oxford University Press.

Bianchi, Eugene C. 1982. *Aging as a Spiritual Journey*. New York: Crossroad.

Bianco, Barbara A. 1996. "Songs of Mobility in West Pokot." *American Ethnologist* 23: 25–42.

Blanco, Tomás. 1975 [1942]. *El prejuicio racial en Puerto Rico* New York: Arno Press.

Boudewijnse, Barbara. 1998. "A Farewell to Mary?: Women, Pentecostal Faith, and the Roman Catholic Church on Curaçao, N. A." In *More Than Opium: An Anthropological Approach to Latin American and Caribbean Pentecostal Praxis*, edited by B. Boudewijnse, A. Droogers, and F. Kamsteeg, 97–118. Lanham, Md.: Scarecrow Press.

Boyarin, Jonathan. 1994. "Space, Time, and the Politics of Memory." In *Remapping Memory: The Politics of Timespace*, edited by J. Boyarin, 1–38. Minneapolis: University of Minnesota Press.

Bram, Joseph. 1972. "Spirits, Mediums, and Believers in Contemporary Puerto Rico." In *Portrait of a Society: Readings on Puerto Rican Sociology*, edited by E. Fernández Méndez, 371–77. Río Piedras: University of Puerto Rico Press.

Brenneis, Donald. 1996. "Telling Troubles: Narrative, Conflict, and Experience." In *Disorderly Discourse: Narrative, Conflict, and Inequality*, edited by C. L. Briggs, 41–52. New York: Oxford University Press.

Brink, Judy, and Joan Mencher, eds. 1997. *Mixed Blessings: Gender and Religious Fundamentalism Cross Culturally*. New York: Routledge.

Brow, James. 1996. *Demons and Development: The Struggle for Community in a Sri Lankan Village*. Tucson: University of Arizona Press.

Brown, David H. 1999. "Altared Spaces: Afro-Cuban Religions in the Urban Landscape in Cuba and the United States." In *Gods of the City: Religion and the American Urban Landscape*, edited by R. A. Orsi, 155–230. Bloomington: Indiana University Press.

Brown, Michael F. 1984. "The Role of Words in Aguaruna Hunting Magic." *American Ethnologist* 11: 545–58.

Brusco, Elizabeth E. 1995. *The Reformation of Machismo: Evangelical Conversion and Gender in Colombia*. Austin: University of Texas Press.

Bryce-Laporte, R. S. 1970. "Urban Relocation and Family Adaptation in Puerto Rico: A Case Study in Urban Ethnography." In *Peasants in Cities*, edited by W. Mangin-Houghton, 85–97. Boston: Mifflin.

Buitrago, Carlos. 1982. "Anthropology and the Puerto Rican Colonial Context:

Analysis and Projections." In *Indigenous Anthropology in Non-Western Countries*, edited by H. Fahim, 97–111. Proceedings of a Burg Wartensteing Symposium. Durham, N.C.: Carolina Academic Press.

Burdick, John. 1998. *Blessed Anastacia: Women, Race, and Popular Christianity in Brazil.* New York: Routledge.

Butler, Judith. 1993. *Bodies That Matter: On the Discursive Limits of Sex.* New York and London: Routledge.

Caldwell, Sarah. 1999. *Oh Terrifying Mother: Sexuality, Violence, and Worship of the Goddess Kali in Kerala.* New Delhi: Oxford University Press.

Calzada Rivera, Joseline. 1988. *Análisis histórico de los procesos político-administrativos, sociales y económicos que propiciaron la separación de los pueblos de Canóvanas y Loíza.* Master's thesis, University of Puerto Rico, Río Piedras.

Camayd-Freixas, Erik. 1997. "The Cult of the Goddess Mita on the Eve of a New Millennium: A Socio-Anthropological Look at a Caribbean Urban Religion." *Latin American Issues: The Caribbean(s) Redefined: A Monograph Series on Contemporary Latin American and Caribbean Affairs.* Vol 13: 1–14.

Castañeda Mache, Yalexy. 1998. "El espiritismo cubano." In *Panorama de la religión en Cuba*, 49–56. Havana: Editora Política.

Castro Flores, Margarita. 2001. "Religions of African Origin in Cuba: A Gender Perspective." In *Nation Dance: Religion, Identity, and Cultural Difference in the Caribbean*, edited by P. Taylor, 54–64. Bloomington and Indianapolis: Indiana University Press.

Chatters, Linda M., and Joseph Taylor. 1994. "Religious Involvement Among Older African-Americans." In *Religion in Aging and Health: Theoretical Foundations and Methodological Frontiers*, edited by J. S. Levin, 196–230. Thousand Oaks, Calif.: Sage Publications.

Chidester, David, and Edward T. Linenthal. 1995. "Introduction." In *American Sacred Space*, 1–42. Bloomington: Indiana University Press.

Clark, Mary A. 1998. "Santería." In *Sects, Cults, and Spiritual Communities: A Sociological Analysis*, edited by W. W. Zellner and M. Petrowsky, 117–30. Westport, Conn.: Praeger.

Clifford, James. 1983. "On Ethnographic Authority." *Representations* 2 (spring 1983): 132–43.

Cohen, Anthony P. 1985. "Chapter 1: Introduction." In *The Symbolic Construction of Community*. London and New York: Routledge.

Coke, Marguerite M., and James A. Twaite. 1995. *The Black Elderly: Satisfaction and Quality of Later Life.* New York: Haworth Press.

Collier, Jane F. 1986. "From Mary to Modern Woman: The Material Basis of Marianism and Its Transformation in a Spanish Village." *American Ethnologist* 13: 100–107.

Collier, Jane F., and Sylvia J. Yanagisako. 1989. "Theory in Anthropology Since Feminist Practice." *Critique of Anthropology* 9: 27–37.

Comaroff, Jean, and John Comaroff. 1993. "Introduction." In *Modernity and Its Mal-*

contents: Ritual and Power in Postcolonial Africa. Chicago: University of Chicago Press.

Connolly, William E. 1991. *Identity, Difference: Democratic Negotiations of Political Paradox.* Ithaca, N.Y.: Cornell University Press.

Cook, Scott. 1965. "The Prophets: A Revitalistic Folk Religious Movement in Puerto Rico." *Caribbean Studies* 4: 20–35.

Cornell, Durcilla. 1993. *Transformations: Recollective Imagination and Sexual Difference.* New York and London: Routledge.

Craig, Susan, ed. 1982. "Sociological Theorizing in the English-Speaking Caribbean: A Review." In *Contemporary Caribbean: A Sociological Reader* 2: 143–80. Maracas: College Press.

Crespo, Edna. 1974. *La estructura agraria en Loíza en el siglo xix.* Bachelor's thesis, Departamento de Estudios Generales, Universidad de Puerto Rico, Río Piedras.

Cruz Monclova, Lidio. 1952. *Historia de Puerto Rico, siglo xix.* Vol. 1. Río Piedras: Editorial Universitaria, Universidad de Puerto Rico. 800–1868.

Csordas, Thomas J. 1994a. "Introduction." In *Embodiment and Experience: The Existential Ground of Culture and Self.* New York: Cambridge University Press.

———. 1994b. *The Sacred Self: A Cultural Phenomenology of Charismatic Healing.* Berkeley: University of California Press.

Cucchiari, Salvatore. 1990. "Between Shame and Sanctification: Patriarchy and Its Transformation in Sicilian Pentecostalism." *American Ethnologist* 17: 687–707.

Davidman, Lynn. 2002. "Truth, Subjectivity, and Ethnographic Research." In *Personal Knowledge and Beyond: Reshaping the Ethnography of Religion,* edited by J. V. Spickard, J. S. Landres, and M. B. McGuire, 17–26. New York and London: New York University Press.

Davies, Douglas. 1994. "Christianity." In *Sacred Place,* edited by J. Holm with J. Bowker, 33–61. London and New York: Pinter Publishers.

Dávila, Arlene M. 1997. *Sponsored Identities: Cultural Politics in Puerto Rico.* Philadelphia: Temple University Press.

———. 2001. *Latinos, Inc.: The Marketing and Making of a People.* Berkeley: University of California Press.

Deiros, Pablo. 1997. *Protestantismo en América Latina: Ayer, hoy, y mañana.* Nashville: Editorial Caribe.

Delaney, Carol. 1995. "Untangling the Meanings of Hair in Turkish Society." In *Off with Her Head!: The Denial of Women's Identity in Myth, Religion, and Culture,* edited by H. Eilberg-Schwartz and W. Doniger, 53–75. Berkeley and Los Angeles: University of California Press.

De Lomnitz, Larissa A. 1975. *Como sobreviven los marginados.* Mexico, D.F.: Siglo Veintiuno Editores.

Derby, Lauren. 1998. "Gringo Chickens with Worms: Food and Nationalism in the Dominican Republic." In *Close Encounters of Empire: Writing the Cultural History of the U.S.-Latin American Relations,* edited by G. M. Joseph, C. C. Legrand, and R. Salvatore, 451–93. Durham, N.C. and London: Duke University Press.

Díaz Quiñones, Arcadio. 1998. "Una España pequeña y remota." In *Vírgenes, magos, y escapularios: Imaginería, etnicidad, y religiosidad popular en Puerto Rico*, edited by A. G. Quintero Rivera, 123–30. San Juan: Centro de Investigaciones Sociales, Universidad de Puerto Rico; Centro de Investigaciones Académicas, Universidad del Sagrado Corazón; Fundación Puertorriqueña de las Humanidades.

Díaz-Stevens, Ana M. 1993a. "La misa jíbara como campo de batalla socio-política en Puerto Rico." *Revista de Ciencias Sociales* 3: 139–62.

———. 1993b. *Oxcart Catholicism on Fifth Avenue: The Impact of the Puerto Rican Migration upon the Archdiocese of New York*. Notre Dame, Ill.: University of Notre Dame Press.

Díaz Soler, Luis M. 1965. *Historia de la esclavitud negra en Puerto Rico*. 2d ed. Río Piedras: Editorial Universitaria, Universidad de Puerto Rico.

Dohen, Dorothy. 1967. *Two Studies of Puerto Rico: The Religion Data and the Background of Consensual Union*. Cuernavaca: Centro Cultural de Documentación.

Drew, Benjamin, and Judith Waters. 1987. "Aging and Work: Perceptions of Low-Income Puerto Rican Adults and High School Seniors." In *Aging and Cultural Diversity: New Directions and Annotated Bibliography*, edited by H. Strange, M. Teitelbaum, and contributors, 131–52. South Hadley, Mass.: Bergin and Garvey Publishers.

Duany, Jorge. 1998. "La religiosidad popular en Puerto Rico: Reseña de la literatura desde la perspectiva antropológica." In *Vírgenes, magos, y escapularios: Imaginería, etnicidad, y religiosidad popular en Puerto Rico*, edited by A. G. Quintero Rivera, 163–213. San Juan: Centro de Investigaciones Sociales, Universidad de Puerto Rico; Centro de Investigaciones Académicas, Universidad del Sagrado Corazón; Fundación Puertorriqueña de las Humanidades.

———. 2002. *Puerto Rican Nation on the Move: Identities on the Island and in the United States*. Chapel Hill and London: University of North Carolina Press.

Duntley, Madeline. 1999. "Heritage, Ritual, and Translation: Seattle's Japanese Presbyterian Church." In *Gods of the City: Religion and the American Urban Landscape*, edited by R. A. Orsi, 289–99. Bloomington: Indiana University Press.

Duranti, Alessandro. 1992. "Language and Bodies in Social Space: Samoan Ceremonial Greetings." *American Ethnologist* 94: 657–91.

Eilberg-Schwartz, Howard. 1996. "God's Phallus and the Dilemmas of Masculinity." In *Redeeming Men: Religion and Masculinities*, edited by S. B. Boyd, W. M. Longwood, and M. W. Muesse, 36–47. Louisville, Ky.: Westminster John Knox Press.

Fabian, Johannes. 1990. "Presence and Representation: The Other and Anthropological Writing." *Critical Inquiry* 16: 753–72.

Fahim, Hussein, ed. 1982. *Indigenous Anthropology in Non-western Countries*. Proceedings of a Burg Wartenstein Symposium. Durham, N.C.: Carolina Academic Press.

Feeley-Harnik, Gillian. 1995. "Religion and Food: An Anthropological Perspective." *Journal of the American Academy of Religion* 63: 565–82.

Fernández, James. 1986. "The Argument of Images and the Experience of Returning to the Whole." In *The Anthropology of Experience*, edited by V. W. Turner and E. M. Bruner, 159–87. Urbana: University of Illinois Press.

Firth, Raymond. 1996. "Religious Belief and Personal Adjustment." In *Religion: A Humanist Interpretation*, 14–47. London and New York: Routledge.

Flores, Carlos. 2001. "Race Discrimination within the Latino Community." *Diálogo*, no. 5 (winter/spring).

Flores, Juan. 2000. *From Bomba to Hip-Hop: Puerto Rican Culture and Latino Identity*. New York: Columbia University Press.

Freston, Paul. 1993. "Brother Votes for Brother: The New Politics of Protestantism in Brazil." In *Rethinking Protestantism in Latin America*, edited by V. Garrad-Burnett and D. Stoll, 66–110. Philadelphia: Temple University Press.

García Leduc, José M. 1994. "Clero católico y esclavitud en Puerto Rico (Siglo XIX)." *Revista/Review Interamericana* 24: 79–103.

Giddens, Anthony. 1991. *Modernity and Self-Identity: Self and Society in the Late Modern Age*. Stanford, Calif.: Stanford University Press.

Giusti Cordero, Juan A. 1994. "Labor, Ecology, and History in a Caribbean Sugar Plantation Region: Piñones (Loíza), Puerto Rico 1770–1950." Ph. D. diss., State University of New York, Binghamton.

Glasser, Ruth. 1997. *Aquí me quedo: Puerto Ricans in Connecticut*. Middletown: Connecticut Humanities Council.

Gobierno Municipal Loíza, Puerto Rico. 1998. "Presupuesto Modelo Año Económico 1997–98, Ferdín Carrasquillo Ayala Alcade."

Godreau-Santiago, Isar Pilar. 1999. "Missing the Mix: San Antón and the Racial Dyamics of 'Nationalism'" in Puerto Rico." Ph.D. diss, University of California, Santa Cruz.

González, José L. 1993. *Puerto Rico: The Four Storeyed Country*. New York: Markus Wiener Publishing.

González, Lydia M., ed. 1993. *La tercera raíz: Precensia Africana en Puerto Rico*. San Juan: Centro de Estudios de la Realidad Puertoni-quena.

González-Wippler, Migene. 1995. "Santería: Its Dynamics and Multiple Roots." In *Enigmatic Powers: Syncretism with African and Indigenous People's Religions Among Latinos*, edited by A. M. Stevens-Arroyo and A. I. Pérez y Mena, 99–111. Program for the Analysis of Religion Among Latinos. Vol. 3. Decatur, Ga.: AETH Books.

Goodman, Jenny. 1999. "Harvesting a Lifetime." In *Spirituality and Ageing*, edited by A. Jewell, 65–70. London; Philadelphia: Jessica Kingsley Publishers.

Griffith, David, Manuel Valdés Pizzini, and Jeffrey C. Johnson. 1992. "Injury and Therapy: Semi-Proletarianization in Puerto Rico's Artisinal Fisheries." *American Ethnologist* 19: 53–74.

Guerra, Lillian. 1998. *Popular Expression and National Identity in Puerto Rico: The Struggle for Self, Community, and Nation*. Gainesville: University Press of Florida.

Gutiérrez, Ángel L. 1997. *Evangélicos en Puerto Rico en la época española*. Río Piedras: Puerto Rico Evangélico, Inc., Seminario Evangélico de Puerto Rico, and Editorial Chari.

Hamilton, Nora, and Norma Stoltz Chinchilla. 2001. *Seeking Community in a Global City: Guatemalans and Salvadorans in Los Angeles*. Philadelphia: Temple University Press.

Harding, Rachel E. 2000. *A Refuge in Thunder: Candomblé and Alternative Spaces of Blackness*. Bloomington and Indianapolis: Indiana University Press.

Harding, Susan. 1987. "Convicted by the Holy Spirit: The Rhetoric of Fundamental Baptist Conversion." *American Ethnologist* 14: 167–81.

Harrison, Faye H. 1988. "Women in Jamaica's Urban Informal Economy: Insights from a Kingston Slum." *New West Indian Guide* 62: 103–28.

Harrison, Simon J. 1985. "Ritual Hierarchy and Secular Equality in a Sepik River Village." *American Ethnologist* 14: 413–26.

Helms, Mary W. 1977. "Negro or Indian?: The Changing Identity of a Frontier Population." In *Old Roots in New Lands: Historical and Anthropological Perspectives on Black Experiences in the Americas*, edited by A. M. Pescadillo, 157–72. Westport, Conn.: Greenwood Press.

Horowitz, Michael M. 1967. *Morne-Paysan: Peasant Village in Martinique*. New York: Holt, Rinehart and Winston.

Hurbon, Laennec. 2001. "Current Evolution of Relations between Religion and Politics in Haiti." In *Nation Dance: Religion, Identity, and Cultural Difference in the Caribbean*, edited by P. Taylor, 118–28. Bloomington and Indianapolis: Indiana University Press.

Ingersoll, Julie. 2002. "Against Univocality: Re-reading Ethnographies of Conservative Protestant Women." In *Personal Knowledge and Beyond: Reshaping the Ethnography of Religion*, edited by J. V. Spickard, J. S. Landres, and M. B. McGuire, 162–74. New York and London: New York University Press.

Jensen, Tina G. 1999. "Discourses on Afro-Brazilian Religion: From De-Africanization to Re-Africanization." In *Latin American Religion in Motion*, edited by C. Smith and J. Prokopy, 275–94. New York: Routledge.

Johnson, Kevin R. 1998. "Melting Pot or Ring of Fire?" In *The Latino/a Condition*, edited by R. Delgado and J. Stefancic, 427–30. New York: New York University Press.

Johnstone, Patrick, and Jason Mandryk. 2001. *Operation World: Twenty-first Century Edition*. Minneapolis: Bethany House.

Kamsteeg, Frans. 1999. "Pentecostalism and Political Awakening in Pinochet's Chile and Beyond." In *Latin American Religion in Motion*, edited by J. Prokopy and C. Smith, 187–204. New York: Routledge.

Kanellos, Nicolás. 1993. *The Hispanic American Almanac: A Reference Work on Hispanics in the United States*. Detroit: Gale Research.

Keith, Jennie. 1980. "The Best Is Yet to Be: Toward an Anthropology of Age." *Annual Review of Anthropology* 9: 339–64.

Kelly, John D., and Martha Kaplan. 1990. "History, Structure, and Ritual." *Annual Review of Anthropology* 19: 119–50.

Kinsbruner, Jay. 1996. *Not of Pure Blood: The Free People of Color and Racial Prejudice in Nineteenth-Century Puerto Rico*. Durham, N.C. and London: Duke University Press.

Kipp, Rita S. 1993. *Dissociated Identities: Ethnicity, Religion, and Class in an Indonesian Society*. Ann Arbor: University of Michigan Press.

Knight, Franklin W. 1990. *The Caribbean: The Genesis of a Fragmented Nationalism*. New York: Oxford University Press.

Koss, Joan D. 1970. "Terapeutica de sistema de una secta en Puerto Rico." *Revista de Ciencias Sociales* 14: 259–78.

———. 1976. "Religion and Science Divinely Related: A Case History of Spiritism in Puerto Rico." *Caribbean Studies* 16: 22–43.

Kottak, Conrad P. 1991. "Television's Impact on Values and Local Life in Brazil." *Journal of Communication* 41: 70–87.

———. 1992. *Assault on Paradise: Social Change in a Brazilian Village*. 2d ed. New York: McGraw-Hill.

LaRuffa, Anthony. 1966. *San Cipriano: Life in a Puerto Rican Community*. New York: Gordon and Breach Science Publishers.

Lawson, E. Thomas, and Robert N. McCauley. 1993. *Rethinking Religion: Connecting Cognition and Culture*. New York: Cambridge University Press.

Levine, Daniel H. 1992. *Popular Voices in Latin American Catholicism*. Princeton, N.J.: Princeton University Press.

Levi-Strauss, Claude. 1963. "The Structural Study of Myth." In *Structural Anthropology*, 206–31. New York: Basic Books.

Lincoln, C. Eric. 1974. "Black Preachers, Black Preaching, and Black Theology: The Genius of Black Spiritual Leadership." In *The Black Experience in Religion*, edited by C. E. Lincoln, 65–69. Garden City, N.Y.: Anchor Press.

López Sierra, Héctor E. 1994. "Un acercamiento desde la sociología de la religión a la relación de raza, política, y religión en Puerto Rico del 1920 al 1930." *Revista/Review Interamericana* 24: 68–78.

Lorentzen, Lois A. 2001. "Who Is an Indian?: Religion, Globalization, and Chiapas." In *Religions/Globalizations: Theories and Cases*, edited by D. N. Hopkins, L. A. Lorentzen, E. Mendieta, and D. Batstone, 84–104. Durham, N.C. and London: Duke University Press.

Low, Setha M. 1994. "Embodied Metaphors: Nerves as Lived Experience." In *Embodiment and Experience: The Existential Ground of Culture and Self*, edited by T. J. Csordas, 139–62. New York: Cambridge University Press.

Machuca, Julio. 1982. *¿Qué es el espiritismo?* Santurce, P.R.: Casa de las Almas.

Maduro, Otto A. 1995. Directions for a Reassessment of Latina/o Religion. In *Enigmatic Powers: Syncretism with African and Indigenous People's Religions Among Latinos*, edited by A. M. Stevens-Arroyo and A. I. Pérez y Mena, 47–68. Program for the Analysis of Religion Among Latinos. Vol. 3. Decatur, Ga.: AETH Books.

Maldonado, David. 1995. "Religion and Persons of Color." In *Aging, Spirituality, and Religion: A Handbook*, edited by M. A. Kimble, S. A. McFadden, J. W. Ellor, and J. J. Seeber, 119–28. Minneapolis: Fortress Press.

Mannheim, Bruce. 1998. "Hacia una mitografía andina." In *Tradición oral Andina y Amazónica: Métodos de análisis e interpretación de textos*, edited by J. C. Godenzzi, 57–96. Cusco: Centro de Estudios Regionales Andinos Bartolomé de las Casas.

Mannheim, Bruce, and Dennis Tedlock. 1995. Introduction to *The Dialogic Emergence of Culture*. Urbana and Chicago: University of Illinois Press.

Mannheim, Bruce, and Krista Van Vleet. 1998. "The Dialogics of Southern Quechua Narrative." *American Anthropologist* 100: 326–46.

Mariz, Cecilia L., and Clara Mafra. 1999. "Family and Reproduction Among Protestants in Rio de Janeiro." In *Latin American Religion in Motion*, edited by J. Prokopy and C. Smith, 205–20. New York: Routledge.

Marrero, María T. 1997. "Historical and Literary Santería: Unveiling Gender and Identity in U.S. Cuban Literature." In *Tropicalizations: Transcultural Representations of Latinidad*, edited by F. R. Aparicio and S. Chávez-Silverman, 139–59. Hanover, N.H.: Dartmouth College Press, University Press of New England.

Matos Salgado, Ramona. 1974. "The Role of the Puerto Rican Spiritist in Helping Puerto Rico with Problems of Family Relations." Ph. D. diss., Columbia University.

Mauleon Benítez, Carmen C. 1974. *El español de Loíza Aldea*. Madrid: Ediciones Partenón.

McCarthy-Brown, Karen. 1991. *Mama Lola: A Vodou Priestess in Brooklyn*. Berkeley: University of California Press.

McGuire, Meredith. 2002. "New-Old Directions in the Social Scientific Study of Religion: Ethnography, Phenomenology, and the Human Body." In *Personal Knowledge and Beyond: Reshaping the Ethnography of Religion*, edited by J. V. Spickard, J. S. Landres, and M. B. McGuire, 195–211. New York and London: New York University Press.

Meyer, Birgit. 1994. "Beyond Syncretism: Translation and Diabolization in the Appropriation of Protestantism in Africa." In *Syncretism/Anti-Syncretism: The Politics of Religious Synthesis*, edited by C. Stewart and R. Shaw, 45–68. New York and London: Routledge.

Míguez, Daniel. 1999. "Exploring the Argentinian Case: Religious Motives in the Growth of Latin American Pentecostalism." In *Latin American Religion in Motion*, edited by J. Prokopy and C. Smith, 221–34. New York: Routledge.

Mintz, Sidney. 1974. *Caribbean Transformations*. New York: Columbia University Press.

———. 1978. "The Role of Puerto Rico in Modern Social Science." *Revista/Review Interamericana* 8, no. 1 (spring): 5–16.

———. 1988. *Taso, trabajador de la caña*. Río Piedras: Ediciones Huracán.

Moore, Robert J. 1999. "Colonial Images of Blacks and Indians in Nineteenth-Century Guyana." In *The Colonial Caribbean in Transition: Essays on Postemancipation Social and Cultural History*, edited by B. Brereton and K. A. Yelvington, 126–58. Barbados: Press University of West Indies.

Morris, Nancy. 1995. *Puerto Rico: Culture, Politics, and Identity.* Westport, Conn.: Praeger.

Muesse, Mark W. 1996. "Religious Machismo: Masculinity and Fundamentalism." In *Redeeming Men: Religion and Masculinities,* edited by S. B. Boyd, W. M. Longwood, and M. W. Muesse, 89–102. Louisville, Ky.: Westminster John Knox Press.

Muñoz Vázquez, Marya. 1986. "The Effects of Role Expectations on the Marital Status of Urban Puerto Rican Women." In *The Puerto Rican Woman: Perspectives on Culture, History, and Society,* edited by E. Acosta-Belén, 110–19. New York: Praeger.

Nasr, Seyyed H. 1990. "The Islamic View of Christianity." In *Christianity Through Non-Christian Eyes,* edited by P. J. Griffiths, 126–34. Maryknoll, N.Y.: Orbis Books.

Negrón-Muntaner, Frances. 2002. "Barbie's Hair: Selling Out Puerto Rican Identity in the Global Market." In *Latino/a Popular Culture,* edited by M. Habell-Pallán and M. Romero, 38–60. New York and London: New York University Press.

Nuñez Molina, Mario. 1990. "Preventive and Therapeutic Aspects of Puerto Rican Espiritismo." *Homines* 13: 267–76.

——. 1994. "Toward an Experiential Approach for Researching Religious Experiences." *Revista/Review Interamericana* 24: 52–67.

Obeyesekere, Gananath. 1981. *Medusa's Hair: An Essay on Personal Symbols and Religious Experience.* Chicago: University of Chicago Press.

Olien, Michael D. 1980. "Black and Part-Black Populations in Colonial Costa Rica: Ethnohistorical Resources and Problems." *Ethnohistory* 27: 267–76.

Olivelle, Patrick. 1998. "Hair in Society: Social Significance of Hair in South Asian Traditions." In *Hair: Its Power and Meaning in Asian Cultures,* edited by A. Heiltebeitel and B. D. Miller, 11–50. Albany: State University of New York Press.

O'Neal, Gwendolyn S. 1999. "The African American Church, Its Sacred Cosmos, and Dress." In *Religion, Dress, and the Body,* edited by L. B. Arthur, 117–34. New York: Berg.

Ortner, Sherry B. 2002. "On Key Symbols." In *A Reader in the Anthropology of Religion,* edited by M. Lambek, 158–67. Malden, Mass.: Blackwell Publishers.

Pérez, Louis A., Jr. 1992. "Protestant Missionaries in Cuba: Archival Records, Manuscript Collections, and Research Prospects." *Latin American Research Review* 27: 105–20.

——. 1994. "Between Baseball and Bullfighting: The Quest for Nationality in Cuba, 1868–1898." *The Journal of American History* (September 1994): 493–517.

Pérez Torres, Rubén. 1997. *Poder desde lo alto: Historia y contribuciones del pentecostalismo en Puerto Rico y en los Estados Unidos Hispanos.* Caguas, P.R.: Editorial MIREC.

Pérez y Mena, Andrés I. 1995. "Puerto Rican Spiritism as a Transfeature of Afro-Latin Religion." In *Enigmatic Powers: Syncretism with African and Indigenous People's Religions Among Latinos,* edited by A. M. Stevens-Arroyo and A. I. Pérez y Mena,

137–55. Program for the Analysis of Religion Among Latinos. Vol. 3. Decatur, Ga.: AETH Books.

Picó, Fernando. 1998. "El catolicismo popular en el Puerto Rico del siglo 19." In *Vírgenes, magos, y escapularios: Imaginería, etnicidad, y religiosidad popular en Puerto Rico,* edited by Á. G. Quintero Rivera, 151–62. San Juan: Centro de Investigaciones Sociales, Universidad de Puerto Rico; Centro de Investigaciones Académicas, Universidad del Sagrado Corazón; Fundación Puertorriqueña de las Humanidades.

Pitts, Walter. 1989. "If You Caint Get the Boat, Take a Log: Cultural Reinterpretation in the Afro-Baptist Ritual." *American Ethnologist* 16: 279–93.

Portes, Alejandro, José Itzigsohn, and Carlos Dore-Cabral. 1994. "Urbanization in the Caribbean Basin: Social Change During the Years of the Crisis." *Latin American Research Review* 29: 3–38.

Privett, Stephen A., S.J. 1988. *The U.S. Catholic Church and Its Hispanic Members: The Pastoral Vision of Archbishop Robert E. Lucey.* San Antonio, Tex.: Trinity University Press.

Puerto Rico, Estado Libre Asociado, Junta de Planificación. 1968. "Informe del estudio para determinar la viabilidad de crear el municipio de Canóvanas, hoy Loíza y restaurar al mismo tiempo el municipio de Loíza, hoy Aldea."

Quinnan, Edward J. 1994. "Life Narrative and Spiritual Journey of Elderly Male Religious." In *Aging and the Religious Dimension,* edited by L. E. Thomas and S. A. Eisenhandler, 147–66. Westport, Conn.: Auburn House.

Quintero Rivera, Ángel G. 1998. "Vueltita, con mantilla, al primer piso/Sociología de los santos." In *Vírgenes, magos, y escapularios: Imaginería, etnicidad, y religiosidad popular en Puerto Rico,* edited by Á. G. Quintero Rivera, 9–100. San Juan: Centro de Investigaciones Sociales, Universidad de Puerto Rico; Centro de Investigaciones Académicas, Universidad del Sagrado Corazón; Fundación Puertorriqueña de las Humanidades.

Ramírez de Arellano, Annette, and Conrad Seipp. 1983. *Colonialism, Catholicism, and Contraception: A History of Birth Control in Puerto Rico.* Chapel Hill: University of North Carolina Press.

Ramos Torres, David. 1992. *Historia de la Iglesia de Dios Pentecostal, M. I.: Una iglesia ungida para hacer misión.* Río Piedras: Editorial Pentecostal.

Rappaport, Roy A. 1999. *Ritual and Religion in the Making of Humanity.* Cambridge: Cambridge University Press.

Rismiller, Arthur P. 1964. *Older Members in the Congregation.* Minneapolis: Augsburg Publishing House.

Rivera Correa, Ricardo R. 1974. *Historia de dos poblados.* Río Piedras: Tipografía Porvenir.

Rodríguez Escudero, Nestor A. 1978. *Historia del espiritismo en Puerto Rico.* Puerto Rico: Nestor A. Rodríguez Escudero.

Rodríguez Toulis, Nicole. 1997. *Believing Identity: Pentecostalism and the Mediation of Jamaican Ethnicity and Gender in England.* Oxford and New York: Berg.

Romberg, Raquel. 2003. *Witchcraft and Welfare: Spiritual Capital and the Business of Magic in Modern Puerto Rico*. Austin: University of Texas Press.

Roof, Wade C. 1993. "Religion and Narrative." *Review of Religious Research* 34: 297–310.

Rosaldo, Michelle. 1982. "The Things We Do with Words: Ilongot Speech Acts and Speech Act Theory in Philosophy." *Language in Society* 2: 203–37.

Rose, Susan D. and Steve Brouwer. 1990. "The Export of Fundamentalist Americanism: U.S. Evangelical Education in Guatemala." *Latin American Perspectives* 17: 42–56.

Rouse, Irving. 1992. *The Taínos: Rise and Decline of the People Who Greeted Columbus*. New Haven, Conn.: Yale University Press.

Rowe, Maureen. 1998. "Gender and Family Relations in Rastafari: A Personal Perspective." In *Chanting Down Babylon: The Rastafari Reader*, edited by N. S. Murrell, W. D. Spencer, and A. A. McFarlane, 72–88. Philadelphia: Temple University Press.

Rubenstein, Hymie. 1987. *Coping with Poverty: Adaptive Strategies in a Caribbean Village*. Boulder, Colo.: Westview Press.

Saavedra de Roca, Angelina. 1969. "El espiritismo como una religión: Observaciones sociológicas de un grupo religioso en Puerto Rico." In *Primer ciclo de conferencias públicas sobre temas de investigación social*, 106–29. Río Piedras: Centro de Investigaciones Sociales, Universidad de Puerto Rico.

Safa, Helen I. 1986. "Economic Autonomy and Sexual Equality in Caribbean Society." *Social and Economic Studies* 35: 1–22.

Said, Edward. 1989. "Representing the Colonized: Anthropology's Interlocutors." *Critical Inquiry* 15: 205–25.

———. 1978. *Orientalism*. New York: Vintage.

Sánchez de León, Carmen. 1994. "Apuntes para una investigación sobre el papel de las mujeres en la Iglesia Protestante puertorriqueña." *Revista/Review Interamericana* 24: 43–51.

Santiago Otero, Horacio, and Antonio García y García, eds. 1986. *Sínodo de San Juan de Puerto Rico de 1645* (by Damián López de Haro). Madrid: Centro de Estudios de CSIC.

Santos Febres, Mayra. 1998. "La raza, la risa, y la rabia." *El Nuevo Día,* Sunday magazine, November 8.

Scarano, Francisco A. 1993. *Puerto Rico: Cinco siglos de historia*. Santafe de Bogotá, Colombia: McGraw-Hill Interamericana.

Scherer, Frank F. 2001. "Sanfancón: Orientalism, Self-Orientalization, and 'Chinese Religion' in Cuba." In *Nation Dance: Religion, Identity, and Cultural Difference in the Caribbean,* ed. P. Taylor, 153–70. Bloomington and Indianapolis: Indiana University Press.

Schilder, Kees. 1994. *Quest for Self-esteem: State, Islam, and Mundang Ethnicity*. Aldershot: Avebury.

Schmidt, Bettina E. 1996. "El encuentro de los muertos orichas: Sincretismo en

Puerto Rico." In *Estudios sobre el sincretismo en América Central y en los Andes*, edited by B. Schmelz and N. R. Crumrine, 33–50. Germany: Bonner Amerikanistische Studien.

Schmink, Marianne. 1986. "Women and Urban Industrial Development in Brazil." In *Women and Change in Latin America*, edited by J. C. Nash and H. I. Safa, 136–64. South Hadley, Mass.: Bergin and Garvey Publishers.

Scott, James C. 1985. *Weapons of the Weak: Everyday Forms of Peasant Resistance*. New Haven, Conn.: Yale University Press.

Sered, Susan S. 1992. *Women as Ritual Experts: The Religious Lives of Elderly Jewish Women in Jerusalem*. New York: Oxford University Press.

———. 1994. *Priestess Mother Sacred Sister: Religions Dominated by Women*. New York: Oxford University Press.

Silva Gotay, Samuel. 1985. "Social History of the Churches in Puerto Rico." In *Towards a History of the Church in the Third World*, edited by L. Vischer, 53–80. Bern: Evangeliesche Arbeistelle Oekumene Schweiz.

———. 1997. *Protestantismo y política en Puerto Rico, 1898–1930*. Río Piedras: Editorial de la Universidad de Puerto Rico.

Simmons, Leo W. 1970 [1945]. *The Role of the Aged in Primitive Society*. Hamdon, Conn.: Archon Books.

Sobo, Elisa J. 1993. *One Blood: The Jamaican Body*. Albany: State University of New York Press.

Solivan, Samuel. 1998. "Interreligious Dialogue: A Hispanic American Pentecostal Perspective." In *Grounds for Understanding: Ecumenical Resources for Responses to Religious Pluralism*, edited by S. M. Heim, 37–45. Grand Rapids: Eerdmans Publishing.

Soto Torres, Edgardo. 2000. "La Bomba: El ritmo que aún negamos." *Diálogo*, San Juan (February): 37.

Spencer, Jon M. 1990. *Protest and Praise: Sacred Music of Black Religion*. Minneapolis: Fortress Press.

Spickard, James V. 2002. "On the Epistemology of Post-Colonial Ethnography." In *Personal Knowledge and Beyond: Reshaping the Ethnography of Religion*, edited J. V. Spickard, J. S. Landres, and M. B. McGuire, 237–52. New York and London: New York University Press.

Spickard, James V., and J. Shawn Landres. 2002. "Introduction: Whither Ethnography? Transforming the Social-Scientific Study of Religion." In *Personal Knowledge and Beyond: Reshaping the Ethnography of Religion*, edited by J. V. Spickard, J. S. Landres, and M. B. McGuire, 1–16. New York and London: New York University Press.

Spickard, James V., J. S. Landres, and M. B. McGuire, eds. 2002. *Personal Knowledge and Beyond: Reshaping the Ethnography of Religion*. New York and London: New York University Press.

Steigenga, Timothy J., and David A. Smilde. 1999. "Wrapped in the Holy Shawl: The Strange Case of Conservative Christians and Gender Equality in Latin America." In *Latin American Religion in Motion*, edited by J. Prokopy and C. Smith, 173–86. New York: Routledge.

Stevens, Cecil E. 1902. *The Village of Loíza in 1902*. San Juan: Puerto Rico Gospel Press.

Stevens-Arroyo, Anthony. 1995. "The Persistence of Religious Cosmovision in an Alien World." In *Enigmatic Powers: Syncretism with African and Indigenous People's Religions Among Latinos*, edited by A. M. Stevens-Arroyo and A. I. Pérez y Mena, 113–35. Program for the Analysis of Religion Among Latinos. Vol. 3. Decatur, Ga.: AETH Books.

Stevens-Arroyo, Anthony, and Ana M. Díaz-Stevens, eds. 1994. *An Enduring Flame: Studies on Latino Popular Religiosity*. New York: Bildner Center for Western Hemisphere Studies.

———. 1997. *Recognizing the Latino Resurgence in U.S. Religion: The Emmaus Paradigm*. World Exploration Series. Boulder, Colo.: Westview Press.

Steward, Julian, Robert A. Manners, Eric R. Wolf, Elena Padilla Seda, Sidney W. Mintz, and Raymond L. Scheele. 1956. *The People of Puerto Rico: A Study in Social Anthropology*. Urbana: University of Illinois Press.

Stewart, C., and R. Shaw, eds. 1994. *Syncretism/Anti-Syncretism: The Politics of Religious Synthesis*. New York and London: Routledge.

Stoll, David. 1990. *Is Latin America Turning Protestant?: The Politics of Evangelical Growth*. Berkeley: University of California Press.

Stromberg, Peter G. 1993. *Language and Self-Transformation: A Study of the Christian Conversion Narrative*. New York: Cambridge University Press.

Summers, Muriel Bishop. 1999. "One Quaker's Perspective." In *Spirituality and Ageing*, edited by A. Jewell, 48–52. Philadelphia: Jessica Kingsley Publishers.

Synnott, Anthony. 1993. "Hair: Shame and Glory." In *The Body Social*, 103–27. New York: Routledge.

Taylor, Lawrence J. 1995. *Occasions of Faith: An Anthropology of Irish Catholics*. Philadelphia: University of Pennsylvania Press.

Tilak, Shrinivas. 1989. *Religion and Aging in the Indian Tradition*. Albany: State University of New York Press.

Torres, Arlene. 1998. "La gran familia puertorriqueña 'ej prieta de beldá' (The Great Puerto Rican Family Is Really Really Black)." In *Blackness in Latin American and the Caribbean: Social Dynamics and Cultural Transformations*, edited by A. Torres and N. E. Whitten, 285–306. Bloomington: Indiana University Press.

Torres Vidal, Nina. 1998. "Buscándole la vueltita a la mantilla: Una vueltita más. . . ." In *Vírgenes, magos, y escapularios: Imaginería, etnicidad, y religiosidad popular en Puerto Rico*, edited by A. G. Quintero Rivera, 105–12. San Juan: Centro de Investigaciones Sociales, Universidad de Puerto Rico; Centro de Investigaciones Académicas, Universidad del Sagrado Corazón; Fundación Puertorriqueña de las Humanidades.

Tweed, Thomas A. 1999. "Diasporic Nationalism and Urban Landscape: Cuban Immigrants at a Catholic Shrine in Miami." In *Gods of the City: Religion and the*

American Urban Landscape, edited by R. A. Orsi, 131–54. Indiana: Indiana University Press.

———. 2002. "Between the Living and the Dead: Fieldwork, History, and the Interpreter's Position," edited by J. V. Spickard, J. S. Landres, and M. B. McGuire, 63–74. New York and London: New York University Press.

Vidal, Teodoro. 1989. *Tradiciones de la brujería puertorriqueña*. San Juan: Ediciones Alba.

Watkins, Joanne C. 1996. *Spirited Women: Gender, Religion, and Cultural Identity in the Nepal Himalaya*. New York: Columbia University Press.

Whitehead, Harriet. 1987. *Renunciation and Reformulation: A Study of Conversion in an American Sect*. Ithaca, N.Y.: Cornell University Press.

Williams, Eric. 1970. *From Columbus to Castro: The History of the Caribbean*. New York: Vintage Books.

Williams, Melvin D. 1974. *Community in a Black Pentecostal Church: An Anthropological Study*. Pittsburgh: University of Pittsburgh Press.

Wuthnow, Robert. 1988. *The Restructuring of American Religion: Society and Faith Since World War II*. Princeton, N.J.: Princeton University Press.

———. 1992. *Rediscovering the Sacred: Perspectives on Religion in Contemporary Society*. Grand Rapids, Mich.: Eerdmans Publishing.

———. 1995. "Syncretism, Popular Religion, and Cultural Identity." In *Discovering Latino Religion: A Comprehensive Social Science Bibliography*, edited by A. M. Stevens-Arroyo with S. Pantoja, 7–12. Program for the Analysis of Religion Among Latinos vol. 4. New York: Bildner Center for Western Hemisphere Studies.

Zaragoza, Edward C. 1995. *St. James in the Streets: The Religious Processions of Loíza Aldea, Puerto Rico*. Drew Studies in Liturgy, no. 2. Lanham, Md., and London: Scarecrow Press.

Zayas Micheli, Luis O. 1990. *Catolicismo popular en Puerto Rico: Una explicación sociológica*. Ponce: L. O. Zayas Micheli.

Zenón Cruz, Isabelo. 1974. *Narciso descubre su trasero: El negro en la cultura puertorriqueña*. Humacao: Editorial Furidi.

Zuesse, E. M. 1975. "Meditation on Ritual." *Journal of the American Academy of Religion* 43: 517–30.

Index

of, xii, 69; and national and socioeconomic identity, 112; neo-Pentecostalism, 84; personal variations within, 94–95; political association with, 86–87; popularity of individual ministries within, 92–93, 150–51; social prohibitions in, 84

Pentecostals: attitude of, toward other Protestants, 36; conservative attacked by moderate, 82; control of media by, xiii; and education, xiv, 80; financial dependency of, on U.S., 78–79; political alliances of, 86–87; Protestants' attacks against, 82; and social action, 79, 93; statistics of, in Las Cuevas (*see* Las Cuevas); statistics of, in Puerto Rico, 69, 253n12. *See also* FLECHAS; Latinos

Pérez, Louis A., Jr., 104, 253n14
Pérez Torres, Rubén, xiv, 69, 77, 92, 252n1
Pérez y Mena, Andrés I., 76, 128, 129
Physical-emotive experience. *See* Religion
Picó, Fernando, 74, 98
Piñones, 11, 36, 48
PIP (Partido Independentista Puertorriqueño), 49, 107. *See also* Loízan political perspectives; Puerto Rican religion
Pitts, Walter, 158
Plena: celebration of, 44, 47; compared with bomba, 23; definition of, 22; in everyday life, 17, 60; popularity in the 1950s of, 24; secular and religious significance of, 22, 23
PNP (Partido Nuevo Progresista): and black sector, 34–35, 49; founding of, 49; and *jíbaro* theme, 49; a progressive version of Puerto Rican national identity, 24; and pro-statehood stand, 97. *See also* Loízan political perspectives; Puerto Rican religion
Ponce: black population and African traditions in, xi, 24, 47; Carnival of Ponce, 24, 47; celebration of abolishment of slavery, 243; cement production, 166, 248; color classifications, 37; and Puerto Rican national identity/culture, 24; first Protestant church, 77
Popular (or folk) Catholicism: Catholic leadership in development of, 126; elements of, 73, 108; expressions of, 71, 102, 105; influence of Spanish folk Catholicism, 73; problems with definition of, 126; as resistance to official Catholicism, 71; Spiritism, Santería, witchcraft, and other religious beliefs, 29, 76, 105, 152; studies of, 7, 108. *See also* Santiago Apóstol (Saint James), festival of
Popular (or folk) Spiritism. *See* Spiritism
Portes, Alejandro, 171
PPD (Partido Popular Democrático): accused of racism against Loízans, 50–51; and Canóvanas, 41; and creation of commonwealth, 9; and land reform, 166; male dominance in leadership, 219; and populist discourse, 20 (*see also* Jíbaro); residential projects in Loíza, 52; and Spanish culture, 50; "subversive" political activities by, 185; and use of culture for political gain, 50; woman leadership in, 52, 204. *See also* Loízan political perspectives; Puerto Rican religion
Privatization. *See* Puerto Rico
Privett, Stephen A., 106
Pro-Independence movement, 10, 17, 72–73, 75. *See also* PIP
Protestantism: centenary celebration of, xiv, 87; and charismatic experience, xiii, 82, 84, 88; and colonialism, 18; doctrine of, 83; establishment of, in Loíza, 102; establishment of, in Puerto Rico, 75, 98; evangelical campaigns in, 90, 177; export of native-born Puerto Rican pastors, 91; identified with North American culture, 107; and individualistic thought, 108–9, 134; and liberation theology, 18, 22; as logical result of U.S. imperialism, 9; missionary work within, 36, 78, 185; mixed with various religious belief systems, 29; neo-(historical)Protestantism, 84; and North American evangelicalism, 92; organization of, 69; political association with, 86–87; and progress; 41; and Puerto Rican national identity, 9; on race (*see* Race); social activities in, 83; social prohibitions in, 84; studies of, 8; supporting colonialism, 18; witnessing within (*see* Witnessing)

on television, 21; against black migrants, 246; within Catholicism, 111–12; Christian church on, 142–44 (*see also* Holy Spirit and Saint Patrick Parish of Loíza; Santiago Apóstol Parish); conflicts between Loízan children related to race and community origins, 35; linguistic expressions of, 38–40, 68; "mild," 11; popularity of topic, 51; in PPD, 50, 51; within population, 49, 51, 59; in Puerto Rican literature, 26; within state government, 48, 49; regarding use and misuse, by Loíza's government, 52; in U.S., 56; against whites, 35. *See also* Church of the Fountain of the Living Water; Latinos; Santiago Apóstol Parish

Raíces (video production), 44, 45, 252n8

Ramírez de Arellano, Annette, 256n1 (ch.7)

Rappaport, Roy A., 5, 6, 97, 138

Re-Africanization, 126

Religion: "acceptance" vs. "belief" in, 97; concept of, 5; disembedding of, 88; experiential approach in study, 8; and family, 88; and identity (*see* Identity); Loízans on concept of, 28, 138, 140; and migration, 97; multilayered (or multidimensional) perspective in study of, 6, 244; on personal, 93–97; physical-emotive experience in study of, 140, 199; religious boundaries, 70; religious competition (or interreligious relationships) in study of, 4, 6 (*see also* Religious pluralism); restructuring of, 85; and ritual and its "doings," 5, 98–99, 120, 138, 202, 254n1; and sociopolitical action, 248, 249–50; and space, 88 (*see also* Space); supernatural (or transcendence) in study of, 6, 7, 8. *See* Puerto Rican religion

Religious competition. *See* Religion

Religious pluralism, 163–64. *See also* Puerto Rican religion

Restructuring (of religion). *See* Puerto Rican religion; Religion

Ray, Richie, and Bobby Cruz, 92

Río Grande, 2, 57, 127, 178, 192, 255n5

Río Grande de Loíza, 2, 165

Rismiller, Arthur P., 241

Ritual. *See* Religion

Rivera Correa, Ricardo R., 255n6

Rodríguez Escudero, Nestor A., 79, 80, 254n20

Rodríguez López, "Geñito," 81

Rodríguez Toulis, Nicole, 8, 97, 163, 200

Rolón, Wanda, 86, 205

Romberg, Raquel, 8, 73–78, 90, 128, 214, 215

Roof, Wade C., 163, 257n3

Roots (TV series), 21

Rosa, Moisés A., 143

Rosaldo, Michelle, 222, 240

Rose, Susan D., 79

Roselló, Pedro, 51, 86, 155, 238, 247

Rouse, Irving, 71

Rowe, Maureen, 163, 206, 219

Rubenstein, Hymie, 167

Rumbones, 160

Saavedra de Roca, Angelina, 7

Safa, Helen I., 201, 208

Said, Edward, 18, 66

Saint Patrick: festival of, as "religious" celebration vs. traditional celebration, 109, 110; origins of devotion to, 99; painted dark, 110; as "real" patron saint of Loíza, 109. *See also* Irish; Santiago Apóstol

Saint Rose of Lima Parish of Fair Haven, 65, 66

Salsa: celebration of, 51; Christian, 92; in everyday life, 17, 60; marketing of, 247; vs. merengue (from Dominican Republic), 22, 59; and religious experience, 22, 23; representing Afro-Puerto Rican element in modern-cultural version, 16; in U.S., 59; women's use of, 204

San Antonio chapel: community and local identity in, 130; festival of Antonio in relation to, 129–30; founding of, 129–31, 201; and Holy Spirit, 132; members of, representing themselves in relation to other Christian churches, 132–33; openness and informality in, 133, 134; origins of devotion to San Antonio, 129; about participants in, 131; and a personal relationship with God, 132–33; physical-emotive experience in, 132; sociopolitical awareness in, 134; on unity and religious tolerance, 133, 134

Sánchez de León, Carmen, 199

of, 58, 243; representing historical version of Afro-Puerto Rican element, 16; studies about, 8, 19, 25; in U.S., 21, 50

Slaves: Christianization of, 72, 73; fugitive, from Caribbean, 2; as labor force, 2, 11, 71, 74, 100; owners of, 44; religion of, 44, 76; religious persecution of, 71; resistance of, through religion, 44; settlements of, 60; significance of ancestry, 67; statistics of, 74; working with free people of mixed color, 73, 74; treatment of, 44, 72

Smilde, David A., 163

Sobo, Elisa J., 173

Socialist party, 49

Sociopolitical action. *See* Religion

Solivan, Samuel, 164

Soto Torres, Edgardo, 23

Soul Train (TV show), 21

Space: and family identities and religion, gendered, 172–74; the sacred through managing of, 196; on sacred, 164; as social and sacred in context of everyday life, 164; sociophysical (*see* Las Cuevas). *See also individual churches*

Spanish colonialism: and Catholicism (*see* Catholicism); critique of, and of genocide of Indians, 17–18 (*see also* Pro-Independence movement); economic and political difficulties of, 74–75; establishment of, 71, 73; resistance to, 72–73, 74–75; treatment of native Indians and slaves under (*see* Slaves; Taínos)

Spanish heritage: critique of overemphasis on, by Puerto Ricans in U.S., 26; folk and popular religion, 27, 73; Latinos and, 38; in Loíza, 43 (*see also* Holy Spirit and Saint Patrick Parish; Santiago Apóstol, festival of); preference for, over other heritage, 20–26, 50; as part of Puerto Rican national identity/culture, 9, 11, 19; among Puerto Ricans in U.S., 38, 64; relationship to *jíbaro* culture, 9. *See also* Holy Spirit and Saint Patrick Parish of Loíza; Santiago Apóstol, festival of

Spencer, Jon M., 254n1

Spickard, James V., 15, 18, 27, 251n3 (ch.1)

Spiritism: central belief system of, 76; and

folklorization of Puerto Rican culture on, 108; folk, 28, 70, 102, 215; hidden by Pentecostalism, 27, 70, 216; influence of Allan Kardec on, 76; and materialism, 214; mixed with Santería, witchcraft, and other beliefs, 28, 69–70, 128, 215; negative use of, 215; official, 28, 75, 215; negative stereotypes of, 31, 214, 216; official establishment of, 75, 77; as opposed to Santería and Vodou, 215; as part of Loízan stereotypes, 17, 18, 27, 94, 214; as part of Medianía Alta stereotypes, 34; as part of Puerto Rican essence, 78; and Protestant individualist ideology on, 108; public attacks and persecution against, 70, 77–78, 80; public and official response to public attacks, 80–81; as scientific and/or philosophical system vs. religious system, 76, 77; Spiritism-Catholicism, 128, 215–16; and Taínos' beliefs and identity, 76, 251n2 (ch.2); and theosophy movement, 75–76; in U.S., 6–7 (*see also* Latinos)

Spiritists: Catholics' and Protestants' attacks against, 80, 108, 216; flexible attitudes toward, 216; and social action, 79 (*see also* Women's religious experience); statistics of, 69–70; statistics of, in Las Cuevas, (*see* Las Cuevas); on stereotypes of, at personal level (*see* Women's religious experience); as witches, 207, 215

Sports: and conflicts based on skin color and community origins, 35; lack of facilities, 104, 175; as means of town identity, 104; for religious purposes, 83–84; as source of social and economic mobility, 83, 104

Steigenga, Timothy J., 163

Stevens, Cecil E., 42, 101

Stevens-Arroyo, Anthony, xii, 7, 8, 42–43, 252n2

Steward, Julian H., 11

Stewart, Charles, 164

Stoll, David, 112, 254n22

Stoltz Chinchilla, Norma, 56, 66

Stromberg, Peter G., 222, 223, 229

Summers, Muriel Bishop, 257n8

Supernatural, the. *See* Religion

After teaching anthropology, religion, and Latino studies, Samiri Hernández Hiraldo is currently conducting independent research on Latino religion. She is also a research fellow of PARAL (Program for the Analysis of Religion Among Latinos).